PRAISE FOR THE BOOK

"Shail Kumar presents a compelling, comprehensive vision for transforming India's higher education system. I am particularly pleased to see his discussion about the key role that technology, MOOCs, and online learning will play in building India's new Golden Age."

–Anant Agarwal
CEO, edX, and Professor, MIT

"Bold, timely, and solutions-oriented book on transforming India."

–Rajiv Bajaj
Managing Director, Bajaj Auto

"Above all, this book is a message of hope for the future of India. It will behoove educational and political leaders and thinkers to read this book to get a better perspective and put some ideas to action."

–Abhay Bhushan
Chairman, Asquare, and Founding President, PanIIT, USA

"This book is an excellent guide for young Indian minds on their path to building a Golden India."

–Gourab Chatterjee
PhD student, University of Washington, Seattle, and
M.Tech and B. Tech, IIT

"I will go home to build this Golden India if there are concrete steps taken in [the book's] direction. This book has revitalized my passion and I'm optimistic about our country's future!"

–Subhamoy Das
PhD, University of Texas, Austin, and B.Tech, IIT

"Shail Kumar's *Building Golden India* is a timely call to action to revamp India's dilapidated education system, leading to accelerated and inclusive development. Must-read for all concerned citizens – students, educators, professionals, and officials – specially the Ministry of Human Resource Development of India."

–Shailabh Kumar
PhD student, University of Minnesota, and M. Tech and B.Tech, IIT

"*Building Golden India* is a must read for those who care about India and its future. Shail Kumar has written a captivating book about how fixing India's higher education system can address many of its largest problems and enable its people to achieve their full potential."

–Arjun Malhotra
Co-Founder, HCL Technologies,
TechSpan/Headstrong, and SPICMACAY

"Educational! Passionate writing supported by extensive analysis. Provides a realistic roadmap to solving India's mega problems. A must read for anyone who cares about a better India."

–Suman Bikash Mondal
PhD student, Washington University, St. Louis,
and M.Tech and B.Tech, IIT

"Very informative and well-researched book, with a concise summary of action at the end. The best part about this book is that one can pick it up anytime, start reading from any page and learn quite a lot just by reading for as less as 10 minutes!"

–Sreeja Nag
Research Engineer, NASA, and MIT and IIT alumna

"Education transforms lives and lifts societies. In an increasingly knowledge intensive economy, quality higher education is a vital national priority. As India approaches the 70th anniversary of its independence, it is time for a forthright assessment of progress in this sector. Shail Kumar has put together a commendable treatise on India's higher education system that offers insightful analysis of current challenges and dilemmas, describes benchmarks for excellence and makes pragmatic suggestions for reforms. An inspiring book and a great read to everyone who dreams of a better India."

–Arogyaswami Paulraj
Professor (Emeritus), Stanford University,
Padma Bhushan awardee, and winner of the Marconi Prize
and IEEE Alexander Graham Bell Medal

"After independence India did a remarkable job in developing world-class education institutions in the area of engineering and technology, primarily at the undergraduate level. However, in the modern times these institutions have not been able to keep pace with their peer institutions around the globe. For India to be competitive in the global economy significant improvement is needed in our education institutions. Furthermore, India lacks excellence in graduate education at PhD and needs a quantum improvement. Indian institutions must establish world-class research facilities and must make an effort to attract best and the brightest students and Faculty to the PhD program. In this book, Shail Kumar has done a remarkable job in painstakingly analyzing the past and present status of this and has given excellent suggestions for improvement. I would highly recommend that both our technical leaders as well as politicians take a closer look at his book."

–Krishna Saraswat
Rickey/Nielsen Chair Professor,
Department of Electrical Engineering, Stanford University

"This book is an excellent amalgam of facts and stories about higher education in India and its potential to lead India to its Golden Age. Every one who is concerned about India's future and wants to affect positive change in its society must read this book."

–Raj Shekhar Singh
Co-Founder, YourAdhikar, and PhD, UC Berkeley, and B.Tech, IIT

"Although the United States has clearly benefited from ambitious Indians seeking quality higher education, the world needs India — as our largest democracy — to craft its own robust higher education system to develop and unleash its considerable talent. *Building Golden India* is a terrific, insightful primer explaining the stark reality of India's flawed current system and providing models and inspiration for needed change."

–Kim Walesh
Director of Economic Development, City of San Jose, and Co-author, *Grassroots Leaders for a New Economy: How Civic Entrepreneurs are Building Prosperous Communities*

BUILDING GOLDEN

GOLDEN

India

BUILDING GOLDEN INDIA

How to Unleash India's Vast Potential and
Transform Its Higher Education System. Now.

SHAIL KUMAR

ONS GROUP PRESS
Fremont
2015

Published by ONS Group Press

ONS Group Press, 47185 Galindo Drive, Fremont, CA 94539, USA

Cover Design by: Fiona Jayde Media
Interior Design by: The Deliberate Page
Author Photo by: Bhavin Nicholas Shah

ISBN 978-0-9966168-0-5

Library of Congress Control Number: 2015916259

10 9 8 7 6 5 4 3 2 1

1. India–Economic Development, 2. India–Higher Education,
3. India–Economic Policy, 4. India–Education Policy

मातृदेवो भव पितृदेवो भव

For my parents – I owe everything to them.

Table of Contents

SECTION 1
The Context: Past, Present, and Future

CHAPTER 1

SECTION 2
The Challenge: Peeling the Onion

CHAPTER 2

CHAPTER 3

CHAPTER 4

SECTION 3
Benchmarking: Learning from the Best

CHAPTER 5

CHAPTER 6

CHAPTER 7

CHAPTER 8

FOREWORD

India has come a long way since getting its independence in 1947. However, with 1.3 billion people living in the country, the country faces both major unseen challenges and opportunities. Building a good higher educational infrastructure will play a big role in whether the challenges or the opportunities will overwhelm the country. There is not much debate over this part. The question is how many and what type of institutions should we build?

Shail Kumar does an excellent job of setting the context for how we should move forward with this task. Over fifteen centuries ago, India built the world's very first higher educational institution. Shail captures the history of that glorious period in India. What is surprising is that what made those institutions great is not that different than what we need to do now; if India was the first in the world to do it, I am sure it can do it again.

Shail starts the book with what India can be a hundred years after its independence. By 2047, there will be 1.8 billion people in the country and it will face huge challenges; food shortage, insufficient clean water, inadequate health care, and lack of skilled workers, to name a few. If the country were to solve these problems, it needs millions of inspired individuals who will come up with innovative solutions and implement them. Shail paints a picture where if we build the appropriate higher educational institutions they will produce graduates who will solve these problems in innovative ways that the world has not seen before. An inspired and innovative individual is the most powerful resource of any country. To produce them in large numbers and create the right fertile ecosystem, we need institutions that graduate students who are not only well skilled and innovative but have a huge compassion for everything around them. These graduates will play a key role in regaining the Golden Age in India.

Shail also makes the point that institutions of higher learning should be multi-disciplinary. Massachusetts Institute of Technology (MIT) started as a technical university 150 years ago in Boston. I have seen it firsthand as a Board Member for the last 15 years as to how it reinvents itself continuously and stays relevant to the world in its ability to make global impact through the students it educates and the new frontiers of knowledge it discovers. Most of the innovation happens at the multidisciplinary boundaries. This is a new phenomenon that we have witnessed in the last 20 years. For example, MIT researchers from biology, civil engineering and economics are all working together to find a cure for cancer. India is still currently focused on building separate institutions for disciplines. Shail makes a compelling recommendation that we should move away from that strategy. Also, India has separated its research institutions from educational institutions in the European tradition. They need to bring them together. To have impact on the country, thinkers have to be "doers" and doers have to be "thinkers."

As Shail points out, universities in the United States are the best in the world and there is a lot that we can learn from them. Educational institutions change very gradually, and in some ways they have not changed that dramatically from the days of Nalanda to the current period. Given the tremendous progress in computing and communications, the way we learn and educate will change dramatically. Over the next 25 years, we will go through the same revolution that mobile phones went through from being suitcase-sized devices to the current smart phones. The fact that education will change is certain, how exactly it will change is not. Educators and technologists in India have to play a key role in this revolution. India has to come up with innovative solutions that are unique to India; India needs scalable, cost effective and simple solutions. The young in India now have the confidence and the capability to solve problems in ways that the world has not seen before.

Thousands of students from India are now going to institutions outside of India for higher education and spending billions of dollars. There is not only the huge unfulfilled need to educate youth in India but also the capacity to pay for it. Several of them are either coming back to India or are engaged with projects in India. We have Indians all over the world playing key roles in leading educational institutions. Forward thinking leaders in India are already putting their ideas into action by building institutions such as Ashoka University. We are all well-networked and will have more tools than ever to take on the task.

I hope this book will be a catalyst in starting this urgent conversation and lead to action in India. I am very hopeful that India will regain its golden years if we implement Shail's recommendations and educate young professionals. This book is an excellent start for students, faculty, university administrators and policy makers who will be a part of building a Golden India; an India where the environment is clean, wildlife is thriving and every living being has an opportunity to live to their full potential.

Gururaj "Desh" Deshpande
Trustee, Deshpande Foundation,
and Life Member, MIT Corporation

PREFACE

Pune, June 1983: My father's excited voice boomed throughout the house. He had just received a call from a relative in Mumbai informing him that I had cleared the Indian Institute of Technology Joint Entrance Examination (IIT JEE) on my first attempt. My father was both excited and relieved at the same time. Mere weeks before, he was late in dropping me at the IIT JEE exam center. I arrived fifteen minutes after the exams had begun and could have easily been disqualified for arriving late. In a tough national competition where a few marks can determine whether you make it into the IITs or not, fifteen minutes meant a lot. The delay had been gnawing at him until he heard the good news. For a middle-class family like ours, it seemed to me like I had won the lottery.

Taking the IIT JEE was a default decision. Two years earlier, when I had topped my school in the tenth board examinations, my family had asked me about my future plans. I had promptly said economics and commerce. A short stunned silence later, there was loud laughter. My father and uncles impressed upon me that a smart student like myself must either become an engineer or a doctor. I respected my father and elders too much to question their advice. I did not like the memorizing that biology seemed to need. Physics, chemistry, and mathematics came naturally to me.

Thus, becoming an engineer was by default as well. It was tough to decide which IIT to attend and which department to select. The IIT JEE rankings played a large part in the decision. Following a trend that has continued over the years, those ranked the highest took computer science, next came electronics and so on. There was a pecking order. I pored over the department catalogs and was more confused than ever.

My father, an army officer, suggested another approach. He wanted me to join the IIT that was the farthest from Pune, which is where he was then stationed. He felt I would grow as a person if I were far from home. I took his advice and joined IIT Kharagpur in July 1983. It was one of the best decisions I ever made.

The four years I spent at IIT Kharagpur are still among the most memorable four years of my life. Those years were also the longest I stayed in any one place in India. Before then, I had moved from one army cantonment to another every one to three years. At IIT, I met some of the smartest and most talented people from around the country. It was also a major reset in my life. I was no longer the class topper. Some of my friends and colleagues were better debaters, artists, writers, and sportsmen than me. I had to find a niche for myself and raise my game to keep up with my classmates in academics and in extracurricular activities. IIT Kharagpur gave me the flexibility to find myself, grow personally and professionally, and mature. I also made friends for life. When I go back to the campus, it feels like a second home. The Scholar's Avenue, buildings, trees, smell, and campus atmosphere evoke priceless and deeply etched memories.

By the end of the four years, I was pleased with my all-around achievements. I played hockey for IIT and Radhakrishnan (RK) Hall, my hostel of four years. I was also president of RK Hall in my final year and was voted the "best secretary" at the end of my second year. I graduated with B. Tech (honors) with a cumulative grade point average of 8.67 on a ten-point scale. Years later, the IIT brand in general and the IIT Kharagpur global alumni network in particular would open doors for me that I could not have even dreamed of in June 1983.

However, during these four years at IIT, I felt underwhelmed by the academics and faculty members. Barring a handful of professors, no one challenged us intellectually. Most would write notes on the chalkboard or share information available in the books. Examinations and assignments were more of the same. If you read the books and diligently solved problem sets, you could do well in the class. There was minimal focus on building things. I was in the mechanical engineering department, where one would have expected a lot of hands-on projects. *Why was it that we, the supposed crème de la crème of students in India, had such an inadequate academic experience? If this was the case in the IITs, then what must go on in the rest of the Indian higher education institutions?* These questions have bothered me since 1983.

Fast-forward to 1991. After working for two years at Eicher Goodearth Ltd. in India and then completing my MBA from Indiana University in Bloomington, I joined a Fortune 500 company in Silicon

Valley. In addition, some friends and I reactivated IIT Kharagpur's Bay Area alumni group chapter. I was interested in how we could not only meet socially but also improve and sustain excellence at IIT Kharagpur. We hosted IIT Kharagpur's director during each of their respective visits and took them to Silicon Valley companies and local universities.

In 1999, Arvind Jain, president of the IIT Foundation and a senior IIT Kharagpur alumnus, asked me to join the IIT Foundation Board. Later, he nominated me to vice president and president roles. Around this time, I, along with Raj Mashruwala and Anil Kshirsagar (IIT Bombay), Abhay Bhushan and Deepak Bhagat (IIT Kanpur), Monishi Sanyal and Partha Ranganathan (IIT Madras), Prashant Fuloria (IIT Delhi), and several others, kicked off efforts to work collectively as IITians for the IITs. Endorsed and supported at the inception by Arjun Malhotra and several other distinguished IIT alumni, this became the Pan IIT alumni movement in the United States. It has since become a global organization (www.IIT.org).

However, I felt that most of our efforts were like a drop in the vast ocean of India's higher education system. *Could I contribute more?*

Since 1991, I have spent thousands of hours volunteering for IIT Kharagpur and the IIT alumni movement. It finally dawned on me that my passion was in higher education and building and sustaining world-class universities. In 2006, I resigned from my role as the senior director of corporate strategic planning at Lam Research, a Silicon Valley–based high-tech firm, to join the University of California at Berkeley as a senior director of external relations. I quit a high-paying corporate job to join a public sector institution with negligible growth prospects and took a huge pay cut. My wife and family were disappointed in me. However, for me, it was another great decision.

UC Berkeley opened new windows and doors in my life. The university leadership and faculty members are a class apart. Their focus on students learning outcomes is astounding. They have fostered active collaborations with industry and government organizations. There is tremendous emphasis on creating, innovating, and starting new ventures. *Why couldn't Indian institutions be similar?*

Then, by sheer alignment of the stars, several Berkeley deans asked me to help establish a research and academic collaboration with IIT Kharagpur. The idea was to start with a summer research program where IIT Kharagpur students would spend eight weeks at UC Berkeley and conduct research. On their return home, they would continue the research with their respective IIT faculty advisers. In time, it was hoped, there would be faculty-to-faculty research collaboration in the fields of biofuels and health.

We hosted close to forty-five IIT students from 2008 to 2011. The majority of them had exceptional experiences in this program. The experience motivated many of them to pursue graduate studies after obtaining their bachelor's degrees. Some recognized that a research career was not for them, and they pursued management degrees or industry jobs. However, we could not establish even one faculty-to-faculty research collaboration. *Why did Berkeley faculty admire and love the IIT students, but most of the IIT faculty members feel the same students were not fit for research? Why, despite organizing faculty visits and providing students an incredibly attractive research experience, we could not establish any research collaborations?*

I also helped organize Kapil Sibal's visit to UC Berkeley when he was the minister for human resource development. He was promoting the Innovations University Bill. I was amazed to learn from his comments that while it was an important initiative he had little budget to bring it to life.

I briefly joined UC San Diego as a senior executive director of development in 2013. In this role, I was leading development for seven colleges and schools. For personal reasons, I resigned and took some time off, during which I volunteered a lot. In July 2013, I co-led an alumni campaign to appoint Partha Pratim Chakrabarti (PPC) as the director of IIT Kharagpur. Selected by the government of India (GOI) nomination committee to be IIT Kharagpur's director, PPC was unable to take charge for almost one year due to GOI-related delays. Coined "PPC for Director," this campaign took me to Arvind Kejriwal, a fellow IIT Kharagpur alumnus. We needed ideas to make a case with the GOI. I was impressed by Kejriwal's suggestions and honest and focused views about removing corruption and improving the lives of the common people in India. After the "PPC for Director" movement closed successfully, I volunteered for the Aam Aadmi Party (AAP). As part of these efforts, I initiated and co-founded a global network of university students for AAP (us4AAP), which expanded to over one hundred universities in four continents.

In June 2014, I decided to clear the deck and write this book full-time — with 100 percent focus and no strings attached. I wanted to answer questions that had been gnawing at me since 1983 and also do my part in transforming India's higher education system. My love for IIT Kharagpur and higher education got me engaged with the "PPC for Director" movement, and my love for a transformed India took me to AAP. This book brings together my love for a transformed India and higher education system. It feels to me that my entire life has been a preparation for this book and related future actions.

To write this book, I have also drawn from thousands of pages of central government and state government reports on higher education. I also attended several talks, presentations, and conferences. Finally, I interviewed over one hundred stakeholders in India and across four continents. These stakeholders include corporate titans, entrepreneurs, university leaders, faculty members, investors, parents, students, and alumni in India, the United States, the United Kingdom, Singapore, New Zealand, and Australia. I have included the list of everyone I interviewed in the Acknowledgments section.

In my book, I write as a concerned Indian citizen who deeply loves his country and wants a brighter future for India and *all* of its citizens. You may notice it in my tone and choice of words.

A few related notes about this book:

1. I have avoided any discussion of matters that divide us. Thus, I do not talk about reservations, which have been used by politicians to divide us on so many fronts for way too long.

2. I also do not speak about financial resources. With several lakhs of crores of rupees squandered repeatedly in many corruption scandals, and with close to US$100 billion siphoned off overseas in black money every year, I believe that there is no funding crisis in the country. (Note: one lakh rupees is equivalent to one hundred thousand rupees, one crore rupees is ten million rupees, making one lakh crore rupees equal to one trillion rupees. At a conservative currency conversion factor of 60 rupees for one US dollar, one lakh crore rupees is equivalent to US$17 billion.)

3. I have used information for India's higher education data from 2011 for two reasons. First of all, when I started writing the book, it was the only data that was considered final and published. Secondly, I could accurately triangulate the per capita metrics with the 2011 census data, which is the most recent official assessment of India's population.

4. Throughout the book, I have woven in stories, anecdotes, and quotes from over one hundred interviews and those who responded to my survey. However, in some chapters, I have deliberately used some fictional characters to make a point. For example, the characters described as being in 2047 are all fictional. Mukund Kapase in Chapter 2, the Mehta family in Chapter 3, Anjana Kapoor and Jayesh Patil in Chapter 4, the Indian students studying in the United States in Chapter 6, and the high school friends in California in Chapter 7 are also fictional characters. Any resemblance to real persons, living or dead, is purely coincidental.

5. I have done my best to attribute works of other people in this book. Please let me know if there are any errors or omissions. I would be happy to correct those in future editions.

I have written this book for the educated youth, the professionals, and those who deeply care about India in India and around the world. I sincerely hope that you will read this book and understand the challenges and opportunities facing us. I believe that the first step toward solving a problem is to acknowledge it.

I also write with hope. India was once called a "Golden Bird." While history can be quite contentious, I hope we can agree that building a Golden India is not just a dream but a vision we can rally around and collectively bring to reality.

What could a Golden India look like? What are the harsh realities of 2015 that we must address? How could we go about building a brighter future? What could we learn from the best? What are the next steps?

Begin reading. Join the conversation. Become part of the movement. #IAmForGoldenIndia

ACKNOWLEDGMENTS

First and foremost, I would like to thank and acknowledge everyone who took the time to meet or speak with me and share their insights and perspectives. I interviewed over one hundred people in India and across four continents. They include people from various walks of life and professions—entrepreneurs, industry leaders, senior corporate executives, university leaders, faculty members, investors, young professionals, and students. Meeting or speaking with all of these people was an extraordinary bonus of writing the book. I had never met most of them before. Their insights added tremendous depth and breadth to my thinking and the book.

Many of the people I interviewed have several titles. I have mostly used one or two of those. This list is sorted by last name.

1. Anant Agarwal: chief executive officer (CEO), edX; professor, Massachusetts Institute of Technology (MIT)
2. Pawan Agarwal: joint secretary, Ministry of Skill Development and Entrepreneurship
3. Mukesh Aghi: president, US–India Business Council; former CEO, L&T Infotech
4. Richard C. Atkinson: president emeritus, University of California
5. Rajiv Bajaj: managing director, Bajaj Auto
6. Ajay Bakaya: executive director, Sarovar Hotels
7. Sujit Baksi: CEO of business services, Tech Mahindra
8. P. Balaram: former director, Indian Institute of Science, Bangalore
9. Chitta Baral: professor, Arizona State University
10. Pranab Bardhan: professor, UC Berkeley
11. Anurag Behar: vice chancellor, Azim Premji University
12. Abhay Bhushan: chairman, Asquare and founding president, PanIIT USA

13. Kunal Chakrabarti: professor, Jawaharlal
    Nehru University
14. Shubhra Chakrabarti: professor, Dyal Singh College,
    University of Delhi
15. Rob Chandra: president and CEO, Avid Park
16. Hang Chang Chieh: executive director, Institute for
    Engineering Leadership and Professor, National
    University of Singapore (NUS)
17. G. Deshpande: trustee, Deshpande Foundation; life
    member, MIT Corporation
18. Parvati Dev: CEO, Innovation in Learning
19. Ashish Dhawan: founder, Central Square Foundation
20. Kalyan Dutta: senior staff scientist, Lockheed Martin
21. Prashant Fuloria: senior vice president, Yahoo
22. Robert Goldman: professor, UC Berkeley
23. R. Gopalakrishnan: director, Tata Sons Limited
24. Pradeep Gupta: chairman and MD, CyberMedia
25. R. Jaikumar: professor, Tata Institute of Fundamental
    Research (TIFR)
26. Sudhir Jain: director, Indian Institute of Technology (IIT)
    Gandhinagar
27. Ashok Jhunjhunwala: professor, IIT Madras
28. Tom Kailath: US National Medal of Science winner;
    professor, Stanford University
29. Anil Kakodkar: former chairman, Atomic Energy
    Commission of India
30. Pradeep Khosla: chancellor, UC San Diego
31. Tsu-Jae King Liu: chair, department of electrical
    engineering and computer sciences, and professor,
    UC Berkeley
32. Anjini Kochar: director, India Programs,
    Stanford University
33. Ranjit Konkar: professor, National Institute of Design
    (NID), Ahmedabad
34. Krishna Kumar: professor, University of Delhi
35. Sanjay Lalbhai: chairman and MD, Arvind Limited
36. Neelam Maheshwari: director of grant making and
    partnerships, Deshpande Foundation, India

37. Anu Maitra: foundation trustee and chair, Council of Presidents, UC Santa Cruz
38. Arjun Malhotra: co-founder, HCL India and TechSpan
39. Raj Mashruwala: serial entrepreneur and investor
40. Paul Matsudaira: head of the department of biological sciences and professor, NUS
41. T. V. Mohandas Pai: chairman, Manipal Global Education
42. Sunil Munjal: joint MD, Hero MotoCorp
43. Narayana Murthy: co-founder, Infosys
44. Bodhibrata Nag: professor, Indian Institute of Management (IIM) Calcutta
45. Roddam Narasimha: professor, Jawaharlal Nehru Centre for Advanced Scientific Research
46. Nandan Nilekani: co-founder, Infosys; former chairman, Unique Identification Authority initiative
47. Alka Parikh: professor, Dhirubhai Ambani Institute of Information and Communication Technology (DA IICT), Gandhinagar
48. David Patterson: professor, UC Berkeley
49. Arogyaswami Paulraj: professor emeritus, Stanford University and winner of the Marconi Prize and IEEE Alexander Graham Bell Medal
50. Deepak Phatak: professor, IIT Bombay
51. Sam Pitroda: former chairman, National Knowledge Commission
52. Sridhar Rajagopal: MD, Educational Initiatives
53. N. S. Rajan: chief human resources officer, Tata Group
54. S. Ramadorai: chairman, National Skill Development Agency
55. Jayanti Ravi: commissioner, Higher Education, Gujarat
56. Aromar Revi: executive director, Indian Institute of Human Settlements
57. Jasper Rine: professor, UC Berkeley
58. Anil Sachdev: founder, School of Inspired Learning
59. Krishna Saraswat: professor, Stanford University
60. Jaideep Sarkar: ambassador of India to Israel
61. Randy Schekman: Nobel laureate; professor, UC Berkeley
62. Janat Shah: director, IIM Udaipur

63. Raghubir Sharan: professor, IIT Gandhinagar
64. Raghu Shevgaonkar: former director, IIT Delhi
65. Ram Shriram: founder, Sherpalo Ventures; vice chair of the Stanford Board of Trustees
66. Pramath Sinha: founder and trustee, Ashoka University
67. Virendra P. Sinha: professor, DA IICT, Gandhinagar
68. Sakti Srivastava: associate professor (teaching) of surgery (anatomy), Stanford School of Medicine
69. Suresh Subramani: executive vice chancellor, UC San Diego
70. S. P. Sukhatme: former director, IIT Bombay
71. Govind Swarup: professor, TIFR
72. Brijendra K. Syngal: former chairman and MD, VSNL
73. Ram Takwale: former vice chancellor, Indira Gandhi National Open University
74. Gautam Thapar: founder and chairman, Avantha Group
75. John Thong: head of the electrical and computer engineering department and professor, NUS
76. Robert Tjian: president, Howard Hughes Medical Institute; professor, UC Berkeley
77. M. Vidyasagar: professor, University of Texas, Dallas
78. Mary Walshok: associate vice chancellor, UC San Diego

I interviewed the following young professionals and graduate students. The list is sorted by last name and includes their college and university affiliations, with the most recent university written first and so on:

1. J. R. Achyuthan: George Mason University; IIT Bombay
2. Bharath Bhat: Stanford University; IIT Kharagpur
3. Sampriti Bhattacharya: MIT; Ohio State University; West Bengal University of Technology
4. Arijit Chakraborty: University of Auckland; Birla Institute of Technology and Science (BITS) Pilani
5. Shouvik Chatterjee: Cornell University; IIT Kharagpur
6. Subhamoy Das: University of Texas (UT) Austin; IIT Kharagpur
7. Anindya De: Princeton University; UC Berkeley; IIT Kanpur
8. Arpit Goel: Stanford University; IIT Delhi

9. Moneisha Gokhale: University of New South Wales; Bausch and Lomb School of Optometry, Hyderabad
10. Sreeta Gorripaty: UC Berkeley; IIT Bombay
11. Suma Jaini: Boston University; IIT Kharagpur
12. Manas Kaushik: Harvard University; London School of Economics and Political Science (LSE); All India Institute of Medical Sciences (AIIMS)
13. Keerthana Kumar: UT Austin
14. Pradeep Lukka: University of Tennessee Health Science Center; UC San Francisco; University of Auckland; Rajiv Gandhi University of Health Sciences, Bangalore
15. Raghu Mahajan: Stanford University; University of Cambridge; MIT (He also spent two years as an undergraduate student at IIT Delhi; he topped IIT JEE 2006.)
16. Vinod Maseedupally: University of New South Wales; Bausch and Lomb School of Optometry, Hyderabad
17. Stuti Misra: University of Auckland; Bharati Vidyapeeth University, Pune
18. Sreeja Nag: MIT; IIT Kharagpur
19. Avinash Nayak: UC Berkeley; IIT Kharagpur
20. Aniket Panda: Duke University; IIT Kharagpur
21. Hetal Parekh: London School of Commerce; St. Francis College for Women, Hyderabad
22. Jagori Saha: University of Washington, Seattle; University College London (UCL); Presidency College
23. Shweta Sangewar: Imperial College London; IIT Kharagpur
24. Rajiv Ratn Shah: NUS; Delhi College of Engineering; JNU; Benares Hindu University
25. Aamod Shanker: UC Berkeley; IIT Kharagpur
26. Akanksha Srivastava: University of Oxford; IIT Kharagpur
27. Smitha Tipparaju: University of Auckland; Calicut University
28. Anshuman Tiwari: Institut Français de Presse; IIT Kharagpur
29. Patralekha Ukil: University of Warwick; Presidency College

Thank you!

In *Building Golden India,* instead of sharing the interviews verbatim, which I felt could get boring or repetitive, I have interwoven their unique insights and quotes where they add the most compelling point, evidence, or inspiration. Doing this, I hope, makes it more interesting and valuable for you.

I also want to acknowledge and thank Raghunath Anant Mashelkar, former director general of the Council of Scientific and Industrial Research (CSIR); Roddam Narasimha; David Patterson, Arogyaswami Paulraj, and S. P. Sukhatme who shared their articles and copies of their lectures on higher education with me.

Close to two hundred and fifty people completed my survey about India's new Golden Age. I was pleasantly surprised by the responses, which came from India, Australia, Canada, France, the Netherlands, New Zealand, Thailand, Singapore, Sweden, the United Kingdom, and the United States. They represented all ages from eighteen to over seventy-five. Thanks to all of them. Special thanks to everyone who gave me permission to include their thoughts in this book.

In addition, a big thank you to everyone who has helped me in my thirty-year journey since joining IIT Kharagpur in 1983 — my wing mates, hall mates, and friends from IIT. They have kept me grounded, helped improve my capabilities, and nudged me to do more. I also want to thank all my family members, friends, professional colleagues, and mentors. I am a better person because of them. I also want to thank all the forty-five IIT Kharagpur students who participated in the UC Berkeley-IIT Kharagpur collaboration and spent eight-weeks at Berkeley conducting research. You are one of the sources of inspiration for this book.

Writing this book was hard work, much more than I had expected. It was also exhilarating, more than I could have ever imagined. Two books altered the trajectory of my book. I would recommend them to all aspiring writers: *Stairway to Earth: How to Write a Serious Book* by Bill Birchard and *APE: Author, Publisher, Entrepreneur: How to Publish a Book* by Guy Kawasaki and Shawn Welch.

Fiona Jayde, who designed the book cover, infused life to the title, sub-title, and the book's spirit. Her creativity and flexibility in working on the design was extraordinary. Thank you Fiona. Tamara Cribley designed the book's interior and gave it the look that you are now reading. Her professionalism and attention to detail is simply outstanding. Thank you Tamara.

I could not have written this book without the extraordinary support of my family, friends, and colleagues. I received advice from a number of friends. Some of them also helped me think about the title and sub-title for the book, a much more difficult task than I had imagined. A few hosted me in various cities in India. Others introduced me to their friends. Some took precious time to review the book and offered valuable suggestions:

Anant Agarwal, Rajeev Agarwal, Sachin Bapat, Pranab Bardhan, Bharath Bhat, Abhay Bhushan, Rob Chandra, Sandipan Deb, Parvati Dev, Kalyan Dutta, Nipun Girotra, Sundip Gorai, Sreeta Gorripaty, Venayak Gupta, Prem Guragain, Anurag Jain, Sudesh Kannan, Rambhagat Kapoor, Sreekanth Kocharlakota, Anil Kshirsagar, Prem Kumar, Pran Kurup, Tsu-Jae King Liu, Rajesh Mashruwala, Stuti Misra, Abha Mital, Rajat Mital, Devika Mittal, Renu Mittal, Nandan Nilekani, Geoff Owen, Asim Parekh, Manjari Dutt Rana, Shyamal Roy, Jagori Saha, Monishi Sanyal, Prashant Sarin, Sonal Sarin, Randy Schekman, Dolly Sheth, Mehul Sheth, Arvind Singhal, Suresh Subramani, John Thong, Savitha Venkateswaran, Venky Venkateswaran and Stu Walesh. Thank you.

Several colleagues, friends, and family members have helped in many crucial ways, and at various stages of the book: Gourab Chatterjee, Subhamoy Das, Robert Goldman, Sudhir Jain, Suma Jaini, Shailabh Kumar, Umika Kumar, Suman Mondal, Sreeja Nag, Arogyaswami Paulraj, Jasper Rine, Krishna Saraswat, Raj Shekhar Singh, Rajni Timbadia, and Kim Walesh. A special thanks to you.

A few have played an instrumental role in my book: Arjun Malhotra for making innumerable introductions and giving sage advice throughout the process; R. Gopalakrishnan for mentoring me on the writing process, introducing me to several people, recommending Birchard's book, and sharing his insights; and Desh Deshpande for encouraging me to visit Hubli and learn more about the Hubli Sandbox, and writing the foreword. Thank you very much.

I want to especially thank Aarti Mittal and Anuraag Mittal. They have been there for me since the inception of the idea and at every step of the book. Finally, thanks to Rajni, my wife, and our two children, Umika and Adi. For a long time now, I have been consumed in writing this book. Their support and patience, explicit and implicit, is the reason this book is seeing the light of day.

SECTION 1

The Context:
Past, Present, and Future

Chapter 1

Destination: India's New Golden Age

You have to dream before your dreams can come true.

— A. P. J. Abdul Kalam, author, scientist,
and former president of India

New Delhi, 2047: Gautama Raju, along with Arjun Das, Meera Gupta, Ziya Khan, Pooja Shah, and Amarjit Singh, were just awarded the National Impact Award from the prime minister. This is indeed a memorable milestone in Gautama's promising life.

Gautama was the first person from his coastal village in Andhra Pradesh to get a college degree. It was just a few decades or so back that Gautama caught the attention of his teachers and parents with his fervent passion for reading and learning. His talent and hard work earned him a prestigious scholarship to attend a nearby high school. Gautama's interest in chemistry, biology, languages, and history grew with each passing day. He represented his school in Sanskrit and Telugu debate competitions and wrote articles for his school's weekly newspaper. For fun, he played soccer and cricket and listened to music. While in eleventh class, he and his friend built a prototype of a new type of solar cell that won the school a first prize in a national science competition.

Based on his high school results, science projects, glowing recommendations from teachers, and thirst for learning, he was given a full scholarship for his undergraduate studies at one of the premier research universities in the world — the National University of India (NUI), Gandhinagar, Gujarat. He completed a dual degree in chemical engineering and Indian history with a minor in Sanskrit. Gautama and his faculty members agreed that pursuing a PhD degree at one of the fifty NUIs matched well with Gautama's loves — learning, innovating, and making an impact in India.

His research work while earning his PhD broke new grounds in solar chemistry. He continued his research after joining NUI Varanasi as a professor of chemistry and chemical engineering. His discoveries and inventions spawned a new homegrown solar cell and storage industry. The National Impact Award, the most prestigious form of recognition from the government of India, includes Rs ten crores (US$1.5 million dollars) in prize money. Gautama Raju received this award for making an impact at a national scale and helping solve India's energy challenge.

Gautama Raju, forty, has a bright future. Raju's journey and accomplishments also bodes well for the over twenty million students who are graduating from colleges and universities in India in 2047. There are many and diverse choices for studying and employment for all. World-class research universities, and master's level colleges and community colleges have become hubs for learning, and making an impact in society. The structural barriers that once held back the engines of economic and employment growth have been addressed. Now, entrepreneurship, research, innovation, and industry-university collaborations are thriving across all fields around the country.

This is India's new Golden Age! This is also the new Golden Age for Gautama, his parents, and their community. Gautama has given his time and money to improve his village. He has also become a role model for the entire community. Kids have hope and high aspirations. So do their parents.

National Impact Award Winners:
Torchbearers of India's New Golden Age

India's 1.8 billion people are participating and contributing to this budding golden era. Those who are making contributions at a national scale are being recognized and rewarded with the National Impact Award. Like Gautama Raju, whose contributions have led to addressing India's enormous energy needs, his fellow awardees are equally stellar in their respective contributions.

Pooja Shah and Amarjit Singh: Revolutionizing Agriculture and Farmers' Profits

The first couple to be awarded, Pooja Shah and Amarjit Singh, have systematically transformed agriculture in India. Their efforts for the last fifteen years have improved farm productivity across the country. Water and energy usage have dropped, storage losses have plummeted, and profits for farmers have quadrupled.

National Impact Award Winners: 2047

1. Arjun Das: home services
2. Meera Gupta: water
3. Ziya Khan: health care
4. Gautama Raju: solar energy
5. Pooja Shah and Amarjit Singh: agriculture

Amarjit grew up in Yuba City, California, and is a fifth-generation Indian American and farmer. He grew up hearing stories about his ancestors in Punjab. The flowing rivers, rich soil, abundant crops, *makkai ki roti aur sarson ka saag* (a favorite meal in Punjab), bhangra, *giddha* (a folk dance), and so much more. He always yearned to go back and see the villages. His heritage and his desire to do something different propelled him to pursue agricultural engineering at the University of California (UC), Davis.

Pooja grew up in Gujarat and wanted to take her interest in gadgets and experimentation further and was admitted to the UC Davis College of Engineering. Pooja and Amarjit met at a Holi festival organized by UC Davis's Indian Students Association.

By the end of his four years at Davis, Amarjit wanted to do something groundbreaking. Pooja wanted to return to India and make an impact. Soon they realized that by combining their interests and strengths, they could achieve their dreams and be together as well. After completing their studies, they moved to India, got married, and joined a family farm in Punjab. Little by little, they started applying their knowledge, skills, and innovations to the family farm. The results exceeded everyone's expectations. The local farms and their friends started asking for their help. Demand for their knowledge and skills grew significantly and quickly. They started a consulting firm. Now, they are recognized experts in the country providing valuable advice to farmers and to those in the agriculture industry.

Ziya Khan: Transforming Health Care IT Services

Grandmother of two, Ziya Khan, was recognized for revolutionizing the health care IT services in India. Born in Meerut, Ziya studied computer science at the Delhi College of Engineering, worked for a few years at Tata Consultancy Services (TCS), got married, and settled in Bhopal. After her kids completed their education, she decided to pursue a master's in computer science. While studying, she became intrigued by the master's in public health program that was being offered at NUI Bhopal. She doubled up and kept the home running while studying. Her husband and kids encouraged her interests and took on some of the chores at home. As part of her master's thesis, she conducted research on health care services in villages and smaller towns. She found that most people depended on word-of-mouth referrals to find doctors and quality health care services. Furthermore, there was no way to ascertain effectively and quickly the quality of the referrals. This problem intrigued her. She discussed this with her faculty members and fellow students.

Soon Ziya came up with a solution. She would create a health care IT service that would fill the information gap. She developed a prototype, recruited some of her colleagues from her TCS days, reached out to some venture capitalists, and received seed capital to finish the product. Her faculty adviser, a renowned MD-PhD, encouraged Ziya and later joined the company's board of directors. The first version was successfully tested out in and around Bhopal, then in Madhya Pradesh (MP). Its adoption was slow and steady. However, customer retention was almost 100 percent. After fine-tuning some feature enhancements and signing some key partnerships, the service went national. The rest, as they say, is history. Now, Ziya's mobile phone–based app is as ubiquitous as the device itself around the nation.

Meera Gupta: Bringing Clean Water to Your Homes 24–7

Meera Gupta won the National Impact Award for developing a water desalination technology that is extensively being used to meet the water needs in the country. She started a company based on this technology and has rapidly grown it into one of the largest and most successful corporations in the nation.

Meera grew up in Mumbai. As a child, she was exposed to acute water shortages. Her parents would wake up at four a.m. to ensure that water for drinking, washing, and cooking was stored in various containers and drums. Her parents and doctors recommended that she drink only filtered water. As a college student, she was aware of the dropping water tables around the country and rising sea levels that could damage the country's vast coastal regions. She decided to do something about these water problems. Thus, she pursued bioengineering, completing her bachelor's from the Indian Institute of Technology (IIT) Delhi, master's from the Massachusetts Institute of Technology (MIT), and a PhD from NUI Trivandrum, which was established in 2020.

Returning to NUI Trivandrum was strategic, as several faculty members from a number of departments and colleges had established an interdisciplinary Water Research Center. They had successfully competed to win grants from a newly introduced GOI research grant initiative. Driven by passion, equipped with knowledge, and enabled by research grants, Meera toiled twelve to fourteen hours a day, seven days a week, for many years before making the breakthrough in the fourth year of her PhD. After building her prototype, defending her thesis, and licensing her technology from the institute, she launched her company. Meera's company has active research collaborations with NUI Trivandrum and a few additional universities. One of the faculty members is on the company's scientific advisory board. Now in its tenth year of existence, her company is closer than ever to achieving her dreams of solving the acute water shortage in India. Thanks to Meera and her company, her family, like most in India today, have a 24–7 water supply.

Arjun Das: Changing the Face of Home Services

The final awardee is Arjun Das. Based in Patna, he is the co-founder and managing director of Home Services Ltd. Home Services is a nationwide service that provides well-trained and certified electricians, plumbers, carpenters, painters, gardeners, maids, cooks, and drivers. Now in its twentieth year, it has become one of the largest employers in the country, boasting some of the highest customer satisfaction rates. Its brand is trusted nationally. And its toll-free number is on most Indians' speed dial.

As a person growing up in a middle-class family, Arjun was struck by how long it took his parents to get anything fixed in the home — whether it was the broken fan, faulty power inverter, or leaky roof. They would call someone, and on the off chance they showed up, they were hours late. Moreover, they did not always fix the problem the first time. He was also amazed to hear from all his uncles and aunties about how much time they spent looking for help such as maids and drivers to work in their homes.

Traditional education options did not catch his fancy, so when he completed secondary school, Arjun joined a local community college. Then one day a lightbulb switched on. He would start a company that would provide well-trained and certified personnel for homes. He would ensure quality, timeliness, and professionalism, and charge a premium. Arjun spoke with his friends, who found the idea very exciting. Arjun put together a business plan, borrowed money from friends and family, and launched his company with two partners. It took years of hard work to perfect the business — finding, training, and retaining the workers, fine-tuning the business model, building the call center, polishing the brand, raising additional funding, and building the management team. The hard work and countless hours have paid off. Home Services is one of the most trusted brands in India and one of the largest employers.

The National Impact Awards in the year 2047 are symbols of a nation that finds itself to be prosperous, peaceful, and vibrant.

India's New Golden Age:
For All Its People and Future Generations

In 2047, one hundred years after its independence, India is a transformed nation. Now, India is well on its way to becoming the Golden Bird once again. Its economy is thriving in urban centers and villages. Foreign trade is robust. National boundaries are secure. Defense forces are strong, well prepared, and well equipped to defend the country. There is peace within. The legal justice system is fair and timely. The police are a respected and trusted force. Rivers, lakes, forests, parks, and wildlife are thriving. Public infrastructure is robust, safe, and adequate. Society has come to terms with its own history, diversity, strengths, and weaknesses. Gender equality is the norm. So is excellence. Making a meaningful impact in all walks of life has become a driving force. Talent, passion, and hard work are valued, nurtured, and rewarded. The education system from early education through higher education is marked by excellence and provides multiple pathways for its diverse people. India's pressing challenges of 2015 have been addressed and are now case studies for historians and writers. India and its neighbors are at peace, and the nation is trusted and respected around the world.

Mahatma Gandhi's vision of a united and prosperous India has been realized. B. R. Ambedkar's spirit of equality and dignity is embedded in society. Rabindranath Tagore's countrymen and women are awake, just as he had hoped for over a hundred years ago when he wrote, "Where the mind is without fear and the head is held high..."

This is India's new Golden Age! It is also a new Golden Age for *all* of its 1.8 billion people.

We can realize this dream. We have the potential, the natural resources, and over sixty-eight years of experience as an independent nation. We can learn from the successes and failures of the various experiments conducted and ideas implemented during this time.

How large is the gap between the dreams and vision of a Golden India and the realities of 2015? What are the challenges that we must overcome to build a brighter future? It may be useful to first acknowledge how far we have come since our independence.

Indian textiles were competitive in cost and quality and were banned in Britain. Indian weavers earned competitive wages: fifty-five to one hundred and sixty pounds of grains per week compared to forty to one hundred and forty pounds of grains earned per week by their counterparts in Britain.

India 2015: Remarkable Progress Since 1947

We have made remarkable progress since 1947, when we became independent after over two hundred years of oppressive and devastating domination by the East India Company and Great Britain. In India's glorious past, over a thousand years ago when it was rich and had a vibrant economy, it was referred to as the Golden Bird. India's economic prosperity, rich natural resources, abundant food, and talented artisans had attracted traders from around the world for thousands of years. "It was to reach this India of fabulous riches that Columbus sailed the seas,"[1] wrote Will Durant, historian and Pulitzer Prize–winning author in *The Case for India*. During that time, manufacturing thrived and India was an exporter of rice. Indian textiles were competitive in cost and quality and were banned in Britain. Indian weavers earned competitive wages: fifty-five to one hundred and sixty pounds of grains per week compared to forty to one hundred and forty pounds of grains earned per week by their counterparts in Britain.[2]

However, India's political weakness and lack of unity attracted invaders. A. L. Basham, historian and author, noted in the *Wonder That Was India* that "the history of the succeeding centuries (after Harsha's death in AD 647) is a rather drab story of endemic warfare between rival dynasties."[3] The invaders included the Bactrians, Greeks, and Huns. Mahmud of Ghazni from 1001 to 1027 carried out seventeen raids. Muhammad of Ghor invaded in 1173, and Qutb-al-Din Aibak, his chief, occupied Delhi, which marked the beginning of the Muslim rule of India.[4] These invaders looted the country and destroyed its symbols of power, knowledge, and worship. During the Mughal Empire, India witnessed a revival in prosperity, arts, and literature, perhaps best epitomized by the building of the Taj Mahal in the seventeenth century.

Durant noted that, "When [the] British came, India was politically weak, and economically prosperous."[5] The British took advantage of this political weakness, playing one king against another, one class against another, one religion against another, and one caste against another to grow and maintain their domination. The divide et impera, meaning "divide and rule," principle was adopted by the British to win and rule India.[6]

Britain destroyed key institutions, and India was left mostly illiterate.[7] They also left us poor. British taxed heavily – up to 50 percent of the produce. British used the same tax revenues to maintain an army to rule India. The exploitation and taxes led to poverty, starvation, and death due to famines and poor nutrition. Close to twenty-five million Indians died during the famines, primarily because they could not afford food. Infant mortality reached its height. In Bengal, close to 50 percent of kids died before they reached the age of eight. India also paid for Britain's wars outside of India. It is estimated that if all the wealth drained from India since 1757 had been invested in India instead, it would have been worth US$400 billion by the early 1930s.[8] According to Angus Maddison, a British economist, in 1700s, around the time of British and East

India Company foray into India, India's share of world GDP was 24.4 percent. In 1950, just after British left, it was a mere 4.2 percent.[9]

Considering our past, especially British rule and how much we lost during those times, we have come a long way.

We are the largest democracy in the world, and ever since 1947, we have had successful transfer of power at the central and state governments. We are one of the fastest growing large economies in the world. Our gross domestic product (GDP) has grown by almost eighteen times since 1950–51, and GDP per capita has grown by more than five times during the same period. The literacy rate in males has climbed from 27 percent to 82 percent and in females from 9 percent to 65 percent. Life expectancy at birth has shot up from thirty-two years to sixty-six years.[10] The media, consisting of about 86,000 newspapers and periodicals and 831 TV channels, is relatively free and active.[11] Thanks to the green revolution and the milk revolution, we are not dependent on imports for survival. Advances in telecom, mobile, and Internet connectivity have significantly improved communication and facilitated commerce. In 2014, there were over two hundred and forty million Internet users[12] and nine hundred million mobile phone users.

"When [the] British came, India was politically weak, and economically prosperous."

Alumni of academic institutions established after 1947, such as the All India Institute of Medical Sciences (AIIMS), the Indian Institute of Technology (IIT), and the Indian Institute of Management (IIM), have done exceedingly well. Many are trailblazers in various walks of life. Nonresident Indians (NRIs) are chief executive officers, chief technology officers, middle managers, and professionals in Fortune 500 companies around the world. NRIs have founded over 13 percent of the Silicon Valley starts-ups.[13] Bollywood has a global presence. The national cricket team is one of the top teams in the world. Several sportsmen and -women have reached the top of the world rankings. A number of corporate houses such as Tata, Infosys, and Wipro have become globally recognized companies.

Since the economic liberalization in 1991, the top 20 percent of the country has seen its living standards improve beyond most people's expectations. There are now ninety billionaires in India, and India's super rich are among the top five in the world in terms of numbers and total wealth.[14]

India's New Golden Age and 2015:
Numerous Mega Challenges Away

Despite significant progress made since 1947, India faces significant challenges, and we are frequently performing well below our potential. Arjun Malhotra, co-founder of Hindustan Computers Limited (HCL), is a pioneer of India's IT industry. He also cofounded Techspan, the Indian School of Business (ISB), and the Society for Promotion of Indian Classical Music and Culture Amongst Youth (SPICMACAY). When I spoke to him about this book, he noted that, "problems are staring in your face." He cited a few examples from multiple sectors: 1) poor infrastructure is resulting in 30 percent loss in food production; 2) poor intergovernmental coordination and execution is contributing to malnourishment and infant mortality; 3) lack of timely action resulted in more people being affected by the 2014 floods in Jammu and Kashmir, and 4) some of the Council of Scientific and Industrial Research (CSIR) labs are completely ineffective.[15] Malhotra is an IIT Kharagpur alumnus and one of the most optimistic and humble people I have met. A Doon School graduate, he walks with a "can-do" attitude and has a sunny personality. Coming from him, the long list was especially disturbing. His sentiments are echoed by most of the industry leaders I interviewed.

India is facing problems on a mega scale, and these problems confront you as you speak with people, walk the streets, ride on a train, or live in the country. They affect hundreds of millions of Indians regardless of their demographics or affiliations. I call them India's "mega challenges."

Poverty

Poverty is striking. According to government figures, 363 million Indians are below the poverty line (BPL). That's close to 30 percent of the population. This official number is based on a rather low BPL benchmark of Rs 47 per person per day for people in urban areas and Rs 32 per person per day for people in rural areas.[16] Some refer to the official BPL line as a starvation line because the group is remarkably poor. For this segment of the society, two complete meals for the family is a challenge, let alone access to warm clothes, health, education, shelter, and sanitary living and work conditions.

The National Council of Applied Economic Research (NCAER) and McKinsey estimate households in poverty to have less than Rs 90,000 (US$1,500) in annual income. Households with income between Rs 90,000 and 200,000 (US$3,333) are considered lower income. According to McKinsey, in 1985, the extremely poor constituted 93 percent and the lower income constituted 6 percent. The McKinsey study that was published in May 2007 estimated that in 2005 the percentage of the extremely poor was 54 percent and the lower income was 41 percent, and by 2015, the extremely poor would be 35 percent and the lower income would be 43 percent. Even though the percentage of the extremely poor has dropped considerably since 1985, 78 percent of India's population is still in the lower income and extremely poor segments.[17]

In May 2015, I attended a talk by P. Sainath at Stanford University. Sainath is the former rural affairs editor of *The Hindu* and the 2007 winner of the Ramon Magsaysay Prize. He spoke about his latest initiative—the People's Archive of Rural India. When I asked him about official poverty figures in India, he remarked that there could be three different official figures for the poverty level, it just depended on the government's political objectives. His talk highlighted the amazing diversity in rural India—833 million people, 780 languages, unique livelihoods, and innumerable stories.[18] It also highlighted the abject poverty in most of rural India. So I started calculating the poverty levels on my own, with data from various sources. According to the 1991–92 National Commission on Farmers (NCF) data, over 85 percent of households in villages had no land, or submarginal, marginal, or small land holdings. This group is poor, and their numbers have increased since NCF data was collected in the early 1990s.[19] Even if we assume 30 percent of the urban population is extremely poor, this would make India's poor in the 60 to 70 percent range. Thus, there are at least seven hundred million living in poverty in India, which is equal to Europe's population.

Thus, there are at least seven hundred million living in poverty in India, which is equal to Europe's population.

While we have made progress in reducing poverty levels, we still have to lift over seven hundred million people out of poverty.

Economy and Global Competitiveness

India's extreme poverty is a reflection on its economy. There are not enough jobs and opportunities for its people. While the population has ballooned from 361 million in 1950–51 to close to 1.2 billion in 2010–11, employment in organized sectors serves a mere twenty-nine million people.[20] New venture creation that is critical for new jobs has grown in the last few years but is just a drop in the ocean. Venture capital investment in the country is a mere 3.7 percent of the global total.[21] Dependence on imports is high, with over 70 percent of capital expenditures spent on imports.[22] There is also an urban–rural GDP per capita imbalance. While 70 percent of the population lives in villages, agriculture accounts for just 18 percent of the GDP.[23]

The World Economic Forum (WEF) periodically assesses global competitiveness of countries on twelve "pillars," which include institutions, infrastructure, macroeconomic environment, health and primary education, higher education and training, goods market efficiency, labor market efficiency, financial market development, technological readiness, market size, business sophistication, and innovation. The index is a measure of an economy's productivity, which is linked directly with the level of prosperity for the nation.[24] In WEF's publication the *Global Competitiveness Report 2014–15*, India is ranked seventy-one among one hundred and forty-four economies.[25]

The table 1.1 highlights select indicators and compares them with the United States, the largest economy in the world; China, the most populous country in the world; Singapore, an island nation that got its independence in 1965; and South Korea, a country that has transformed from one of the poorest countries in 1960s to one of the richest today.

Table 1.1: Key Indicators: India vs. USA, China, Singapore and South Korea					
Select Indicators	India	USA	China	Singapore	South Korea
Total Population *(in millions)*	1,252.1	316.2	1,357.4	5.4	50.2
Gross Domestic Product (GDP) *(in constant 2005 US$, billions)*	$1,458.7	$14,450.3	$4,864.0	$199.2	$1,119.9
GDP per capita *(in constant 2005 US$)*	$1,165	$45,710	$3,583	$36,897	$23,892
Select Health Indicators					
Life Expectancy at birth (years)	66	79	75	82	81
Infant mortality rate *(per 1000 live births)*	41	6	11	2	3
Immunization, DPT *(% of children ages 12-23 months)*	72%	94%	99%	97%	99%
Improved sanitation facilities *(% of population with access)*	36%	100%	65%	100%	100%
Corruptions Perception Index (Rank)	85	17	100	7	43
Global Competitive Index (Rank)	71	3	28	2	26

Sources: Global Competitive Index is from The World Economic Forum; Corruptions Perception Index is from Transparency International; all others are World Development Indicators, World Bank based on the latest 2010-2014 data (last accessed on March 22, 2015)

Table created by Shail Kumar

We have to significantly increase our productivity to deliver economic prosperity to all the Indians.

Urban Migration

The abject poverty facing rural India has led to one of the most significant movements of people in history— urban migration. The people are moving to urban centers with the hope of a better future for themselves and their families. They are expecting better employment, education, and living conditions. The scale and speed

Over four hundred million people, a number that exceeds the United States population by one hundred million, are expected to move from villages to cities in the next thirty-five years.

of the migration has created a host of issues around infrastructure, such as housing, roads, transportation, health, and education. Close to 50 percent of the people in Mumbai are living in slums.[26]

In 1951, the urban population in India was sixty-two million people, 17 percent of the total population. By 2011, it was 377 million, or 31 percent. It is expected that by 2025 the urban population will be 42.5 percent, and by 2050, it will be close to 50 percent or 800 million.[27] Over 400 million people, a number that exceeds the United States population by one hundred million, are expected to move from villages to cities in the next thirty-five years.

Energy – Water – Food – Health – Environment

The basic needs of the people—food, water, energy, health, and environment—are interconnected in many important ways. We need energy and water to grow food. For good health, we need nutritious food, clean and safe drinking water, energy, and a clean environment. For water and energy, we need forests, rivers, glaciers, and reliable rainfalls. The interconnected issues of energy, water, food, health, and environment are rapidly reaching crisis mode. India now ranks last among one hundred and thirty-two countries in air pollution.[28]

Healthy people make a healthy nation. However, around 42 percent of children under the age of five suffer from malnutrition. Furthermore, over 50 percent of Indian households do not have attached toilets and have to defecate outside in the open. Matters are made worse by the grossly inadequate (in quantity and quality of) public services related to education and health. Public Health Centers (PHC) are the first line of defense for the poor for their health care needs. PHCs have worker absenteeism of 38 to 58 percent, only approximately 36 percent have a regular power supply, only 20 percent have a telephone, and only 12 percent enjoy regular maintenance.[29] As a result of poor services, India's record on immunization, infant mortality, and nourishment is lagging behind most nations.

Lack of 24-7 energy is a serious issue affecting farmers, industry, and people. Currently, 56 percent of the population has no access or has only four to six hours of intermittent access to electricity in their homes.[30] Very few cities in the country enjoy a 24-7 power supply. Most of the country has become accustomed or resigned to irregular power supply and blackouts. There is a huge gap between energy demand and current energy supply.

There is also a significant water demand and supply mismatch in the country. Agriculture drives around 90 percent of the demand for water, and the rest is driven by home and industrial consumption. Approximately 30 percent of the rural population lacks access to drinking water, and of the twenty-nine states in India, only seven have full availability of drinking water for rural inhabitants. None of the thirty-five Indian cities with a population of more than one million distributed water for more than a few hours per day. India depends heavily on monsoons and groundwater for its water supply.[31] Yet, due to several factors, we are not making the most of the water in our vast river system and water received during monsoons. The water-storage systems can hold just thirty days of rainfall compared to nine hundred days in developed countries. India is tapping just 20 percent of the hydroelectric potential compared to 80 percent in the advanced nations.[32] The water distribution system is also inadequate, encouraging individuals to dig private wells. The policy of giving free electricity for agriculture has also led to wasteful use of groundwater. The polluted rivers have also increased dependence on groundwater. As a result, groundwater levels are dropping to crisis levels, and around 21 percent of communicable diseases in India are linked to unsafe drinking water.[33] The urban migration is taking people to more water-strapped cities, which will make the situation worse.

According to Asit Biswas — winner of the Stockholm Water Prize, which is considered to be the most prestigious prize in its field — and Cecilia Tortajada, "If the country (India) continues with its past and present practices, the country will face an unprecedented water crisis around 2030, the magnitude and extent of which no other earlier generation had to face."[34] Since energy, water, food, health, and the environment are interrelated issues, Biswas and Tortajada's warning applies to all of them.

Climate Change

Climate change is a global phenomenon and is expected to affect everyone. However, it is likely to affect some nations and communities more than others, especially the poor. It is forecasted that there will be more extreme weather patterns, such as extreme rains and extreme droughts. It is also forecasted that glaciers will melt more quickly and sea levels will rise.

Rising sea levels will affect India's 7,517 kilometer coastline. The wealthy countries and communities have the resources to adapt to rising sea levels by building seawalls and moving critical infrastructure away from harm's way. People along India's coastlines are mostly poor and depend on sea and land for their livelihoods. Climate change induced rising sea level has the potential of a significant disruption, especially to India's 170 million people who live in coastal districts.[35]

Extreme rains and drought cycles will further pressure India's fragile agriculture-based livelihoods, economy, and food production. The faster melting glaciers in the Himalayas will affect India's famous rivers, the water supply, and the waterways. It is expected to become another source of geopolitical tension, especially with its neighbors, particularly China. This has the potential of impacting most of India's 1.3 billion people.

Gender Inequality and Women's Security

There are a number of important issues related to gender inequality and women's security facing the nation. One metric in some ways sums it all up. The female-male ratio in the zero to six years has fallen from 927 girls per 1,000 boys in 2001 to 914 girls per 1,000 boys in 2011. Haryana has the worst record with a mere 819 girls per 1,000 boys. The world human sex ratio is 1.07 male/female at birth, while in India it is 1.12 male/female.[36] The Indian society values male life over female. Parents and grandparents take extreme measures to ensure a male birth. There are horror stories about sex-selective abortion.

In 2013, the tragic death of a female student after a brutal rape in Delhi highlighted the issues with women's security in India. The BBC's documentary on this tragedy, which became famous on social media with the hashtag #IndiasDaughter, was banned by the Indian government.[37] Those who supported the ban and those who believe that BBC's coverage was harsh missed the central point. Women's security, despite India not being the rape capital based on per capita rape figures, is a serious problem. Mothers, sisters, daughters, and female friends are strongly urged not to travel alone in the evening. They are scared for their safety. If they take a taxi, they check the number plate before boarding, message friends and relatives, and inform them after reaching the destination safely. Physical, mental, and emotional harassment of girls and women is endemic.

Over five hundred million Indian women of all ages are directly and indirectly affected. So are many of their male family members.

Law and Order

To enable a robust economy, peaceful society, and a united nation, a fair and just law and order system is critical. The laws have to be the same across the country for all people, and justice has to be timely. Justice delayed is justice denied. In 2014, there were 31.3 million pending cases in the lower courts, of which four million were in the high courts and sixty-four thousand in the Supreme Court.[38] The cases can take decades to close.[39] In April 2015, Chief Justice of India H. L. Dattu cited judicial vacancies as the primary reason for the delays.[40] India has 1.2 judges for every one hundred thousand people, compared to three in Canada, four in Australia, and 10.8 in the United States.[41] Cases on a "fast track" usually take several years. In addition, a person without access to power or influence has little or no chance of getting justice. The police force is considered to be mostly in the pockets of the rich, the famous, and the politicians. It is feared by most of the poor and the middle class and honest and law-abiding citizens.

In May 2015, Bollywood superstar Salman Khan was found guilty of killing a person while driving under the influence of alcohol. Several other men were also hurt. The accident occurred in September 2002.[42] Following several twists and turns, a guilty verdict was announced thirteen years after the accident. Social media was buzzing with Bollywood stars and Khan's fans crying foul and asking for leniency. The tragic death of Nurullah Sharif and its impact on his family mostly took a backseat. Also, Ravindra Patil, a policeman and prime witness against Khan, was forgotten. Patil was fired from service several years back and died from tuberculosis, a poor and abandoned person. Is this case an exception, where a poor person killed while sleeping on a footpath gets justice? Or is this yet another case where the rich and privileged person never steps in jail despite committing a crime? The case is unfolding, and history is still being made. However, it is clear that justice has been delayed for Sharif's and Patil's families, and thus justice has been denied to them.

Not only are the aggrieved parties affected, their respective families are also impacted. Thus, close to 170 million Indians are affected by the slow-moving justice system. The malfunctioning justice system also turns away people from seeking a legal remedy or pursuing an extrajudicial solution. Finally, the poor legal system also encourages and enables corruption, which affects the entire nation.

Corruption

Corruption is endemic and affects most parts of society. Gurcharan Das's *India Grows at Night* primarily revolves around this topic. Transparency International, a global coalition against corruption, compares corruption around the world. In their 2014 *Corruptions Perception Index,* India is ranked eighty-fifth and is considered one of the most corrupt countries in the world.[43] Most transactions that need certification or services from the government require bribery. These include basic services, such as getting a driver's license, marriage license, death certificate, ration card, or passport. At the highest levels, there are scams involving political leaders, bureaucrats, and the government running into lakhs of crores. Some of the prominent ones are the Coal Scam, Spectrum Scam, Commonwealth Games Scam, and Land Scam, to name just a few.

The Association for Democratic Reforms, which was established in 1999 by a group of professors from IIM Ahmedabad, reported on the Lok Sabha elections of 2014. They found that 34 percent of the winners, or one hundred and eighty-six out of the five hundred and forty-one elected, had declared criminal cases against themselves. Furthermore, 21 percent had serious criminal cases declared against themselves, such as murder, attempted murder, communal disharmony, kidnapping, and crimes against women.[44]

In the FICCI-Pinkerton India Risk Survey 2015, corruption, bribery, and corporate fraud were ranked as the topmost risks to the entire economic system of the country.

Das's eloquent comment sums it all up: "And lo and behold, a lawbreaker has become the lawmaker." It is also becoming a family business or dynasty rule. Patrick French in *India: A Portrait* notes that every member of parliament (MP) under the age of thirty and over 67 percent of MPs under the age of forty have inherited their seat.[45]

In the Federation of India Chambers of Commerce and Industry's FICCI-Pinkerton India Risk Survey 2015, corruption, bribery, and corporate fraud were ranked as the topmost risks to the entire economic system of the country. In a recent report by Global Financial Integrity, black money that left India is estimated to have jumped from US$10 billion in 2003 to US$94.7 billion in 2012. The actual amounts are likely to be higher. The impact of corruption is not just in lost revenues. Corruption favors nonmeritorious factors for business deals, promotions, and awards. It is making India unattractive to some of the best and the brightest people. It is also attracting the wrong people to vital roles and positions. Finally, funds are not reaching areas where they could be making a significant impact on people's lives, such as food, health, energy, water, environment, infrastructure, and education.

Education

Education at all levels is yet another mega challenge facing India. According to the Government of India's Census 2011:[46]

- Approximately 900 million people, accounting for 75 percent of its population, are forty years of age or younger

- 630 million people, accounting for 52 percent, are twenty-five years of age or younger

- 470 million people, accounting for 39 percent, are eighteen years of age or younger, and

- Close to 70 percent of India's population is rural

Potentially, there are twenty-six million kids to be taught in *every* class for the foreseeable future. The sheer magnitude pales everything else in comparison. Furthermore, the public schools are marked by teacher absenteeism of 20 percent and student absenteeism of 33 percent. The Program for International Student Assessment (PISA) placed India at the bottom of the seventy-four countries it assessed. The ASER Survey of 2011 found that 58 percent of children enrolled in classes three to five could only read at a class one level. The India Human Development Survey (2004–05) found that only 50 percent of all children aged eight to eleven years enrolled in a government school were able to read a simple paragraph with three sentences. The Wipro-Educational Initiatives Quality Education Study (2011) noted that reading and math skills of class-four pupils in India's "top schools" are below the international average.[47]

Higher education or postsecondary education, including vocational education, is also facing several challenges. The gross enrollment ratio (GER), which is a globally accepted indicator of students enrolled in the higher education system, is merely 20 percent.[48] GER is the total number of students between the ages of eighteen and twenty-three enrolled in higher education institutions divided by the total number of people in that age bracket. According to various surveys, depending on the sector, 60 to 90 percent of the graduating students are considered unemployable.[49] India does not have even one world-class comprehensive research university. Finally, there is just one Indian institution in the top 500 in one of the world university rankings.[50]

These are India's mega challenges. We must address these challenges urgently to create our new Golden Age. We must build a bridge to cross this chasm. We have much to do.

Building a Golden India:
One Student, One Professional, and One Teacher at a Time

To build our new golden era, the seeds of transformation must be sowed now, which means making this happen in the context of our twenty-first-century realities. The world as we know it is smaller, more connected, and fiercely competitive.

To lift over 700 million people from poverty, the nation's economy has to be more vibrant, multifaceted, and sustainable. We need millions of new start-ups that will create new jobs. We have to significantly increase productivity in all our sectors. Most of the mega challenges are complex and multidisciplinary. Increasing productivity and solving mega challenges would require large numbers of experts in every field. They would also need to collaborate and experiment with many ideas. The successful ideas must then be scaled effectively, efficiently, and quickly. Thus, the research and innovation ecosystem has to be significantly expanded. The situation also demands large numbers of well-prepared and educated professionals in all walks of life—armed forces personnel, artists, bureaucrats, businessmen and -women, doctors, engineers, farmers, humanists, lawyers, politicians, police force members, researchers, scientists, service and manufacturing industry workers, and teachers.

"Education was thus perceived as the chief agency for accomplishing the great moral agenda of colonialism."

Finally, close to 900 million people are forty years of age or younger and represent the potential of a "demographic dividend."

20

India's young population has dreams and aspirations of a better future for themselves and their families. They are also looking for social and income mobility.

Education is also the only systematic and proven way to unleash people's passion, power, and potential and to prepare them for a productive life and career. The importance of education in improving the economy, health, and people's lives is well recognized. Education continues to play a critical role in the United States' knowledge-based and innovation-driven economy. Countries such as South Korea, Singapore, and Finland have transformed themselves from poor nations to among the wealthiest countries in the world based on a systematic transformation of their education system. The twelve pillars in WEF's Global Competitive Index include two pillars on education—health and primary education and higher education and training. All other pillars are directly or indirectly affected by education.

Education has historically been important to Indians. We may be one of the few societies where there is a god and goddess of knowledge, intellect, and wisdom. Takshashila and Nalanda Universities were among the first universities in the world, established over a thousand years before the first Western university was founded. The teachers were among the most revered in the society. People in villages and towns, alongside kings and merchants, used to financially support the teachers and educational institutions. There are innumerable stories and anecdotes from history where the king would rise from his throne and come down to welcome the learned gurus and *acharyas*.

"Give a man a fish and you feed him for a day. Teach a man to fish and you feed him for a lifetime."

Those who invaded India in the twelfth century and the imperial rulers knew the importance of education. The invaders destroyed educational institutions such as Nalanda, burning its libraries and killing most of the teachers. And Britain, during its imperial rule of India, used education as a way to further subjugate us and serve their colonial objectives. Krishna Kumar—professor of education at Delhi University, former director of the National Council of Educational Research and Training, and author of *Politics of Education in Colonial India*—notes in his book, "Education was thus perceived as the chief agency for accomplishing the great moral agenda of colonialism."[51]

21

The schools and universities started by the British and the missionaries were meant to instill British and Christian values and create a cadre of Indians who could interact with the British rulers and be intermediaries with their countrymen and -women. The British centralized curriculum and teachers' compensation related decisions. As a result, teachers and the curriculum got disconnected with their respective local community and teachers also lost their status in society.[52]

Rabindranath Tagore aptly captured India's malaise under the British rule: "In my view the imposing tower of misery which today rests on the heart of India has its sole foundation in the absence of education."[53] Many have heard the wise words of Maimonides, a Spanish philosopher: "Give a man a fish and you feed him for a day. Teach a man to fish and you feed him for a lifetime." Tagore's views and Maimonides's wisdom are shared by almost everyone in independent India. It is the only known way for the 99 percent who are not in the 1 percent privileged class to move up socially and economically. Improved education also improves the health of the individuals, the families, and the community.

Rajan grew up in Bapatla, a village of forty thousand people in Andhra Pradesh. His early education was in a one-wall school with Telugu as the medium of instruction. Then his father got transferred and Rajan moved to a new school. Recognizing Rajan's talent, the principal of the new school recommended that Rajan be moved to a better school. At that time Rajan was in the seventh class and he faced two challenges simultaneously—a higher standard of education and English as the medium of instruction. On his first day of class, he could not understand a word. Too anxious to speak to his father about his predicament, Rajan did what every motivated and hardworking kid in India does—he doubled up on his studies. Every day after school, he taught himself. He started with class one books and worked his way up. By the time he reached tenth class, he came in second in an English debate. His confidence grew, and he realized that he could learn anything. He went on to earn his undergraduate degree in economics from Loyola College, an MBA from Xavier Labor Relations Institute (XLRI) in Jamshedpur, and most recently a PhD from IIT Delhi.

Meet N. S. Rajan. He is Tata Group's chief human resources officer and a member of Tata's executive council. Prior to joining Tata, he was a partner of E&Y Consulting and head of its human resources practice worldwide.[54]

N. S. Rajan's inspiring story exemplifies the transformative impact of education, the value of motivation and hard work, and a family's commitment to their child's education. There are numerous stories of how parents are sacrificing to ensure their children get a good education. It is estimated that middle-class families are spending almost one-third of their monthly income on private tuitions and coaching classes so that their children can compete successfully in examinations for selection into higher education institutions. Many eat one meal per day so that they can send their children to school.

India's young population could potentially power India's economic engine for the near future and set the stage for the future generations. But before they can add higher value to the economy and the society, they all need to be educated and prepared for living and working. Narayana Murthy, in his book *A Better India: A Better World,* notes, "Progress is based on dreams and requires change. Change requires learning. Education is about learning to learn. Education is therefore the main instrument a nation has to achieve progress."[55]

Thus, transforming our education system is the most effective, efficient, and time sensitive way forward for the government and the people. The stages include early, primary, and secondary school education, higher education, and continuing education. While the entire education system needs to be transformed, higher education, including vocational education, offers India an incredible leverage.

Higher Education: One Key That Opens All Doors

Higher education is at an intersection of preparing young adults for working life and affects every aspect of our lives and careers. Its importance to the individual, society, and the nation is similar as the starting sample for making yogurt, seeds for cultivating crops, or seed crystal for preparing semiconductor wafers. To make yogurt at home, the starting sample determines the sweetness and thickness of the yogurt. In agriculture, the quality of the seed is considered critical for crop yields that eventually affect farmers' profits. In semiconductor manufacturing, the purity of the seed crystal ultimately drives the quality of the wafer, the plant productivity, and a firm's profitability. Similarly, preparation of the next generation of schoolteachers, faculty members, and professionals is critical for building and sustaining schools, higher education institutions, research and innovation ecosystem, new venture creation engine, corporations, and the government.

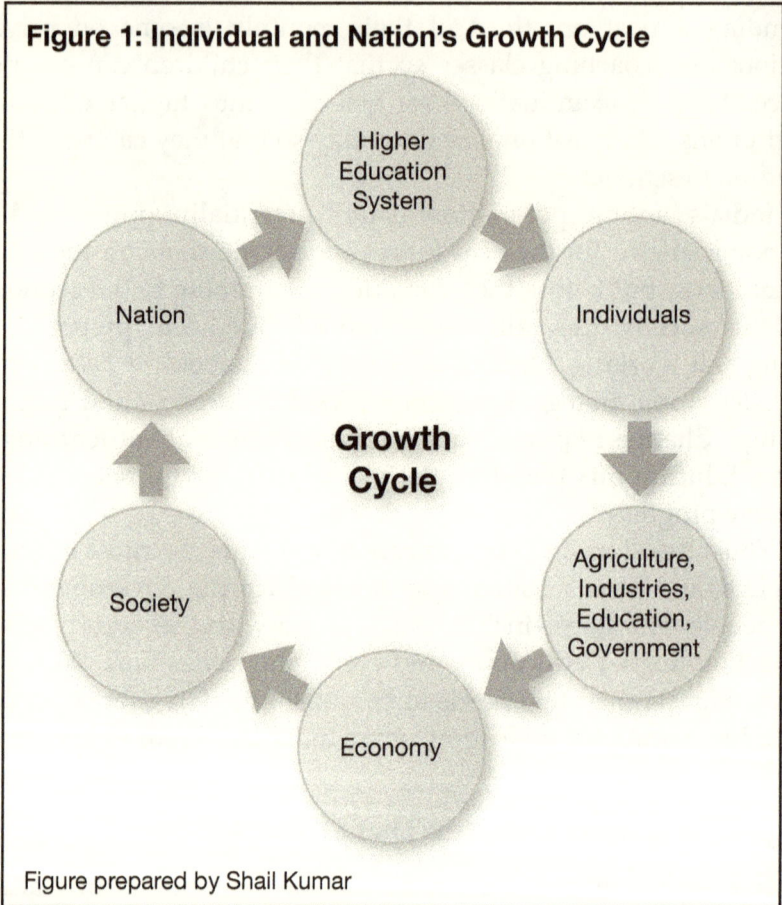

Figure 1: Individual and Nation's Growth Cycle

Higher Education System

Individuals

Nation

Growth Cycle

Agriculture, Industries, Education, Government

Society

Economy

Figure prepared by Shail Kumar

The Individual and Nation's Growth Cycle, as I like to call it, above, captures the importance of the higher education system to the individuals, economy, society and nation. Universities and colleges provide education to individuals and prepare them for life and careers. These well-prepared individuals add value in their professions in all walks of lives. As a result, productivity increases, services and solutions are more effective and efficient, mega challenges are addressed, and research, innovation and entrepreneurship are spurred. This makes the economy more vibrant, increases the tax revenues, and creates more jobs. Individuals, their families, and communities benefit from gainful employment, increases in income, and more dignified living. Society as a whole will become more peaceful and prosperous. The nation, as a result of improved economy, will be able to provide additional resources to enhance and sustain excellence in higher education system. This is a virtuous Growth Cycle.

Anand Kumar is the founder of Super 30, which provides free coaching for the Indian Institute of Technology Joint Entrance Exam (IIT JEE) to children of extremely low-income families. Super 30 also provides free lodging and boarding for the selected thirty students. IIT JEE is an entrance exam for the Indian Institutes of Technology. Less than 2 percent of students who take exam are selected by one of the IITs. In 2014, Kumar spoke at Stanford University, where I met him. His success is legendary — 308 students out of the 360 he has taught since 2002 have joined IITs. Considering the odds, Kumar's success percentage of close to 86 percent is off the charts. He shared several stories where he coached the students from extremely poor families. All of them, after joining IITs, went on to do really well in life. These students' successes not only transformed their life and their immediate family's lives, it also transformed their communities. The students also became role models for others in the community.

Sanjay Lalbhai, chairman and managing director of Arvind Limited, believes that "education is the single biggest tool for people, society, and the nation." He has seen the value being created in front of his eyes. His father and grandfather were catalysts and enablers in establishing several colleges and universities in Gujarat. Lalbhai currently serves on the board of governors of several educational institutions such as IIM Ahmedabad, Ahmedabad Education Society, and Ahmedabad University.[56]

Early and K–12 Education

The primary and secondary schoolteachers get their specialized degrees in all subjects, such as civics, geography, history, languages, mathematics, and science in the colleges and universities. They also earn their teaching credentials and a bachelor's in education (BEd) degree in a college or university. Thus, they receive their content expertise and teaching skills in higher education institutions. What is expected in higher education institutions significantly influences what teachers teach and students focus on at the school level. Knowledgeable teachers who inspire, mentor, and provide excellent education to their students are the most important factor in students' learning and future success. Anand Kumar is one of the inspirational teachers. There are many others who are touching the lives of students in positive and important ways.

Raghu Mahajan topped IIT JEE in 2006. In a meeting at Stanford University, where he is completing his PhD in physics, he recounted how three teachers were instrumental in his life and career choices and success. Until class tenth, he counts his father for his love for learning mathematics. He credits Arvind Chauhan, who he met when he joined Chauhan's IIT JEE coaching classes in Chandigarh, for his love for physics. During high school, Mahajan participated in Physics Olympiad training for three years. There he met his third influential teacher — Vijay Singh, then professor at IIT Kanpur and convener of the Physics Olympiad, who mentored and encouraged his love for physics.[57]

By his own admission, Rajiv Ratn Shah was not a good student until the seventh class. Then he was fortunate to be taught by some good teachers in a local school in Varanasi. Thanks to those teachers, he became interested in science and math. This propelled him to better grades in high school. He ended up joining Benares Hindu University (BHU). Currently, he is pursuing his PhD in computer science from the National University of Singapore (NUS).[58]

Growing up in Hyderabad, Suma Jaini had similar experiences. She was an average student until the eighth class. Thanks to her brother, she enrolled in Prasanthi Niketan coaching classes. The teachers ignited her mind, and she became fascinated with science and math. Two years later, she passed an entrance examination to join Ramaiah Coaching Institute. Jaini found the Ramaiah teachers outstanding as well. Thanks to the teachers at these coaching institutes, she got better and better in her studies. She went on to graduate from IIT Kharagpur with a bachelor's and master's in biotechnology. Jaini recently received her PhD from Boston University.[59]

There are innumerable stories about how great teachers have made an impact in a student's life. Teacher preparation that is fundamental to transforming early and K–12 education happens in higher education institutions. Thus, transforming higher education would also transform the K–12 education system by preparing well-educated and well-prepared teachers.

Higher Education and Continuing Education

Faculty members who will prepare the next generation of students for life and professions, including in academia, also get educated and prepared in colleges and universities. Thus, the higher education system keeps the cycle of learning and teaching moving forward. There is a significant skills shortage in the country. Vocational colleges provide valuable education and skills training, and prepare people for higher paying jobs. Midcareer professionals and senior leaders receive valuable retraining, continuing education, or specialized education in higher education institutions. Thus, transforming higher education will significantly improve the quality of faculty members and professionals.

Economy and Mega Challenges

The nation's economic productivity and competitiveness depends on people's productivity and creativity. Almost all professionals in all walks of life at various stages of life and career receive their education at higher education institutions. Thus, higher education impacts the nation's economy and vitality. The research and innovation that could occur in colleges and universities have the potential of addressing the mega challenges and also spurring entrepreneurship and the economy. We not only need job seekers but also job creators. We need millions of people like Gautama Raju, Arjun Das, Meera Gupta, Ziya Khan, Pooja Shah, and Amarjit Singh, the National Impact Award winners in 2047.

Thus, transforming higher education is the key to unleashing India's vast potential, providing valuable means to all people for personal and professional growth, transforming the K–12 education system, spurring the economy, and addressing India's mega challenges. It is the one key that opens all doors. It is the *Kamadhenu*[i] of modern times.

---

i   *Kamadhenu:* In *Vedas*, Kamadhenu, or Surabhi, is considered to be the mother of all cows who gives its owner whatever he or she desires.

So how is India's higher education system? How well is it serving the nation's, the society's, and the individual's needs? The next section and the three chapters analyze the system; the key issues facing students, parents, industry, society, and the nation; the impact the system has on all of its stakeholders; and the factors that are contributing to the current state of the system.

SECTION 2

The Challenge:
Peeling the Onion

Chapter 2

The Current System:
Broken and Disconnected

If I write at all it is not only because I feel deeply about India, but because life cannot wait till knowledge is complete. One must speak out, and take sides before the fight is over.

— Will Durant, historian, Pulitzer Prize–winning writer, author of *The Case for India*

Pune, 2014: Mukund Kapase recently joined an automobile company as an assembly-line worker after his dreams of joining the IT industry were repeatedly crushed. He was deemed "unemployable" by the IT companies even after receiving several degrees. India's higher education system has let Mukund and his family down. His story is similar to millions of India's youth graduating from colleges and universities across the country.

As the second son of a farmer in a village in Maharashtra, Mukund was the "chosen one" to attend the local college. His elder brother was "kept" in the village so he could take over his father's farm. His two younger sisters dropped out after eighth class. His parents did not want them to take a bus to a high school hours away from the village; there were too many instances of physical and emotional harassment to worry about, not to mention the lack of sanitary women-only restrooms. Mukund completed his twelfth class at a high school where teachers rarely showed up. When they did, they mostly read from the book or scribbled on the blackboard. Mukund's father paid for private tutoring so Mukund could pass the state board examinations and pursue a higher education.

After passing the twelfth-class exams, Mukund enrolled in one of the state's affiliated colleges. Like the majority of the affiliated colleges in Maharashtra and the nation, the college was owned and operated by a politician and his family members. The faculty members were mediocre and poorly paid, the infrastructure was decrepit, and the library and computer infrastructure were practically nonexistent. Unknown to his father, who had taken loans for Mukund's higher education, there was no incentive for Mukund to attend classes at the college. Everyone passed and got their degrees. Reality struck when he did not get any job offers after completing his three-year degree program. On a friend's recommendation, Mukund enrolled in a well-known one-year Information and Communication Technology (ICT) program. His father sold part of his land to finance this program. That did not help either, as none of the IT companies offered him a job. Frustrated, he finally joined a manufacturing company as an assembly-line worker. Ashamed that he did not live up to his father's dream, Mukund hardly visits his village. He is saving all he can to pay off his father's debts.

Is something fundamentally wrong with Mukund and millions of Indians graduating with one or more degrees? Or are the colleges and universities failing the youth? What is the state of India's higher education system? In this chapter, I address these and related questions.

India's higher education has come a long way since 1947. Based on 2013 and 2014 information, there were over 700 universities, 37,000 affiliated colleges, 11,400 stand-alone institutions, and several open- and distance-education universities.[1] Online programs are catching on for students and for teachers' training. In 2011, approximately 27.5 million students were

Key Numbers

- Global Rankings[1]: just **one** institution features in the **Top 500** (IISc ranked in 301–400)
- Total number of higher education institutions[2]: **732 universities, 37,204 colleges, 11,445 stand-alone institutions and several open- and distance-education universities**
- Student enrollments[3]: **27.5 million**
  - Affiliated Colleges: 74.3%
  - Open and distance: 12.1%
  - Stand-alone: 11.3%
  - Universities: 2.2%
- Gross Enrollment Ratio[3]: **19.4%**

Source: [1]www.shanghairanking.com, [2]www.mhrd.gov.in (provisional data for 2013 and 2014), [3]All India Survey of Higher Education (AISHE) data (2010–2011) published in 2013

enrolled in the system. Affiliated colleges accounted for approximately 74 percent of student enrollments, open- and distance-education 12 percent, stand-alone institutions 11 percent, and universities just over 2 percent.[2] In the immediate years following independence, large numbers of outstanding faculty members joined the higher education system, especially the newly established institutions, such as the IITs and IIMs, and also led the atomic and space efforts. Compared to many developing nations and where we were in 1947, we have done remarkably well.

However, the higher education system has fallen short of India's enormous potential—a country of 1.3 billion people and home to great thinkers, spiritual leaders, scientists, writers, and artists. Several leading thinkers such as Hermann Keyserling, Max Müller, and Mark Twain noted India's immense contributions to the world.

Not only has India fallen from its glorious past, its higher education system does not serve the needs and aspirations of its people. The over one billion people of India want to progress socially and financially. They want to reap the benefits of a free nation and a country rich in natural resources. They also want to overcome the daily challenges of easy access to water, health, education, and electricity. Finally, they want well-paying jobs and opportunities to prosper personally and professionally.

It was striking to me that almost everyone I interviewed felt that India's higher education was in crisis. India's higher education system is broken and disconnected. It is broken on all fronts that matter and is disconnected with the needs and aspirations of the students, parents, industry, society, and the nation. There are five key dimensions to the problem:

1. **Enrollments**: There is inadequate enrollment in the system. A mere 20 percent of the students in the eighteen-to-twenty-three-year-old age group are currently enrolled in higher education institutions.

2. **Excellence:** There is a severe shortage of excellent institutions. The few islands of excellence serve a small fraction of the population and have also fallen short of their potential.

3. **Structure and Scope:** Colleges and universities are inadequately preparing students for their careers and lives. Furthermore, there is no emphasis on conducting research and making an impact.

4. **Faculty Members and University Leaders:** There is a severe shortage of well-prepared faculty members and university leaders.

5. **World-Class Comprehensive Research University:** There is not one in the country and just one institution is in the top 500 of global rankings.

Taken together, these five dimensions capture the essence of India's current higher education system.

1. Enrollments: Grossly Inadequate

GER, as I noted earlier, is a metric used to measure access to higher education. In 2011, India's official GER was 19.4 percent, and 27.5 million students were enrolled in higher education. This implies that over ninety-three million Indians in the eighteen-to-twenty-three-year-old age bracket were *not* enrolled in higher education. India's GER also compares unfavorably with the developed world where it is between 50 percent and 95 percent.[3]

For the foreseeable future, on average, 26 million children could be part of India's education system *every year*. Thus, potentially 26 million children could graduate from high school and pursue higher education *every year*. At this population flow and 100 percent GER, the colleges and universities must be able to enroll 130 million students at any given point—a whopping 375 percent increase from the 2011 level. At a more realistic GER of 40 percent, the system must be able to enroll fifty-two million students, a 90 percent increase from the existing capacity. If we want to achieve a GER comparable to the developed world, our GER has to be in the 60 to 80 percent range. For those GER levels, the colleges and universities must have a capacity for 80 million to 105 million students, a substantial increase in capacity from the 2011 level.

We are not able to provide adequate access to colleges and universities to our youth today and have a huge catch-up to do to reach the standards of a developed nation. To achieve our new Golden Age, we need the higher education system to prepare and train hundreds of millions of Indians at any given point. The enrollments are clearly falling short.

In addition, even those who currently get access, like Mukund, are shortchanged.

2. Excellence: A Few Tiny Islands That Are Falling Short of Their Potential

India's higher education landscape is highlighted by a few small islands of excellence that are serving a tiny fraction of its population. Furthermore, they are falling short of their potential. AIIMS, IIMs, IITs, Indian Institutes of Sciences (IISc), and a few additional higher education institutions are the shining stars of India's higher education system. These select institutes have an attractive brand name, are relatively well resourced, and their infrastructure, governance, faculty, and processes tend to be much better than the rest. Thus, these institutions are the destination of choice for aspiring students, faculty members, and employers. Beyond these premier institutions, there is a sharp drop in the brand name, infrastructure, quality of faculty, and available resources.

This assessment is widely shared across India from high-ranking bureaucrats responsible for the higher education system to heads of institutions and employers. In 2011, IITs, which make up the largest premier system in India, had an intake of 7,678 undergraduates, 7,152 master's students, and 1,799 PhD students for a total of 16,629.[4] The total IIT enrollment accounted for less than 0.2 percent of the total enrollment in the higher education system and less than 2 percent of the enrollments in engineering.

This situation is pervasive and not just limited to engineering. For example, for the longest time, AIIMS selected just fifty students per year for its highly coveted bachelor of medicine and bachelor of surgery (MBBS) program. According to India's Best Colleges — the 2013 rankings, as reported by *India Today* — the total number of seats in the top fifty colleges in arts were a mere 18,587 with the top ten having just 5,010 seats. The capacity in the top fifty colleges for commerce was a meager 23,510, with the top ten having just 4,447 seats. The table below is indicative of the inadequate capacity even within the top colleges in every field.

Table 2.1: Available Seats in Top Colleges in 2012		
	Top 10	Top 25
Engineering	11,403	24,771
Arts	5,010	11,445
Commerce	4,447	13,654
Source: India Today: India's Best Colleges - 2013		
Table created by Shail Kumar		

In addition, even the premier institutions have fallen short of their potential. They are able to attract the best and the brightest students from around the country. However, they are *not* providing the best learning experience for these students. In 2007, Thane Richard, a student at Brown University, came as a visiting student to St. Stephen's College in Delhi, one of the premier colleges for economics and commerce in India. He wrote an article about his seven-month experience at St. Stephen's. He found the classes to be a waste of time except for one. One of the faculty members just read from his notes. Some classes were suddenly canceled. After experiencing the academics, he realized why most of St. Stephen's students were planning to pursue a second bachelor's degree overseas.[5]

Presidency College in Kolkata is yet another prestigious college in the country. Nobel laureates C. V. Raman and Amartya Sen and many well-known freedom fighters, researchers, scientists, and leaders count Presidency College as their alma mater. Jagori Saha and Patralekha Ukil received their bachelor's degrees in economics from Presidency College. It is another really difficult college to get into. In 2007, when Saha joined, approximately 9,000 students took the entrance examination for a mere 40 seats. Saha and Ukil shared many of the same experiences that Thane Richard experienced at St. Stephen's. Most of the faculty members did not

"Since the contributions of M. S. Swaminathan, Vikram Sarabhai, and Sam Pitroda in the 1970s and 1980s, the country has not seen any major scientific and technical adaptations. Not a single major invention has emerged from India over the past fifty years."

care about the students and most of them taught from old notes. Classes got canceled randomly and without notice. Sometimes exam papers got lost and students received incomplete grades. Evaluation of exams was also inconsistent. The number of pages of written text mattered more than the quality. Saha studied at University College London for her master's, and Ukil studied at the University of Warwick. Thanks to their stronger math backgrounds, hard work, and dedication, they were able to graduate with merit. However, both felt that Presidency had not prepared them well for the master's programs. They had colleagues from various leading economics programs in India such as St. Stephen's, SRCC, and Lady Shri Ram College for Women. All of their colleagues from India struggled, and some even failed.[6]

Most of the IIT friends and colleagues I have spoken with believe that they could count outstanding faculty members on their fingertips. That would be 5 to 10 percent of the faculty members. The numbers and percentages were notably higher when IITs were first established and have been going downhill ever since. They are also becoming more regional in their character. When IIT Kharagpur was first established in 1951, its faculty members came from around the country. Now most of the faculty members are increasingly from West Bengal, Odisha, and the eastern region. This trend toward the regionalization of faculty members is a slippery slope for all institutions. These institutions are not attracting the best and the brightest faculty members from around the country or the world. It would be uncomfortable and perhaps even an unwelcoming place to work for those not from that region.

The premier institutions have also fallen short in making an impact in their local communities and the nation. In May 2015, *Nature*, the internationally reputed science journal, published a special report on India's science and research situation. India is spending competitive amount of funds per researcher. However, it lags behind in all metrics that are normalized by population and GDP such as full-time researchers, papers published, scholarly citation impact, and number of patents.[7] Infosys's Murthy notes, "Since the contributions of M. S. Swaminathan, Vikram Sarabhai, and Sam Pitroda in the 1970s and 1980s, the country has not seen any major scientific and technical adaptations. Not a single major invention has emerged from India over the past fifty years."[8] While

Nature and Murthy are talking about the entire country and its higher education system, the premier institutions carry a larger burden of responsibility. They do, after all, have the best students and relatively better faculty members and financial resources to make an impact.

3. Structure and Scope: Misaligned with Needs and Aspirations

The affiliated colleges and stand-alone institutions account for around 86 percent of the student enrollments in the country. They are specialized around a few fields or professions, and do not have a critical mass of faculty to provide a broad education. A handful of exceptions aside, they do not conduct research. The colleges and universities are narrow in scope, and there is little focus on making an impact. Curriculum is also outdated and inflexible. Thus, the learning opportunities for the students are limited and restrictive.

Affiliated College System: The Bane of Undergraduate Education

The affiliated colleges account for the bulk of undergraduate enrollment in India. India copied the nineteenth-century affiliated college model from the British. In this system, affiliating universities focus on postgraduate education and research. They also establish the curriculum, academic schedule, fee structure, and exam papers for the affiliated colleges. Currently, some universities in India have over 1,000 colleges affiliated to them. These affiliating universities get a fee for each student enrolled in the affiliated colleges. The affiliated colleges confer degrees on behalf of the university. By mandate, the affiliated colleges do not conduct research. Thus, most of the students in India get their first degree in institutions that conduct *no* research. This has created two serious issues: 1) with no research, the curriculum has become mostly stagnant and is not benefitting from the innovation that research enables and 2) with no research expectations, many of the college faculty members are holders of only a bachelor's degree.

- Average number of students enrolled in a college: **720**
- Student faculty ratio: **26.4**
- Average number of faculty per college: **27**

Source: AISHE data (2010–2011) published in 2013

Furthermore, it is estimated that approximately 96 percent of affiliated colleges have enrollments of less than 3,000 students and the average enrollment per college is about 720 students. With an average teacher-to-student ratio of 1:26, these colleges on average have just 27 faculty members each.[9] With narrow specialization and small faculty strength, the colleges offer limited learning opportunities for the students.

The situation in state universities and affiliated colleges is alarming. Like many others, P. Balaram, professor and former director at IISc Bangalore, has thought deeply about India's higher education and is extremely concerned about the situation. He believes that "the higher education system at the state level has become deeply politicized; the governance structure is in shambles; academics is the lowest priority; and domicile, caste, and political affiliations play a significant role in appointments of faculty members." There is no guarantee that classes or exams will be held on schedule. The degrees and the grades have no credibility as all the students graduate and one can pay to change their grades.[10] With the affiliated colleges dominating the state higher education system, the focus, scope, excellence, and incentives are perversely connected to a race to the bottom.

Single Field Institutions: Inadequate Preparation for Life and Career

Most of Indian higher education institutions are narrowly specialized in one the following fields or professions: agriculture, animation and gaming, business, dentistry, engineering, fashion technology, handloom technology, hotel management, law, medicine, mining, nursing, pharmacy, public health, science, teacher training, or veterinary medicine. This has created artificial boundaries and inhibited creativity, research, and innovation. These disadvantages also fundamentally limit the learning experiences of our youth. We are missing key opportunities to unleash their aspirations, capabilities, and energy during their formative years. This is a huge loss for individuals,

"The higher education system at the state level has become deeply politicized; the governance structure is in shambles; academics is the lowest priority; and domicile, caste, and political affiliations play a significant role in appointments of faculty members."

their respective families and communities, as well as the industry, economy, society, and nation.

The premier institutions are narrowly focused as well. Established after independence, IITs were designed to focus on engineering, AIIMS on medicine, and IIMs on business. In fact, we have started making our institutions even more narrowly specialized — the Indian Institute for Science and Engineering Research (IISER) and National Institute of Science Education and Research (NISER) were recently established and focus on science only. This is despite the fact that science and engineering are integral to each other, and science is integral to a liberal arts education. There are similar narrowly specialized institutions that the government and various ministries continue to build, such as the Indian Institute of Information Technology (IIIT), Indian Institute of Public Health, (IIPH), Institute of Handloom Technology (IHT), Indian Statistical Institute (ISI), National Institute of Design (NID), National Institute of Fashion Technology (NIFT), National Institute of Pharmaceutical Education and Research (NIPER), Nursing Institutes, the School of Animation and Gaming, and Teacher Training Institutes.[11] This list is too long and the fields too narrow.

Research: Disconnected from Teaching

Also, research in most institutions is almost nonexistent. As I noted earlier, affiliated colleges, by design, conduct no research.

A long time ago, the decision-makers made the choice to conduct scientific and engineering research in government labs such as CSIR, the Department of Science and Technology (DST), and the Department of Biotechnology (DBT). Thus most institutions, by design, including IITs and IIMs, were focused on teaching. Only recently has there been a shift toward research in some of these institutions. And even in institutions that conduct research, a segment of the faculty believes that they could either teach or conduct research but not do both. "[There is a] strangely divided notion that teaching and research are different," says Anurag Behar, vice chancellor of Azim Premji University. Behar, also the chief sustainability officer at Wipro, is an outspoken thought leader on higher education reforms.[12]

With no research expectations, many of the college faculty members are holders of just a bachelor's degree.

Even when research is conducted, it is mostly below average or has little impact on the local community or the nation. Satish Deshpande teaches sociology at Delhi University and wrote an essay called "Declining Simplistic Narratives" in the book *Beyond Degrees: Finding Success in Higher Education* (edited by Ira Pande). Talking about the state of Indian social science research, he wrote, "The institutions are weak, the research looks bad, and the researchers are all below average."[13]

Scope: Limited to Academic Preparation and Credentialing

Another shortcoming of the higher education system is inadequate preparation for life. In a nation and a world that are more connected and competitive than ever, certain skills and knowledge have become critical. Unlike the twentieth century, it is expected that in the twenty-first century that a person will change jobs, industries, or even their career path multiple times. Thus, they will need mental agility and an ability to learn new subjects and work with different types of people. Most professions require a certain level of mastery in the chosen field and in skills such as communication, project management, problem solving, time management, critical thinking, and leadership.

In addition, corporations and start-ups in India and around the world place a premium on a commitment to values, a smart mind in a healthy body, and the ability to work with people from all walks of life. Values such as honesty and integrity, open communication, respect for others, and ownership and accountability are sought after. In this world, self-awareness and self-confidence to do an outstanding job, taking initiative, admitting mistakes, asking questions, and seeking advice when necessary are also important.

Most of the colleges and universities take a fairly narrow view of their scope—academic preparation and credentialing. They do not offer any specialized courses or cocurricular or extracurricular opportunities for students to learn and hone their skills and knowledge. This is usually left to a student's initiative. Some institutions like the IITs, IIMs, and AIIMS have a culture where students pursue valuable cocurricular and extracurricular activities, including sports, drama, debate, music, and art. There is also significant exposure to national and international artists and speakers. However, for the most part, the nonacademic aspects are ignored altogether.

Furthermore, there is no focus on the "whole" person. The mind-body-soul connection is completely forgotten. Abhay Bhushan—IIT Kanpur and MIT alumnus, entrepreneur, and activist—emphasized that we need "strong bodies and sharp minds."[14] Time for reflection, physical exercise, and spiritual growth is often taken as a matter for each student to pursue on their own or not at all. Physical infrastructure for meditation, yoga, sports, and entertainment is typically lacking.

Curriculum: Stagnant and Disconnected from Needs

With narrowly specialized institutions, there is no access to faculty members from other fields. Thus, the institution's narrow specialization and the small faculty size make it impossible for students to have an adequate depth and breadth of learning at their college.

In addition to mastering a field or profession, obtaining critical skills, and developing the whole person, it is important to learn about additional subjects that expand our knowledge and appreciation of the world around us. Thus, exposure to history, music, art, religions, languages, and subjects not covered for the mastery in the field or profession must be covered. Such a holistic education experience is unavailable in India right now.

In addition to the inadequate depth and breadth in curriculum, it is also stagnant. Pranab Bardhan, faculty member at UC Berkeley, was educated at Presidency College, Kolkata, and Cambridge University. Before joining UC Berkeley, he was a faculty member at MIT, ISI, and the Delhi School of Economics. He mentioned how faculty members he knows at Delhi University (DU) have been teaching from the same notes for the past twenty years.[15] The story of using dated notes is repeated across the Indian education system.

Rajiv Bajaj, managing director of Bajaj Auto, is an easy person to like. He is approachable and friendly. He is also sharp and has a unique understanding of the issues at hand. Bajaj is engaged with a number of Industrial Training Institutes (ITI), is a member of the board of directors of IIM Udaipur, and is an alumnus of the College of Engineering at Pune and the University of Warwick. A fan of homeopathy and yoga, he brings a holistic and systems thinking to the conversation. He mentioned that in 1990 at Bajaj Auto 23,000 people manufactured 900,000 vehicles. In 2007, just 850 people are making the same number of vehicles. His point is that the Indian industry has changed dramatically, and that different skill sets are now needed from diploma holders and engineers.[16]

Tata's N. S. Rajan shares this view and thinks that there is a wide gap in what is being taught and what is needed in the industry. "Just 5 percent of what is studied in the colleges and universities is used in the industry," Rajan noted.[17]

The world is moving forward fast, knowledge is evolving rapidly, and the industry is either leading or adapting to this competitive landscape and global reality. The curriculum, unfortunately, is lagging behind in India and not aligned with what is needed for a fulfilling life and career.

If Mukund, after joining his local college, wanted to change his field, he would practically have no chance as a result of the limited and restricted structure and scope. The ability to learn across disciplines is impossible. Many of my friends, fellow IITians, after joining IIT, realized that engineering was not their core passion, and they were more interested in journalism, advertising, business, or some other field of engineering. They had no choice except to complete their degree and change paths after graduation. And many did. This trend continues. Take Akanksha Srivastava's story for example.

Srivastava's recent journey took her from a bachelor's in architecture to a master's in computer science. Even as a student in high school, she was interested in computer science and was among the best programmers in her school. She qualified for IIT and was accepted in the architecture department based on her IIT JEE rank. At IIT, she continued to take computer science classes, and in the common first year class in computer science and data structures, she did better than even the computer science students. However, the IIT system did not allow her to change her field or get a minor in computer science. Undeterred, she wrote to hundreds of faculty members around the world and was accepted to a computer science lab at the Nanyang Technical University in Singapore (NTU) after her second year. After her third year, Srivastava spent a summer in École Polytechnique in Paris, also doing computer science research. During her fourth year compulsory architecture-field-related summer training, she wrote a paper, again on computer science, and presented it at a conference in Cambridge. Five years after joining IIT Kharagpur, she finally joined the field she loves the most—computer science at the University of Oxford.[18]

4. Faculty and University Leadership: Acute Expertise Shortage

Excellence in higher education institutions is created and sustained by outstanding faculty members and university leaders who deeply care about their field, the research, making an impact, and student learning outcomes. There is an acute shortage of qualified faculty members and academics who can lead higher education institutions. It is said that 30 percent to 50 percent of faculty positions are vacant in most institutions.[19] This shortage has created a vicious cycle where the standards are quickly dropping to the bottom.

Gautam Thapar, founder and chairman of the Avantha Group, is deeply knowledgeable about higher education and its impact on students, the school system, and industry. He is also the president of Thapar University and is on the board of governors of the Doon School. I met him in Thapar House in New Delhi when he shared many experiences. One stood out.

Recently, he was on the search committee to select a director of a prominent higher education institute. They wanted an academic who had also published extensively. They reviewed over one hundred applications and found only two who had any meaningful research papers and citations to their credit. Many of the applicants had labeled their conference talks as published papers. Thapar was disappointed by the tiny pool of qualified candidates but not surprised. He mentioned, "Teaching has lost its attraction—now the bottom 3 to 4 percent join the faculty. People are [also] coming out of a system that is missing an ingredient [research]. So we cannot expect something vastly different when they reach the top."[20]

"Teaching has lost its attraction—now the bottom 3 to 4 percent join the faculty. People are [also] coming out of a system that is missing a key ingredient [research]. So we cannot expect something vastly different when they reach the top."

Thapar's view that the teaching profession is the last choice is widely shared by current and former university leaders and those in the industry. Industry salaries have outpaced those in the higher education field. Thus, those who can either join industry or go overseas for higher education or take up government jobs. Pursuing a PhD is not a financially attractive option. As a result, the engine that creates the next generation of faculty members is stagnant and inadequate. This shortage in turn, is attracting professionals with just undergraduate degrees to teach as temporary, part-time, or full-time faculty in colleges and universities.

The majority of the students I interviewed, who studied in India and then studied overseas, found the faculty quality lacking in India in four significant ways: 1) faculty members did not care if the students learned, 2) they also did not provide context on why students must learn concepts and theory in that class, 3) they taught from decades-old notes and slides, and 4) there was no application to real-world problems.

A large number of students echoed Aniket Panda's comments that "quality of faculty at IITs was mixed — there were some exceptional faculty members, some were bad, and some were really bad." Panda, an IIT alumnus, is pursuing an MBA at Duke University.[21] Shweta Sangewar, an alumna of Imperial College in London and IIT, mentioned that the IIT faculty might as well be teaching "rocks" — they do not seem to care and have no interactions with the students.[22] Shouvik Chatterjee, another IIT alumnus now at Cornell University, recalls one of his faculty members remarking, "If I teach or not, it does not matter."[23] The situation is similar in other premier institutions and worse in the rest of the higher education system.

"Top-class students are taught by second-class faculty."

The severe shortage of qualified faculty members has created a situation where "top-class students are taught by second-class faculty," says Govind Swarup. He is a professor at the Tata Institute of Fundamental Research (TIFR), Mumbai and one of the pioneers of radio astronomy.[24] The faculty-student mismatch continues at all levels and has created unfortunate and damaging behavior on both sides. Students skip classes because they can learn more efficiently on their own. Teachers skip classes to avoid students' questions. When they do teach, they read from their dated notes and administer strict disciplinary codes to ensure no one asks questions. Rote teaching and learning are fostered. There are no projects or assignments that integrate the various topics, subjects, or fields. Furthermore, there are no group or collaborative projects or ones that focus on solving real-world problems. The exam questions are repeated year after year, which students prepare for and pass. This becomes a win-win situation for teachers and students. Teachers can claim that they are teaching and that their students are learning. Students can pass the exams and get their degrees without much effort. This is yet another way the higher education standards in India are racing toward the bottom.

The focus on exam preparation is affecting the kind of books that get placed in the libraries. DU's Krishna Kumar was asked to assess a college affiliated to the University of Allahabad in Uttar Pradesh. At one time, the University of Allahabad was considered to be one of the premier education institutions in India. It has slipped several notches from that lofty reputation. Kumar mentioned to me that on the site visit, he requested to visit the college library a number of times. After much probing, they relented. There were two sections in the library. One was closed to preserve older books and the other was used primarily to store exam guides.[ii] It became evident to Kumar that the college administrators did not want him to see that their library was filled with exam guides rather than scholarly books.[25]

Pranab Bardhan mentioned his experience with libraries and the culture that comes with recruiting and then retaining below average faculty members. He met a head of department at a university in Bihar who kept the department's library books locked under his supervision. He did not want any of the department's faculty members to read those books lest they get better than him.[26]

The shortage of qualified and capable faculty members, librarians, and university leaders manifests itself in a number of ways. Some of these positions are vacant for several months or even several years. Many of these are filled with underqualified or unqualified faculty on a temporary basis. Many states and institutions have started hiring "temporary" faculty members. These contracted faculty members are paid well below what the sixth pay commission guidelines. Some of the temporary teachers are paid daily.

During the absence of a vice chancellor (VC) or a director, there is complete paralysis in decision-making. No faculty members are hired and no important projects are initiated. From July 2012 to June 2013, IIT Kharagpur was without a full-time director. It

---

ii   Exam guides are books with likely questions to be asked in the exams along with their answers. Instead of reading and understanding the subject, the students merely read the exam guides and memorize the questions and answers.

was finally filled after its alumni launched a nationwide protest under the banner "PPC for Director." In 2014, when IIT Patna's director's appointment was not renewed, IIT Kharagpur's new director was appointed as interim director of IIT Patna as well. It is tough enough to lead one institution. IIT Patna's director was finally selected in April 2015. Several leadership positions in CSIR, DBT, and DST institutes also have gone vacant for many months. Vacancies and asking one person—no matter how competent—to lead two institutions suggest that there is a severe shortage of capable leaders.

The acute shortage of outstanding faculty members and university leaders is also reflected in what's not happening. Most of the institutions and the hundreds of millions of students and hundreds of thousands of faculty members have *not* made a significant impact in their respective local communities, regional economy, or national society, either as part of the curricular or extracurricular activities. The linkage between government, industry, and universities for fundamental research and applied research is weak. This weak connection also deprives students of meaningful exposure to problems that must be solved.

Several quotes sum up India's higher education system from a student's perspective:

"Wasted four years [academically at IIT]."[27]

—Bharath Bhat, IIT alumnus, who subsequently completed a master's at Stanford University

"[We] studied to score [marks] as opposed to studied to learn."[28]

—Arijit Chakraborty, Birla Institute of Technology and Science (BITS) Pilani alumnus, who is now completing a PhD from the University of Auckland

"Nonacademic life [at IIT] was excellent. There were only a few great faculty members. Industry lures the best of them, and only a handful are ready to sacrifice those perks."[29]

—Sreeja Nag, MIT and IIT alumna

*"Everyone [students] knows that no one is going
to teach them [at Presidency College]."[30]*

—Jagori Saha, Presidency College and University
of Warwick alumna, now pursuing a PhD at the
University of Washington, Seattle

5. World-Class Comprehensive Research University: None; Institutions in the Top 500 of Global Rankings: One

Even though India has over 700 universities, 37,000 affiliated colleges, and 11,400 stand-alone institutions, there is not a single world-class comprehensive research university in the country. Increasingly, innovation and new ideas are coming at the intersection of multiple disciplines. For example, medical doctors collaborating with science and engineering faculty are developing new cost-effective diagnostics and surgical devices. Engineering faculty members are working with law, economics, and business faculty members to develop innovative solutions for energy and water challenges. Artists and humanists are working with architects, city planners, business school, and engineering faculty members to create more innovative products, workspaces, and city designs. The traditional boundaries, which had created artificial restrictions in the past, have given way to impact-oriented mind-sets, collaborations, and interdisciplinary research and innovation. These collaborations are fostered in institutions that have outstanding faculty members and students in multiple disciplines located on one campus. They can easily interact with like-minded faculty members and students in classrooms, labs, hallways, hostels, or cafeterias. They can also share expensive research facilities and libraries, and explore and test new ideas together.

By design, we do not have these opportunities to learn, research, and innovate even in our premier institutions. By design, we are not giving students chances to find their passion or to change paths. And, by design, we are falling behind the world and losing ground on solving our own complex and multidisciplinary mega challenges.

As a result of all of the shortcomings in our higher education system, we have only one institution in the top 500 of the world university rankings. IISc Bangalore placed in the 301–400 category in the 2014 Academic Ranking of World Universities (ARWU) conducted by the Center for World-Class Universities at Shanghai

Jiao Tong University. The rankings are a measure of excellence in teaching, research, learning opportunities, outcomes, and the impact that the institution's faculty, alumni, and students are making. All the rankings have some limitations, but they are valuable benchmarks to assess excellence and impact. India's higher education system fails to measure up in such rankings. The table below shows the rankings in comparison to the United States, China, Singapore, South Korea, and the United Kingdom. I have added the United Kingdom to this comparison since it attracts the second highest number of students from India for higher education.[31]

Table 2.2: Number of Universities in Top 500	
USA	146
China	44
UK	38
South Korea	10
Finland	5
Singapore	2
India	1

Source: www.shanghairanking.com, ARWU Ranking 2014
Table prepared by Shail Kumar

This is clear and compelling evidence that the land of the Bhagavad Gita, Buddha, Mahavira, Chandragupta, Ashoka, Kalidasa, Aryabhatta, Tansen, Guru Nanak, C. V. Raman, Tagore, Gandhi, and A. P. J. Abdul Kalam is punching well below its potential in higher education.

Exceptions: Silver Linings in the Dark Clouds

A nation as vast and complex as India has exceptions. There are silver linings in the dark clouds.

Several philanthropists and successful executives have started new higher education institutions. Some of these include the Ashoka University, Azim Premji University, BML Munjal University, Indian School of Business (ISB), Mahindra École Centrale (MEC), and Shiv Nadar University.

These new colleges and universities are increasing learning opportunities for students and providing a much-needed boost to the capacity in the system. They are also raising the bar for students and faculty members. Some, like Ashoka University, are offering a liberal arts education—a bold adventure in India where most philanthropists in the past have opened colleges in the tried and tested fields of engineering or ICT.

Many of them have established active collaborations with foreign universities. These relationships foster innovation in the curriculum and exchanges of faculty and students. They also enable the creation of a culture of excellence. Some, on the other hand, have also established active collaborations with industry. They are also experimenting with new designs for classrooms and physical spaces.

Sunil Kant Munjal is the joint managing director of Hero MotoCorp. He is also the chancellor of BML Munjal University (BMU). In the interview with me, he was excited about the various innovations the university has adopted. The session for students starts with a one-week "joy of learning" program, which is all about igniting young minds. There is tremendous focus on industry experiences. Each student is expected to visit three to four industries per year. Collaboration with Siemens enables BMU and its students to work on the latest research equipment. They have also redesigned their classes. As Munjal noted, when we work in companies, there is no lecture room seating anywhere. There are boardrooms, conference rooms, and office spaces. To replicate the "real-life" setting, the classes have square tables and students face one another. They can interact with one another, collaborate, and solve problems together. They also have an academic collaboration with Imperial College London, a leading university in the world.[32]

In addition, there are practices and innovations that are positive steps in the right direction. Medical colleges and institutions in allied fields of medicine are providing relevant and valuable experiences to future doctors and practitioners. IITs and IIMs are speaking a lot more about conducting research and making an impact. IIT Kharagpur is working with several villages to improve farm productivity and farmers' earnings. A few newer IITs, like IIT Gandhinagar, are trying new ideas to add compelling value to student learning. IIM Udaipur, one of the recently established IIMs, is "leveraging its newness to its advantage," noted Janat Shah, its director. IIM Udaipur's leadership is creating a unique selling point that leverages its location in Rajasthan. They have also made research their number one priority and are encouraging the young faculty to publish in reputed journals. Instead of involving the faculty in the administration, which is time-consuming, Shah is engaging faculty in the institute's governance. IIM Udaipur is also reinvesting close to 20 percent of its funds in faculty development.[33]

For J. R. Achyuthan, the Solar Decathlon competition was the high point in his IIT Bombay experience. A civil engineering student, he participated in an interdisciplinary project with students from energy, civil engineering metallurgy, mechanical engineering, and control systems to design and build an energy efficient home. These thirty-five to forty students, which included a few from the architecture school, competed and were selected to join the final competition in France. He learned more from this hands-on experience than anything else he could have done. Achyuthan is now pursuing a PhD at George Mason University in the United States where he is using machine learning to develop a novel approach to automate the structure design process. Building energy efficient homes is an outstanding example of a hands-on, interdisciplinary, and collaborative group project that is needed in all our educational institutions.[34]

Deepak Phatak is a professor of computer science and engineering at IIT Bombay. Phatak and I first met when I was the co-chair of the education program at the IIT Global Conference 2013 in Houston. The second time was in his Powai office. He recalled his days as an undergraduate student at Shri Govindram Seksaria Institute of Technology and Science (SGSITS) Indore. He told me that for the first exam he diligently studied all the topics. Then he realized that he could cover just six of the ten topics and still do well. Shortly thereafter, he realized that exam questions were being repeated from previous years and he could just review past exam papers. Fortunately for IIT students and the industry, he did not take his SGSITS experience forward. Phatak takes special pride in setting question papers that are never repeated. Currently, he is the principal investigator (PI) for the Massive Open Online Courses (MOOCs) initiative in India. He is a passionate and self-driven person, and his eyes light up as he shares the impact that the MOOCs and the Teachers Training initiatives are making.[35] He is also the architect behind the Akaash project for building low-cost tablets. Phatak is one of the exceptional faculty members in India.

Ashok Jhunjhunwala, professor of electrical engineering at IIT Madras, is another exceptional faculty member. Hailing from a generation of Gandhians, he is driven to make an impact in villages around the country. His previous efforts have been telephony and the Aakash tablet. Now, he is also focused on the nation's energy challenge. In addition, he is leading the efforts to establish and grow the IIT Madras Research Park, which is increasing industry–university research collaborations and encouraging intellectual property (IP)–based start-ups.[36]

Academics such as Ashok Jhunjhunwala at IIT Madras and Deepak Phatak at IIT Bombay highlight the value of exceptional faculty members. They are educating students, conducting research, establishing meaningful industry-government-university collaborations, and having an impact in the local communities and around the country. People like Jhunjhunwala and Phataks, unfortunately, are currently few and far between.

Exceptions exist and they prove the rule. The higher education system is broken and disconnected. And Mukund Kapase, his parents, and people around the country are paying a heavy price. How is the higher education system affecting its stakeholders—students, parents, industry, economy, society, and the nation? The next chapter focuses on this question.

CHAPTER 3

Bottom Line: A Hefty Price Tag for All

The only thing necessary for the triumph of
evil is for good men to do nothing.

— Edmund Burke, Irish philosopher

San Francisco, 1994: Anand and Poonam Mehta and their two young children just finished their green card processing at San Francisco International Airport's immigration desk. They have come a long way from India. Anand and Poonam want a bright future for their kids, so they are immigrating to the United States. Their story is similar to hundreds of thousands, if not millions, of families who have left India to escape the broken higher education system and the burden it places on students and families.

Back at the airport, the family is palpably excited about starting their new life. Anand's elder brother is waiting at the arrival area for their final step—picking up their bags from the baggage carousel. Prior to leaving India, Anand was a midlevel corporate executive in Mumbai. With a bachelor's degree in engineering from Jadavpur University and an MBA from XLRI in Jamshedpur, he was looking forward to working his way up the corporate ladder. It was looking good for him. He had just been promoted to be a general manager of marketing in one of the business units. However, he and Poonam frequently worried about their kids' future. Getting into engineering, medicine, or business was getting tougher. Coaching costs were getting higher. Most of all, they were petrified to learn that their friends' kids had started taking tuition classes in eleventh class to prepare for the entrance examinations. While Riti and Rishi were smart and hardworking kids, there was a lot of uncertainty and anxiety clouding their higher education opportunities.

Then a few years ago, an offer came from the United States. Anand's brother offered to sponsor him for a green card, which would allow them to immigrate. Anand knew leaving India would mean taking a step down in his own career, perhaps several steps down. His degrees and business experiences would not be as valued in the United States. Poonam had completed her BA and MA in history from Kolkata but had never worked. She might have to work as well. But a brighter future for Riti and Rishi outweighed all other concerns, and in 1994, they took the plunge to leave India for the United States.

Now, two decades later, Anand and Poonam are well settled in California. They miss their family and friends in India dearly. They go as often as they can. They have found peace with their career and lifestyle changes and couldn't be more satisfied with their decision to leave India in the mid-1990s. Based in Silicon Valley, Riti is now working on her second start-up. She did her computer science degree at the University of Illinois at Urbana-Champaign and then joined one of the earlier social media companies before launching her start-up. Their son is now Dr. Rishi Mehta — he completed his BS from UC Berkeley and his medical training at the University of Michigan in Ann Arbor. He is now working at a leading research and teaching organization where he is running a cancer research project. Riti and Rishi are doing great and are making an impact in the United States.

Families are making a statement with their wallets by sending their children overseas and with their feet (like Anand and Poonam) by emigrating from India. And the money is *not* on our higher education system. At this point, we have looked at enrollments, excellence, structure, scope, faculty, and university leadership in India's higher education. But how is the broken and disconnected higher education system affecting its stakeholders — students, parents, industry, economy, society, and the nation?

1. **Hyper-Competition for Premier Institutions:** There is hyper-competition for the few islands of excellence. This has escalated the costs and time needed to prepare for entrance examinations and led to several unintended social costs.

2. **Overseas Education:** With students going overseas for higher education, the country is losing financial resources in the short term. It is also losing valuable human resources for decades, generations, and in some instances forever.

3. **Unemployable Graduates:** Many students graduating from the majority of the colleges are considered unemployable. This is also forcing the students and parents to invest additional time and money for more certificates and degrees.

4. **Hyper-Competition for Talent:** There is hyper-competition to find the employable. Thus, industries are spending considerable amounts of time and resources on recruiting, training, and retaining the employable candidates. This is increasing labor costs and decreasing the country's cost competitiveness.

5. **The Nation's Competiveness, Mega Challenges, and the Future:** The nation and society are paying a heavy price. India's economy is *not* firing on all cylinders. The innovation and entrepreneurship engine is a drop in the ocean. India's mega challenges are going unsolved. The next generation of students, professionals, teachers, and faculty members are at risk. The nation's future is being mortgaged.

Directly or indirectly, everyone is paying a heavy price. Let's take a closer look.

1. Hyper-Competition for Premier Institutions: Among Students (and Parents)

Escalating exam preparation time and costs

The severe shortage of high quality colleges and universities has created hyper-competition for the premier institutions. The stakes are high—join one of the premier institutions and a professional career is on the right trajectory. Getting an internship, a job, or a scholarship for graduate studies becomes almost certain. Society puts you on a pedestal. Marrying well becomes easier. Life is set. Thus, admission into one of the premier institutions is highly coveted by students and families alike. Everyone wants to get on this narrow highway. The entrance is, not surprisingly, clogged.

- AIIMS selected just under 0.1 percent, or seventy-two students, for its MBBS program from the 80,000 to 100,000 who took the exam, making it the most selective institution in the country.

- Just 1.9 percent of the 512,000 thousand students who took the IIT JEE exam in 2012 got selected for one of the IITs.

- In 2012, the cutoff percentage to get into St. Stephen's College in arts was 96 percent and Shri Ram College of Commerce in commerce was 96.5 percent.

- In 2015, the National Law Universities (NLU) are expected to select a mere 4.3 percent, or 1,700 students, from a pool of about 40,000 students who took the Common Law Admission Test.[1]

> - In 2012, the cutoff percentage to get into St. Stephen's College in arts was **96%** and Shri Ram College of Commerce (SRCC) in commerce was **96.5%**[1].
> - AIIMS admitted **0.1%**, IITs **1.9%**, and NLUs **4.3%** of those who took the entrance exams.[2]
>
> Source: [1] India Today: Best Colleges -2013, [2] various

This has unleashed a coaching "arms race" in India. Consider this: in the 1950s and 1960s, a smart and hardworking student would prepare for the secondary school exams and then take the IIT JEE. This student would have a decent chance of getting a good rank in the IIT JEE and then choosing one of the IITs. In the 1980s, when I took the IIT JEE, it had become the norm to take either Agrawal Classes or Brilliant Tutorials or both. These correspondence courses cost approximately Rs 1,000 for an entire year. Most of my fellow IITians studied in a "nose-to-the-grindstone" mode in twelfth class, a one-year effort, and made it to the IITs. In 2014, to enter the IITs, most students have begun studying in the "nose-to-the-grindstone" mode at least by the ninth class. The most recent trend is to start preparing as early as sixth class. The coaching options have mushroomed. There are private tutors specializing in chemistry, physics, and math available locally. There are national chains, such as FIITJEE, with coaching centers around the country. Finally, there are residential programs such as those in Kota. Students can enroll in coaching classes and live and breathe studies 24–7 for one or more years. Many students, after completing twelfth class, are enrolling in such classes in Kota. As the admissions have become hyper-competitive, the costs have ballooned.

For a two-year preparation for IIT JEE, it could cost anywhere from Rs 2.5 to 4 lakhs. (US$4,167 to US$6,667)

- Tuition classes in eighth class could cost Rs 80,000 (US$1,333), and in sixth class, Rs 30,000 per year. (US$500)

- Private tutors charge from Rs 1,000 to Rs 4,000 (US$17 to US$67) per hour per student on a one-to-one basis, while group tuition costs Rs 1,000 to Rs 6,000 (US$17 to US$100) per month.

Reputed coaching programs have become stepping stones to premier higher education institutions. Now, there are even coaching classes to get into premier coaching programs.

Hyper-competition, the coaching arms race, and escalating costs have made it really tough for children of lower income families. People like Anand Kumar, founder of Super 30, are doing yeoman service by providing free coaching for IIT JEE and engineering exams to children of extremely low-income families. Anand Kumar's extraordinary success, high visibility, and immense popularity with the masses have made him the target of the "coaching mafia." Recently, Bihar's government assigned two commandos as full-time protection for him. Coaching is a large and lucrative business, and Kumar is giving it away for free and is the most successful of all of them. Thus, it is also not surprising that the coaching industry does not like him and his model.

In June 2013, a survey by the Associated Chambers of Commerce and Industry of India (ASSOCHAM) titled "Business of Private Coaching Centers in India" revealed that 87 percent of primary school students and 95 percent of high school students in metropolitan cities received private tutoring. According to the survey, "a majority of the middle-class parents have been spending one-third of their monthly income on private tuitions for their wards to do better in their examinations and prepare them for competitive entrance exams for professional courses." It estimated the size of the private coaching industry in India to be Rs 1,41,416 crores (US$23.7 billion). It is projected that the coaching industry will skyrocket to Rs 2,38,677 crores (US$40 billion) by 2015.[2]

Social Costs: Unintended and Widespread

The coaching "arms race" has many implications. The most obvious is the amount of time and money the students and families are investing to improve their chances of entering one of the premier education institutions. Often, this is forcing families to use up all their savings or even take loans, like Mukund's father did. It is inordinate and painful. Unfortunately, in today's broken and disconnected system, the parents feel that investing in private coaching is the only way to improve their children's chances of a better life and career. Loss of savings or taking on debt comes with its own direct and indirect costs for the families. In cases like Mukund's where the return on family investment

- **87%** of primary school students and **95%** of high school students in metros receive private tutoring.

- Estimated size of the private coaching industry in India: **US$23.7 billion** (Rs 1,41,416 crores) in 2013. It is projected to reach **US$40 billion** (Rs 2,38,677 crores) by 2015.

Source: "Business of Private Coaching Centres in India," ASSOCHAM, Indian Express

is likely to be negative, his father may end up selling additional land, his mother's jewelry, or both to pay for their daughters' weddings.

Excessive coaching and exam preparation is also taking away from a more holistic development of young children. Instead of playing games, learning new skills, or developing hobbies, the children are focusing on exam preparation. Sudhir Jain, director of IIT Gandhinagar, is a new and small breed of academic leaders in India—young, ambitious, and bold. He completed his bachelor's in engineering from Roorkee University (now IIT Roorkee) and got a PhD from Caltech. Subsequently, he taught at IIT Kanpur prior to joining IIT Gandhinagar as the founding director. To address the burnout and narrow preparation of students entering the IITs, he has created a five-week boot camp for incoming first-year students. The boot camp focuses on five points: physical activity, creativity, teamwork, values and ethics, and societal awareness. The first-year students undergo an intense exposure to music, sports, community service, and lectures on a wide range of topics. Jain believes that this is an important step toward decompressing the students from years of debilitating pressure and IIT JEE exam preparation, and toward providing a more holistic preparation for their lives and careers.[3]

As the preparation time has increased over the years, students have had to decide earlier about their chosen field or profession. It was tough enough to make the decision about my professional path in twelfth class. I shudder to think students have to make that decision by ninth class. Making the same decision in sixth class is just ridiculous. At that young age, students hardly even know themselves let alone how they want to spend the rest of their lives.

On another level, increasing time and costs has skewed the playing field, favoring the middle class and the rich. Coaching costs are out of reach for the poor. This is also creating a more nonhomogeneous student community in premier institutions. Now the student community primarily includes students from upper- and middle-class families. This is in sharp contrast to just a few decades back when coaching costs were negligible. The student community at an IIT, IIM, or AIIMS represented the society. They all shared some common traits — these students were all smart, hardworking, and self-driven. Now, in addition to having these qualities, their parents must be able to afford the coaching classes necessary to get into the colleges.

Not "making" it into the premier institutions leaves students and families shaken and disappointed. Each year millions of students are made to believe that they are not good enough. However, the smart, hardworking, and self-driven traits do not magically disappear at the AIIMS, IIT, IIM, St. Stephen's, or SRCC cutoffs. "Everyone is good at something," notes S. Ramadorai, chairman of the National Skill Development Agency.[4] Unfortunately, the exams merely test one dimension of the person's capability — an ability to prepare for and take exams well over a few days. It does not test for passion, aptitude, or commitment to the field or profession. It also discounts the multidimensionality of the student and what he or she brings to the college and university.

Many students lose self-confidence and self-esteem, unjustly so. Some lose yet another year preparing for the exams. Since the student and their family invested so much in their exam preparation, many students pursue fields and careers that they are not truly passionate about. The students are also burned out by the time they enter the college. Many students find the whole coaching and related investment intimidating and drop out before or just after completing high school. Many, like Anand and Poonam Mehta, emigrate from India for their children's education, and others who have the means leave for higher education overseas.

2. Overseas Education: A Huge Outflow of Precious Financial and Human Resources

Overseas education, when students from India leave to pursue higher education in some other country, is yet another indicator of a broken and disconnected higher education system. It is also costing India precious financial and human resources. It costs anywhere from several thousand rupees in tuition per year in a local college to up to six lakh rupees in a new private institution, which includes tuition, meals, and living in residence halls. It costs anywhere from thirty lakhs to forty lakhs per year to study in the United States. So compared to India, it costs 5 to 4,800 times more to study in the United States. The table below highlights the cost differential between higher education in India and the United States.

Table 3.1: India-US: Cost Comparison of a Four-Year Undergraduate Degree (in US Dollars)
$282,400
USA: Private research university, e.g., Stanford
$242,400
USA: Public research university, e.g., UC San Diego
$40,000
India: Residential, private college, e.g., Ashoka University
$10,000
India: Residential, public institution, e.g., IIT
$60
India: Non-residential, public college, e.g., Presidency College
Source: www.ucsd.edu, www.stanford.edu, discussions with various people in India Table prepared by Shail Kumar

A significant pull, push, or both is needed for a student to leave family and friends and go thousands of miles away from home as a young eighteen-year-old. The magnets that pull most of the students who pursue overseas education at the undergraduate level are many and vary by the individual. Some of the attractions include: an excellent education; opportunities to explore different disciplines and fields; flexibility to conduct research and do hands-on projects; the halo effect of a degree that is well recognized in India and around the world; a global network of friends; and an international experience. Some are also attracted by the opportunity to work overseas after completing their degree and the chance to emigrate from India.

The push to leave India is primarily driven by the hyper-competition of getting into premier institutes, several years of "nose-to-the-grindstone" coaching, and studying with no certainty of a successful outcome. Many talented students are turned off by the lack of opportunities, lack of flexibility of pursuing unconventional paths, and/or the lack of ability to change fields after a year or two.

Keerthana Kumar recently completed her undergraduate from the University of Texas (UT) at Austin. She studied in Chennai and was selected for a two-month summer program at IIT Madras after her eleventh class. This is a wonderful program where she took classes and participated in projects at IIT Madras. She also took the opportunity to discuss her interest in pursuing research as an undergraduate. The IIT Madras faculty adviser, to his credit, suggested that she explore getting an undergraduate degree in the United States as her chances of conducting research as an undergraduate at an IIT were low. Thus, even though Keerthana cleared the IIT JEE exams, she elected to join UT Austin. She graduated with a major in computer science and biology, and thanks to her recent research experiences, has found a particular interest in neuroscience. She is planning to pursue those interests by either starting a company or enrolling in a PhD program.[5]

Despite the cost differential, close to 100,000 Indian students in 2012 pursued higher education in the United Sates. While a number of students received fellowships or financial assistance, particularly for graduate studies, the majority funded their own education. Another 90,000 Indian students are spread throughout the United Kingdom, Canada, Australia, New Zealand, Germany, and over one hundred other countries.[6] Six countries accounted for 85.7 percent of Indian students overseas. See the table below for a detailed breakdown.

Table 3.2: Indian Students Studying Overseas		
Country	Number of Students	% of Total Indian Students Overseas
United States	97,120	51.3%
United Kingdom	29,713	15.7%
Australia	11,684	6.2%
United Arab Emirates	8,247	4.4%
Canada	8,142	4.3%
New Zealand	7,248	3.8%
Source: UNESCO Institute for Statistics, 2012		
Table created by Shail Kumar		

At a cost of Rs 36 to 42 lakhs per student per year in the United States (assuming there are no scholarships), families in India are spending approximately Rs 35,313 to 41,140 crores (US$5.9 to US$6.9 billion) in overseas education just in the United States every year. This is a wonderful investment in a student's education. However, if India's higher education system were comparable to universities around the world, a significant percentage of these students would be studying in India. India would benefit from having smart, hardworking, and self-driven students in the Indian higher education system. The local and national economy would also benefit from the investment the family makes in paying for their child's tuition, fees, and living expenses.

The demand for overseas education is affecting high schools in India. There are secondary schools in India that are primarily preparing students for overseas education. They offer the international baccalaureate (IB) program that is more widely accepted by universities around the world than the Central Board of Secondary Education (CBSE), the Indian Certificate of Secondary Education (ICSE), or other indigenous programs. Most of these schools cater to children of the upper- and middle-class families who can afford an overseas education. Some schools, like the Doon

School, offer students the option of taking either the IB or the ICSE. According to Gautam Thapar of the Avantha Group, Doon School students and parents are encouraged to benefit from one of the most extensive counseling programs in India before enrolling in the IB program. Almost 50 percent of the recent graduating class of ninety-two students at the school took the IB with an eye toward studying overseas.[7] Recently, around 95 percent of the graduating twelfth class from the Dhirubhai Ambani International School in Mumbai went overseas for higher education. Those who stay in India felt "peer" pressure to leave India.

Students also leave India to pursue graduate studies in foreign universities. Students are attracted to overseas graduate programs for similar reasons as undergraduate programs. Several additional factors play a role. Some want to become an expert in a field and are attracted by the leading researchers in leading universities outside of India. Most who leave believe that the quality of research in India is not at the cutting edge. Some others go overseas to pursue a field that they really wanted to pursue but could not during their undergraduate studies in India.

Take Manas Kaushik for instance. He completed his MBBS from AIIMS and wanted to pursue a specialization in public health. When he was deciding, public health in India was not considered a worthwhile option for brilliant students like Kaushik. At AIIMS, it was among the lowest in pecking order for specializations. He also did not find any worthwhile options in India. The worldview of faculty members in India, including AIIMS, was limited, and there was little research in public health being conducted. So he applied and was accepted to the London School of Economics and Political Science (LSE) where he completed a master's in health economics and health policy. Kaushik decided to further his interests and joined Harvard University where he completed his doctoral degree in public health.[8]

Pursuing graduate studies in foreign universities is not limited to the alumni of premier institutions. Students who are talented, hardworking, and self-driven from colleges and universities in every field and from across the country are leaving for graduate studies in foreign countries.

Sampriti Bhattacharya always wanted to be an engineer and build things. Based on her twelfth class and entrance examination results, she joined West Bengal University of Technology (WBUT) in Kolkata. WBUT is a public college established by the West Bengal state government in 2001. A go-getter with a steely resolve, Bhattacharya found no opportunity to build things at WBUT. She started attending conferences and in one such meeting met a researcher from the Fermi Lab in the United States. She impressed the researcher and was accepted to a fully paid summer research program at the lab. She fell in love with the United States. The gender discrimination and hierarchy that she felt was constraining her in India was negligible in the United States. At the Fermi Lab, she was a valued member of the research team and her ideas mattered. Long story short, after WBUT, and after briefly working at the Fermi Lab, she completed her master's at Ohio State University. She is now completing her PhD at MIT. She is building robots that will be part of an underwater sensor network. She has started a company to take the idea forward. In addition, Bhattacharya has started a nonprofit organization to give Indian students an opportunity to get hands-on experiential learning, just like she was fortunate to receive at the Fermi Lab.[9]

Stories like Kaushik and Bhattacharya are unfolding in India and around the world. Stuti Misra completed her bachelor's in optometry from Bharati Vidyapeeth in Pune and then went to the University of Auckland for her higher studies.[10] Vinod Maseedupally and Moneisha Gokhale completed their bachelor's degrees from the Bausch and Lomb School of Optometry in Hyderabad and went on to pursue graduate studies at the University of New South Wales in Australia.[11] Hetal Parekh first went to St. Francis College in Hyderabad and then studied at the London School of Commerce.[12] Arijit Chakraborty, after completing a master's in vision science from BITS Pilani, is currently completing his PhD at the University of Auckland in visual neuroscience.[13] Rajiv Ratn Shah got multiple degrees in India before he joined a PhD program at the National University of Singapore.[14] Each of these students wanted something more and better and found it in Australia, New Zealand, Singapore, the United Kingdom, and the United States.

There is a second order of costs to students leaving India. Many of these smart students fall in love, with another student or with the country they studied in or both. Then life happens. These students get jobs, get married, have kids, and settle overseas, only to visit

India for vacations, family events, or business. In most cases, their expectations and mind-set change.

Smitha Tipparaju grew up in Chennai and then studied botany at Victoria College in Palakkad, an affiliated college of Calicut University in Kerala. After marriage, she and her husband moved to New Zealand. Tipparaju pursued graduate studies in molecular medicine at the University of Auckland. She loves her life in New Zealand and mentioned, "I can never live in India ever again." She attributes this view on India to change in her mind-set.[15]

After completing his postdoctoral studies at the University of Tennessee Health Science Center, Pradeep Lukka is planning to join a pharmaceutical company in New Zealand. Lukka completed his bachelor's from the V.L. College of Pharmacy, a college affiliated with the Rajiv Gandhi University of Health Sciences in Bangalore. Subsequently he completed his master's and PhD in pharmacology specializing in anticancer drug development from the University of Auckland. He then completed a postdoctoral stint at UC San Francisco. Going back to India is an option for Lukka. However, India would have to change a lot, especially in faculty salaries.[16]

Anand and Poonam are now US citizens and are not planning to return to India. Riti and Rishi are unlikely to ever call India home or ever settle in India. Their collective wisdom, hard work, wealth, and knowledge creation will have the highest impact overseas. India will get minimal to no benefit of the impact they make in the United States.

3. Graduates: "Unemployable"

As the economy has improved, the demand for well-prepared professionals has gone up. This has resulted in a sharp increase in the number of colleges and universities in India. However, due to poor education in most colleges, the number of well-trained professionals has not gone up in proportion to the capacity growth—almost 75 to 90 percent of graduating students are considered "unemployable" by industry.

Ill-prepared faculty members, limited and outdated curriculum, a blind focus on rote learning, no access to libraries, computers, or the Internet, and not having to attend classes to get a degree play a significant role in students' lack of employability. They are ill prepared for the working world at almost all levels. They lack knowledge and skills, and have no experience in asking questions, being creative, or applying their knowledge to make an impact. The National Association of Software and Services Companies' report "Perspective 2020: Transform Business, Transform India" (based on research conducted by McKinsey & Company) mentioned that "low employability of existing talent with only 10 to 15 percent employable graduates in business services and 26 percent of employable engineers in technology services continues to be a major bottleneck."[17]

Unemployability is forcing students to seek additional degrees.

Crutches for Poor Education: More Time and Money!

It has become common for a motivated student who joins a local college to simultaneously enroll in a supplemental program. Programs or correspondence courses with perceived market value in fields such as ICT and finance and accounting are in high demand. So when these students get their bachelor's degrees after three years, they can demonstrate better knowledge and skills than their colleagues. Others who are unemployed or underemployed after their first degree, like Mukund who works on an automobile assembly line, enroll in an ICT or another professional program to add to their credentials.

In 2013, I moderated a panel at the IIT Global Conference in Houston where Gururaj "Desh" Deshpande was a speaker. He is one of the most impressive people I have met. His worldviews are unique, optimistic, and solution-oriented. Founder of several successful start-ups, Deshpande is also a life member of the MIT Corporation and trustee of the Deshpande Foundation. The Deshpande Foundation funds many initiatives such as the Akshaya Patra Foundation and the Hubli Sandbox. The Akshaya Patra Foundation serves hot meals as part of the midday meal program to 1.4 million children in 10,661 schools across ten states in India. When he suggested that I visit Hubli to learn more about the Hubli Sandbox, I jumped at the opportunity. Visiting the Akshay Patra Kitchen, which is the purest expression of compassion and wisdom working together for the future of the country, was a bonus.[18]

Hubli Sandbox is a novel concept where the vision is to prepare "difference makers." Students learn work ethics, communication skills, computer skills, and get transformative experiential learning. Their daily schedule includes morning yoga, classes, project work, computer time, and additional reading and work time. Students work in small groups to find solutions to pressing local problems. Neelam Maheshwari, director for grants and programs, Deshpande Foundation in India calls it the "Silicon Valley for social entrepreneurship." They are creating an ecosystem and talent pool to solve local problems. She kindly took me to one of the classes. The students were engaged and eager to answer questions. I was also struck by how many of them had already completed their master's degrees. They were at the Hubli Sandbox because it offered (finally!) a compelling gateway to a more satisfying career and life. Many of its alumni have joined nongovernmental organizations (NGOs) or have launched start-ups, and all are pursuing more fulfilling professional careers. Their starting salaries, according to Maheshwari, are 40 percent more than those with comparable education and experiences. Equally important, the students are forever touched by Deshpande's spirit of hard work, work ethics, and finding solutions to local problems that matter. They are no longer job seekers; they are "difference makers."[19]

Arming themselves with multiple degrees is an appropriate response for students and families to make themselves more employable. But it comes at a huge cost—students are spending more time and money earning more degrees and credentials. Parents are investing more of their income and savings for their children's education. Many are taking loans and selling their assets.

Industry is also paying a heavy price for the current higher education system.

4. Hyper-Competition For Talent: Among Corporations

Recruiting and Retention Engine:
Finding the Gem in a Haystack and Keeping It

A few years back, I visited TCS in Hyderabad. Jasper Rine, a UC Berkeley faculty member, and I had gone to discuss a potential TCS–UC Berkeley collaboration. We met Ananth Krishnan, chief technology officer (CTO) at TCS, and several TCS R&D team members. As I recall, Krishnan, after sharing pertinent details about TCS, remarked that TCS is a human resource company and a recruiting engine since it recruits tens of thousands of professionals every year and employs several hundred thousand employees globally. It turns out, several industries and companies have established recruiting engines at a different scale than TCS in their own companies to combat the tremendous shortage of well-prepared professionals.

Anil Sachdev, one of the leading experts in the field of human resources management and founder of the School of Inspired Learning (SOIL), noted that, "There is extremely high cost and cycle time for hiring talent."[20] Thapar of the Avantha Group also believes that the current situation has made the cost of a bad hire too high.[21]

Thus, most companies review thousands of résumés to hire one person. They have multiple recruiting firms constantly scouring résumés for trained professionals. The hiring is a year-round and always-on process. HR managers are constantly reviewing short-listed résumés sent by the recruiting firms. Select employees within the company are periodically interviewing short-listed candidates on the phone and in-house. The final few candidates, who end up being highly sought after, are offered a job. Frequently, they get multiple offers, and the top few candidates might accept another firm's offer.

Because well-prepared professionals are in short supply, these few are heavily recruited by search firms to change companies. This has created several related problems—higher turnover, higher turnover-related costs, and salary inflation for recruitment and retention. The *Economic Times* published an article on January 16, 2015. It mentioned that Cisco, a multinational company in India, had increased the compensation for its top employees with a specific objective of reducing attrition. The compensation increases created 132 *crore patis* (one crore is equivalent to approximately US$167,700, six crores would be equivalent to US$1 million) in 2014, compared to three in 2013.[22]

Higher salary and bonuses to attract and retain well-prepared professionals is a win-win outcome for the individual and the company. However, in the context of India's demographics, higher compensation packages caused by an inadequate supply of talented professionals is unacceptable and avoidable. In the short term, higher recruiting and turnover costs and increasing salaries are reducing the profitability and pricing flexibility for the companies. In the long term, it has the potential of reducing market share and revenue growth for companies and the overall cost-competitiveness of the nation.

Training Enterprise: Recruiting and Polishing the Gems

One of the must-visit sites in Bengaluru is the Infosys campus. Infosys is both a trailblazer and one of the most respected companies in India. The co-founders, N. R. Narayana Murthy, K. Dinesh, Nandan Nilekani, Ashok Arora, S. D. Shibulal, Kris Gopalakrishnan, and N. S. Raghavan, have raised the bar for good governance and succession planning. Infosys has created thousands of millionaires, and its investors, customers, and community have benefited from its commitment to its stakeholders. Furthermore, Infosys is famous for establishing Infosys University, which may be the largest training center of its kind in India, training over 30,000 Infosys employees at any one point. This makes it bigger than any premier education institution in the country.

Like Infosys, many companies have invested in in-house training centers for their new recruits. The purpose of Infosys University and similar training centers is simple — make the newly employed professionals ready for the working world. They are filling the gap left by the current education system. This also costs a lot of financial and human resources that could have been deployed elsewhere.

Sujit Baksi, chief executive of the business services group at Tech Mahindra, mentioned that his company typically invests sixty days of in-class training and assigns a new employee for billing, revenue-generating projects, after one hundred and eighty to two hundred and forty days of hiring.[23] "One of the biggest complaints we receive from our customers is that our employees [more recent graduates] do not ask questions and do not make creative suggestions," noted Mukesh Aghi, former CEO of L&T Infotech. "They are so used to rote learning and passing exams in schools and college, that they are used to following directions," Aghi added. Thus, they invest six to twelve months to prepare recent graduates for productive work.[24] This is a significant investment of resources to ensure that a fresh college graduate is ready for productive work.

This is not just an IT industry phenomenon. Ajay Bakaya, executive director of Sarovar Hotels & Resorts, is a hospitality industry veteran. He has spent over thirteen years at the Oberoi Hotel and over nineteen years at the Sarovar chain of hotels and resorts. Recalling his days at the Oberoi, he mentioned how Oberoi had started a program with a hotel management institute to ensure students coming out of the institute were ready for employment in the hospitality industry. In this program, students would spend six months in the institute, followed by six months at Oberoi, another six at the institute, and then six more at Oberoi.[25]

All industries, with varying degrees, are compensating for inadequately prepared workers by investing more in their training programs.

The nation is also paying a heavy price.

5. Nation's Competiveness, Mega Challenges, and the Future: Paying a Price Today and Mortgaging the Future

Innovation and Entrepreneurship: A Drop in the Ocean

The culture of mediocrity, the focus on rote learning and exam preparation, the reverence of seniors, and a hierarchical culture have taken the oxygen out of being creative, challenging existing notions, and pursuing bold ideas. We are still paying a price for License Raj, which stifled competition and innovation in the country. As a result, the companies and the nation are paying a price with inadequate new venture creation and product innovation. In 2013, US$48.5 billion of venture capital (VC) funding was invested globally. India accounted for just 3.7 percent of the global total. See the table below. In the last decade more start-ups have been created, which is a positive trend. However, for the scale of the nation's need, the current innovation and entrepreneurship engine is a mere drop in the ocean.

Table 3.3: Venture Capital Investments in 2013		
Country	Amounts (US$ in Billions)	% of Global Investment
USA	$33.1	68.2%
China	$3.5	7.2%
India	$1.8	3.7%
Global Investments	$48.5	

Sources: Dow Jones VentureSource 2014, EY Global Venture Capital Insights and Trends 2014

Table created by Shail Kumar

In July 2015, I attended the IIT Global Leadership Conference. One of the panels was on new venture creation in India. It included venture capitalists and successful India-based entrepreneurs. One of the biggest headaches for the entrepreneurs was finding talent in India. Talent acquisition and retention took up a significant part of the panel discussion. These founders are experimenting with unique solutions to finding talent for their respective companies. The ideas include recruiting fresh graduates from colleges and universities and training them, finding talent overseas and incentivizing them to return to India, or establishing business processes that enable them to seamlessly integrate talent who live overseas with their India-based operations. A country of 1.3 billion people is short of well-prepared professionals, and it is affecting rapid expansion of start-ups and large companies.

Innovation and entrepreneurship drive growth, and not having them in full force is adversely affecting economic growth and job creation. The economy is not firing on all cylinders. Everyone is impacted by inadequate job growth. Additional funds that the government could have earned from a higher tax base could be deployed to address many of the nation's mega challenges.

Mega Challenges: Unsolved Problems

India is facing numerous mega challenges outlined in detail in Chapter 1. These are complex and multidisciplinary problems, which need to be addressed at many levels. Significant research has to be done. Ideas have to be brainstormed, discussed, and short-listed. Experiments have to be conducted thoughtfully and cost-effectively. Winning solutions have to be piloted. The most effective and efficient solutions have to then be scaled quickly. Most importantly, young, energetic, and smart minds must be applied to these problems.

Almost 100 percent of India's undergraduate students get no exposure to research. Almost all the education institutions have no focus on making an impact in the community. Thus, we are losing the opportunity to unleash the passion, power, and potential of tens of millions of our youth to solve our own problems. And we are missing the opportunity to address these problems cost-effectively and quickly.

Economy and National Security: Overdependence on Imports

The lack of research and innovation has another costly impact on the economy and the nation: lack of new products and product-based companies. To make the economy more sustainable and robust, we need more start-ups, more homegrown product-based global companies, more export orientation, and more manufacturing. And to be successful in the global markets, these products have to competitive. Not having a vibrant research, innovation, and entrepreneurial engine is leading to missed opportunities and lost potential for the economy. The result is heavy dependence on imports. From 2013 to 2014, India imported approximately US$450 billion of goods, of which oil accounted for 40.3 percent and precious and semiprecious gems 13 percent. At least 33 percent of imports, approximately US$150 billion, are high-technology-related goods where there is a significant contribution of research, innovation, and manufacturing.[26] The dependence on imports is even more striking in capital expenditures. From 2010 to 2025, India is expected to spend US$200 billion on capital expenditures. Currently it spends 70 percent of the capital expenditures on imports.[27]

This does not just affect our current account or foreign exchange reserves—it affects our national security. Could our Internet be brought down? Could satellite or wireless communication be blocked? Could desalination technology be restricted? Could drought resistant seeds be stopped from entering India? Could the much-needed drug to combat an epidemic be too expensive for the masses? Do we have enough IP, research, and manufacturing resources to ensure our 1.3 billion people's futures are not compromised? In case of a military conflict, could key technologies be restricted by the enemy, which could affect the outcome for India?

The broken and disconnected higher education system poses a risk for the nation and society today. It also severely impacts future generations of students and professionals and our nation's competitive position.

The Next Generation of Faculty Members, School Teachers, and Professionals: At High Risk

Higher education, including vocational education, is at the intersection where young adults are prepared for working life.

72

Higher education institutions are where people from all walks of life and professions are educated and prepared for their life and careers. The primary and secondary school teachers are also getting their specialized degrees in various subjects and the BEd degrees in the colleges and universities. Faculty members, who prepare everyone for life and careers, including teaching, are also getting educated and prepared in colleges and universities. Today's higher education system is falling short in preparing the next generation of faculty members, schoolteachers, and professionals. The nation's competitive position is at risk.

The problems of the higher education system are staring us in our faces. One way or another, everyone is paying a hefty price. Before we can solve the problems, it is critical to know how we got into such a messy situation. As someone wise remarked, "To get out of the ditch and then stay out of it, it is really important to know how we got into the ditch in the first place." My next chapter tackles that in detail.

CHAPTER 4

Contributing Factors: An Inside Job

*When a crime occurs, half the punishment goes to the guilty, a quarter to
his ally, and another quarter falls to those who remain silent.*

—Rishi Kashyapa, Mahabharata

Bengaluru, 2013: Anjana Kapoor and Jayesh Patil returned to India
after completing their PhDs at UT Austin. At UT Austin, they got
hooked on research, teaching, and each other. For family and
personal reasons, Jayesh and Anjana wanted to return to India. For
professional reasons, they both really wanted to work at either an
IIT or IISc. Life had other plans for them, and they ended up joining
a multinational company (MNC). Higher education institutions in
India, including premier institutions, continue to lose the best and
the brightest talent to industry.

In 2007, Jayesh completed his B.Tech. from BITS Pilani and
Anjana her B.Tech. from the National Institute of Technology (NIT) in
Trichy. They joined UT Austin on research scholarships. Jayesh and
Anjana also shared a passion for making a difference in India and
met at an Association for India's Development (AID) Austin chapter
event. Founded in 1991, AID supports grassroots organizations in
India and has approximately 800 volunteers and thirty-six chapters
in the United States. AID's Run for India program caught Anjana
and Jayesh's fancy, and they started preparing for the marathon and
raising funds for several grassroots organizations in India. At the
same time, they also got hooked on research, she in bioengineering
and he in analytics of large-scale data. They both also enjoyed teaching

undergraduates. After years of running together, organizing and attending AID-Austin parties, raising funds for India, and talking about their hopes and dreams, they realized they loved each other as well. With their family's blessings, they soon got married.

Shortly thereafter, the two started planning their return to India. IITs and IISc showed interest, and they received multiple offers. With their friends' urging, they had also sent out feelers to a few MNC R&D organizations in Bengaluru. They were pleasantly surprised that the offers from MNCs were several times more than the IITs. MNCs also offered significant incentives for them to relocate to India and join their research teams. The final factor that pushed them to accept the MNC offers were the amazing pools of talent with similar backgrounds, experiences, and a culture similar to UT Austin's — fast-paced, open, collaborative, merit based, and impact oriented.

By now, you know that transforming India's higher education is pivotal to addressing its numerous mega challenges, spurring the economy, and unleashing the potential, power, and passion of hundreds of millions of Indians. You also know that it is broken on all fronts that matter and is disconnected with the needs and aspirations of its people and nation. Finally, directly or indirectly, everyone is paying a price for the system. Why are we not attracting the best and the brightest talent to higher education? What has made India's higher education system broken and disconnected? How did we get into this ditch? Before we address the problems, we must answer these questions.

Since independence in 1947, we have designed, managed, and regulated our higher education system. Thus, only we are responsible and accountable for the outcomes. There are several key reasons for the current state of India's higher education:

1. **Regulations and Regulatory Bodies:** There is a multiplicity of regulatory bodies at the central and state levels. The regulations are prescriptive and heavy-handed, which has made the system unattractive to the best and the brightest people.

2. **Corruption:** It is rampant and rising. It is also stoking nonmeritorious reasons for hiring, awards, promotions, and selection to faculty and leadership positions.

3. **Governance:** Politicians and bureaucrats hold key positions in governing bodies of public colleges and universities. They have mired the institutions and processes in red tape and made them more political and regional.

4. **Faculty Salaries and Incentives:** Faculty salaries and incentives have lagged behind that of industry. As a result, the best and the brightest students are either flocking to industry and not joining academia, or leaving India altogether.

5. **Leadership and Vested Interests:** Politicians directly and indirectly own the majority of private and affiliated colleges. For them, colleges and universities have become "money-making" factories. Thus, they resist any effort to reform the higher education system.

Let's consider each of these five factors in more detail.

1. Regulations and Regulatory Bodies: Fragmented and Prescriptive

The University Grants Commission (UGC) and other regulations and regulatory bodies were the most mentioned issue in my interviews with over seventy-five industry titans, entrepreneurs, investors, corporate executives, university leaders, faculty members, and thought leaders. Roddam Narasimha, DST Year-of-Science Professor at the Jawaharlal Nehru Centre for Advanced Scientific Research (JNCASR) and former faculty member at IISc Bangalore, aptly captured the viewpoint of all when he said, "Today it [UGC] is a body that overregulates and undermanages the system. It is less interested in outcomes and more in rules."[1]

"Today it [UGC] is a body that overregulates and undermanages the system. It is less interested in outcomes and more in rules."

Regulatory bodies in India are fragmented. There is a regulatory body for technical education, another for medical, and yet another for law and so on. There are regulatory bodies at the central government level and then there are similar ones at the state level. Thus, if a philanthropist or organization wanted to establish a multidisciplinary university, they would either need an act of parliament or be approved by a state act. In addition, they would need to follow the provisions laid out by UGC and the All India Council for Technical Education (AICTE), the Indian Council for Agricultural Research (ICAR), the Indian Nursing Council (INC), the Bar Council of India (BCI), the Central Council of Homeopathy (CCH), the Council of Architects (CoA), the Dental Council of India (DCI), the Distance Education Council (DEC), the Medical Council of India (MCI), the National Council for Teacher Education (NCTE), the Pharmacy Council of India (PCI), and the Rehabilitation Council of India (RCI).[2] The National Knowledge Commission in its *Report to the Nation* (2006–2009) noted that:

> The present regulatory system in higher education is flawed in some important respects. The barriers to entry are too high. The system of authorizing entry is cumbersome. There is a multiplicity of regulatory agencies where mandates are both confusing and overlapping.[3]

> First, in India, it requires an Act of Legislature of Parliament to set up a University. The deemed university route is much too difficult for new institutions. Entry through legislation alone, as at present, is a formidable barrier. The consequence is a steady increase in the average size of existing universities with a steady deterioration in their quality.[4]

> There are several instances where an engineering college or a business school is approved, promptly, in a small house of a metropolitan suburb without the requisite teachers, infrastructure or facilities, but established universities experience difficulties in obtaining similar approvals. Such examples can be multiplied. These would only confirm that the complexity, the multiplicity, and the rigidity of the existing regulatory structure is not conducive to the expansion of higher education opportunities in India.[5]

Regulatory bodies in India are also prescriptive. The founder(s) and operators of the university have to follow strict guidelines on the curriculum, fee structure, infrastructure, governance, number of students, faculty salaries, and student to faculty ratio. The regulatory bodies' influence continues after approval. UGC, by law, can inspect and ensure compliance with the prescribed guidelines.

In 2007, AICTE served notice to over two hundred institutes in the country for offering technical education courses without obtaining prior approval. They published names of these institutes on their website, recommended that students not join them, and demanded the institutes seek their approval. One of these two hundred institutes was the Indian School of Business (ISB). The ISB did not care about AICTE approval. Neither did its students, founders and promoters, or employers.[6] For context, ISB, according to its website, was the first business school in south Asia to be recognized by the Association to Advance Collegiate Schools of Business (AACSB), which is earned by less than 5 percent of the world's business schools and is considered one of the premier management schools in the country and the world.

In August 2014, UGC directed IISc Bangalore to stop its four-year undergraduate program... It was like an umpire (UGC) walking down to the cricket pitch and telling Sachin Tendulkar (IISc) how to bat.

In August 2014, UGC directed IISc Bangalore to stop its four-year undergraduate program.[7] IISc was established in 1909 as a culmination of Jamsetji Nusserwanji Tata's dream and has since established itself as a premier research and teaching institute. In 2014, IISc was the only Indian institution to be ranked in the top 500 in global rankings of universities. The UGC, as a matter of context, was officially established in 1956. It was like an umpire (UGC) walking down to the cricket pitch and telling Sachin Tendulkar (IISc) how to bat. Enough said.

Furthermore, if someone wants to establish a university in multiple states, they would have to get approvals from each state. Nandan Nilekani, co-founder of Infosys, and fellow collaborators are planning to establish the Indian Institute of Human Settlements (IIHS), a research and teaching institution focused on urban planning and related topics. IIHS is a novel concept and much needed in light of one of India's mega challenges–urban migration. They are waiting for the approval of a legislation known as the "Innovation University bill" that would make it easier for them to establish such a university in multiple states and reduce the regulatory burden.[8] Nilekani, the IIHS board, and its promoters are influential and likely to get regulatory approval sooner than most people. However, they have already waited for over two years.

T. V. Mohandas Pai, chairman of Manipal Global Education and former chief financial officer at Infosys, made a striking point: "UGC and additional regulatory bodies focus on input factors such as the area of the land, built square footage, total number of students, student-teacher ratio, number of hours a day of teaching, and constituency of the board of directors, and not on the outcomes."[9]

The overprescriptive and fragmented regulation that focuses on inputs and not on outcomes has attracted mostly corrupt operators. It has also kept most of honest and well-meaning people and organizations away from the sector. It is common to hear stories about inspectors visiting a college for assessment or accreditation and the college administration preparing their college for the inspection by renting books, computers, and even teachers for the day. There are businesses that provide services for passing the inspection. As long as the college operators can demonstrate that inputs are consistent with the regulations, even for a day, they are good until the next assessment cycle. Once the inspection is completed, the rented books are taken to the next college. In many cases, if not all, inspectors know about this practice.

We have a License Raj in higher education. Gurcharan Das in *India Unbound* captures the impact of the License Raj: "The endless delay in clearing applications discourage the entry of efficient and honest entrants and rewarded wily, inefficient producers who could manipulate the system. It raised costs, brought delays, arbitrariness, and corruption, and achieved nothing. We killed at birth any hope for an industrial revolution."[10] Das was talking about License Raj in industry. He may as well be speaking about higher education.

2. Corruption: Rampant and Increasing

The License Raj epidemic has resulted in rampant corruption in higher education. According to many "old-timers," it is increasing at an alarming rate. The vice chancellor (VC) posts are being bought and sold for tens of crores of rupees. Prestigious awards are being given to favored candidates rather than the most deserving. Faculty positions are also being marketed. Once in a VC position of an affiliating university, VCs are known to ask for and get bribes from the owners of affiliated colleges. The capitation fees, which are voluntary or coerced donations to secure admissions, collected in cash, are additional means of generating black money and influence for those in power. Pawan Agarwal, an Indian Administrative Service (IAS) officer who spent several years in the Ministry of Human Resource Development (MHRD) and later was an adviser on higher education to the Planning Commission, wrote a book in 2009 titled *Indian Higher Education: Envisioning the Future.* He wrote, "Private deemed universities are mostly family-run institutions. These are either families that play important role in politics themselves or earn political patronage by dispensing favors like out-of-turn admissions. It is therefore not surprising that they wield great influence in the shaping of policy on private education."[11]

Higher education has largely become a business, and many call colleges and universities "money-making factories." The founders and operators of the colleges and universities, which are run under nonprofit laws, have found ways to channel the funds into their private accounts. Thanks to India's demographics, there is a tremendous demand for education. Through License Raj, politicians have successfully kept the supply of outstanding education institutions low. Customers (students) keep coming as they have limited or no options. The faculty, administrative, and related expenses are kept low by hiring inadequately trained faculty or having faculty on short-term contracts. The regulators, who report to the politicians one way or another, are kept from harming their business interests. Revenues and profits are predictable and risk free. For the unscrupulous and corrupt, this business proposition is incredibly compelling.

Many involved in this case, including one journalist, have died mysteriously. As a result of the national debate and discussion and increasing concerns, in July 2015, the Supreme Court of India asked the Central Bureau of Investigation (CBI) to take over investigation of all the cases related to the Vyapam scandal.

The Vyapam scandal currently rocking the nation is yet another glaring example of deeply rooted corruption. So far, hundreds of students and parents have been booked and many politicians, officials, and middlemen have been arrested. The Madhya Pradesh

(MP) former education minister is one of those arrested. On February 25, 2015, MP's governor resigned after a First Information Report (FIR) was registered against him.[12] Many involved in this case, including one journalist, have died mysteriously. As a result of the national debate and discussion and increasing concerns, in July 2015, the Supreme Court of India asked the Central Bureau of Investigation (CBI) to take over investigation of all the cases related to the Vyapam scandal.[13] While the flurry of allegations and cover-ups are still going on, it is evident to all that a massive scam has occurred. It included politicians, bureaucrats, police officers, government officials, parents, and students.

Vyapam is short for MP Vyavsayik Pareeksha Mandal, also known as the MP Professional Examination Board (MPPEB). It is a self-financed autonomous body incorporated by the MP government. Vyapam's governing body includes several top state bureaucrats, vice chancellors of several colleges, and state political leaders. It has the responsibility of conducting entrance examinations for admission to various colleges in the state, such as the PreMedical Test (PMT) for entrance to the state's medical colleges and the PAT for entrance to B.Tech. (agricultural engineering), BSc (Ag.), BSc (forestry), BSc (horticulture), and BSc (Ag. and entrepreneurship). It is a powerful body for all aspiring students interested in professional education and their parents. Its website makes that message explicit:

> It is worth mentioning that only on the basis of these tests one can get admission to the courses recognized by national level bodies like All India Council for Technical Education (AICTE), Medical Council of India (MCI), NCTE New Delhi etc. against seats available in various institutions of the state.[14]

Parents of the students aspiring to become doctors gave bribes to be selected in the Vyapam-managed PMT exams. For these particular students, fake test takers were allowed to take the exams on their behalf. Some of them were allowed to sit next to a fake test taker and copy their answers. Some received high marks fraudulently. It is also alleged that key people in Vyapam, the state's ministry, the bureaucracy, the police, and the exam officials were involved to pull off this scandal at a massive scale.

Another instance of corruption occurs in faculty hiring. As part of the sixth pay commission salary increases, it was also required that a person must have a PhD to be eligible for an assistant professor position at a college or university. For most of the population, faculty positions offer a decent income and secure lifetime employment. Thus, they are in high demand in the section of the population that is unable to compete in private sector jobs, go overseas, or get another government job. Now, PhD theses and degrees are being purchased for a fee, and PhD degrees are being completed in two to three years, suspiciously quicker than the global averages. In addition, faculty positions are being sold and bought or made on factors that do not involve merit.

As a result of such rampant corruption, students, learning outcomes, having a culture of excellence, and making an impact have taken a backseat. Those who are making money through corruption are illicit beneficiaries, and everyone is paying a price for this rampant corruption.

Politicians and bureaucrats run and manage regulatory bodies and decide on regulations that affect the entire higher education system. Central and state governments fund the institutions. Furthermore, access to youth and their associated power and influence is an added incentive for politicians to interfere with the colleges and universities. As a result, politicians and bureaucrats are extensively engaged in the governance of the system at the college and university levels.

3. Governance: Politicians and Bureaucrats Damaging the Institutions and Processes

The central government not only funds many universities, it also ends up having the final say on major issues such as pay scales, career progression of faculty, and appointment of the leadership. Pawan Agarwal notes, "Central government makes key appointments in all central universities, other central institutions of higher education, and central regulatory agencies. This enables the central government to have a final say on major issues."[15]

The chancellor for all state universities is the state's governor. Governors, typically, serve at the pleasure and confidence of the central government. However, the state government has significant interest and stake in the universities. If the central and state governments are not allies, then it is a source of tension in the running of the university.

Caste and regional considerations have crept up in the appointments of vice chancellors, other key leadership positions, and faculty members.

"Our universities are now among the last remaining holdouts of the top-down state, where the government's word passes down the ranks, and is carried out by its bureaucrats,"[16] wrote Nandan Nilekani. The chapter title "Institutions of Sands: Our Universities" in his book *Imagining India: The Idea of a Renewed Nation* itself conveys a lot.

In a scathing criticism of the bureaucracy inflicting India's higher education Philip G. Altbach, professor at Boston College and an avid writer on international higher education, and N. Jayaram, professor and dean, School of Social Sciences, Tata Institute of Social Sciences (TISS) in Mumbai, wrote:

> India is world famous for sclerotic bureaucracy, and higher education fits into that mold. Few decisions can be made without taking permission from an authority above, and the wheels of decision making grind slowly. Fear of corruption or of a loss of control entrenches bureaucracy. Teachers and academic leaders and colleges and universities have little incentive to innovate higher education–indeed quite the opposite.[17]

Scandals like Vyapam, instances of unnecessary meddling by regulatory agencies, and the overall inept vision and management of the higher education system over the past sixty-eight years have killed any confidence in the political and bureaucratic leadership. The iron grip of regulations and regulatory bodies, corruption, and poor governance have practically robbed India's academia of any luster. The faculty members are no longer held in high esteem by the society as they once were. Inadequate faculty salaries and incentives are outcomes of these factors and a contributing factor as well.

4. Faculty Salaries and Incentives: Dysfunctional

Much like Jayesh and Anjana, every smart student faces a fork at the end of each stage of their education. The salaries, incentives, and cultures play a significant role in these decisions. Currently, students graduating with a B.Tech. from an IIT or a postgraduate diploma in management (PGDM) from an IIM are receiving pay packages in the crores of rupees per year. While most of these high-profile cases are rare even for IITs and IIMs, the pay scale is several times higher than higher education institutions. Thanks to the sixth pay commission, salaries and benefits have increased for all government employees, including faculty members. The table below is a snapshot of faculty compensation.

Table 4.1: Entry-level Compensation for Faculty Members in India		
(Based on sixth-pay commission)		
	Annual Compensation (Rs.)	Annual Compensation (US$)	% increase from one level to the next
Professor	1,621,200	$27,020	11%
Associate Professor	1,457,520	$24,292	35%
Assistant Professor	1,080,000	$18,000	41%
Assistant Professor(Contract)	766,896	$12,782	-

Note: Compensation includes salary, academic grade pay (AGP), dearness allowance (DA), traveling allowance (TA), and house rent allowance (HRA); Foreign Exchange @ Rs. 60/$

Source: IIT Gandhinagar, www.iitgn.ac.in

Table created by Shail Kumar

Faculty salaries and benefits lag behind salaries in industry, and what the best and the brightest faculty members might get in countries with welcoming immigration policies, such as the United States. A professional in a corporation, after around fifteen years of experience, currently makes Rs 45–70 lakhs compared to Rs 15–16 lakhs in academia. The industry compensation also has a higher variation for above- or below-average performance. Thus, it is possible for an executive with over fifteen years' experience to make over Rs 1 crores. It is evident from the table that there is not much of a jump in compensation from assistant professor to associate professor and than to professor. After working over thirty years as a faculty member, the best one could expect is a 60 percent raise from when they first started. In industry, the comparable increase is more likely to be 1,000 to 2,000 percent.

In addition, after a one-year probation, everyone is confirmed as a permanent faculty member. The difference in compensation for a high-performing and low-performing faculty member is trivial. Finally, unless they break the law in a rather egregious manner, every faculty member can expect a full pension benefit. This means that the upside for a high-performing faculty member is negligible and the downside for a low-performing faculty member is also negligible. Thus, the incentive structure in academia is clearly dysfunctional.

As a result, the best and the brightest students in India are either headed to industry or for higher education overseas. The pay scale in the IT industry is so attractive that it is drawing students from all engineering disciplines such as mechanical, civil, and mining. Pursuing a PhD in India is one of the last options for bright students today. This problem is affecting even ICT program organization, as the better software developers are taking IT jobs. The trainers at these programs, like where Mukund Kapase studied, are the ones who could not get IT jobs.

5. Leadership and Vested Interests: The Ultimate Stranglehold

Do the central and state leaders and bureaucrats believe that there is no problem in the higher education system? Or do they believe that higher education is not important for the people, economy, state, or nation?

There have been a number of national committees that have extensively reviewed the higher education system. Some of the recent ones include: *Taking IITs to Excellence and Greater Relevance: Report of Dr. Anil Kakodkar Committee* (April 2011), *Report of the Committee to Advise on Renovation and Rejuvenation of Higher Education* (the Yashpal Committee, 2009), and the National Knowledge Commission's *Report to the Nation* (2006–2009). All of them have made recommendations to reform. Industry leaders and industry organizations, such as the Confederation of Indian Industry (CII) and FICCI, have also repeatedly appealed for changes. Higher education plays a critical role in addressing our mega challenges, making our economy sustainable, and preparing our youth for their careers and lives. All evidence points toward the fact that the importance of higher education is ingrained in our society.

This, then, suggests that vested interests are coming in the way of making changes to the current system. The vested interests care about private gains and not about the country and its people. Political interference in colleges and universities creates significant short-term gains for the political parties and leaders. People are filling their personal bank accounts by running substandard educational institutions, receiving bribes in exchange for seats and degrees, and issuing licenses to open new institutions. Keeping the system shackled

CONTRIBUTING FACTORS: AN INSIDE JOB

and broken helps substandard institutions, the coaching industry, the brokers who profit from supply-and-demand shortages, the overseas educational institutions, and perhaps many more individuals and organizations, which all benefit from a weak and dependent India.

In this mix of overregulation and corruption, the politicians are thriving. According to some reports, 50 to 80 percent of colleges are owned directly or indirectly by politicians and their families. "Politicians have emerged as the singly largest provider of new higher educational institutions," note Devesh Kapur and Pratap Bhanu Mehta.[18]

"We have created an election system where there is actually an incentive for our politicians to keep our people poor, helpless, and illiterate."

Narayana Murthy captures this misalignment between the public's interest to be well educated and well prepared for life and the politicians' private vested interests: "We have created an election system where there is actually an incentive for our politicians to keep our people poor, helpless, and illiterate."[19] Again, enough said.

This concludes the three chapters that assess our current higher education system. To make the stories of Gautama Raju, Amarjit Singh, Pooja Shah, Meera Gupta, Ziya Khan, and Arjun Das a reality and to stop repeating stories like the ones of Mukund Kapase, Anand and Poonam Mehta, and hundreds of millions of other Indians, we must transform our higher education system.

Bad news: We have designed, managed, and regulated our higher education system, and the outcomes are inadequate.

Good news: Since we have designed and are managing and regulating the system, we can transform it as well. Now.

To make the transformation effective and efficient, it is necessary to conduct an honest evaluation and learn from others. Could we learn from our glorious past when we built universities over a thousand years before the first modern university was built in Europe? Could we learn from the nations and institutions that are currently leading the world in higher education? What are those lessons? The next section and the five chapters are devoted to learning from Nalanda University in ancient India, the United States, the state of California, the University of California (UC) in Berkeley, and Stanford University.

SECTION 3

Benchmarking:
Learning from the Best

CHAPTER 5

Nalanda University:
The View from 1,400 Years Ago

*If there is one place on the face of the earth where all the dreams
of living men have found a home from the very earliest days when
man began the dream of existence, it is India.*

— Romain Rolland, Nobel laureate,
French scholar

Nalanda Vihara, between 629 and 645 CE: Xuánzàng, a renowned
scholar from China, arrived in India. The objective of his historic
visit was to learn about the Buddhist principles and doctrines,
see India's famous shrines, and gather sacred texts. He traveled
extensively and spent several years at Nalanda University.
Xuánzàng was one of many scholars who visited India from
around the world, especially China, Indonesia, Korea, Mongolia,
Sri Lanka, and Tibet, who were attracted by India's religious and
intellectual advancements and higher education institutions such
as Nalanda University.[1]

During this time, Nalanda University was the center of higher
learning in the country and the world. The University of Bologna,
one of the earliest universities in the western world, would be
established in 1088,[2] over four hundred and fifty years after
Xuánzàng's visit to India. The University of Oxford was established
in 1096.[3]

Xuánzàng was famously preceded to India by Faxian, a Chinese scholar, who traveled in India between 399 and 414 CE. Upon Xuánzàng's arrival at Nalanda, Xuánzàng was received with honor and respect and escorted by four of its most distinguished teachers, as was the practice when welcoming well-known scholars. He formally met Shilabhadra, the head of Nalanda, and expressed a desire to learn Yoga Shastra from Shilabhadra. He was admitted to Nalanda and given appropriate residence, food, supplies, and assistants befitting his stature as a respected scholar.

Sixteen years after first arriving in India, Xuánzàng returned to China carrying with him 657 sacred books of Buddhism and images of the Buddha and his saints in gold, silver, crystal, and sandalwood. Twenty horses were needed to carry all of this.

Thanks to scholars such as Xuánzàng, Faxian, and Yijing, we have a recorded history of ancient and medieval India, including Nalanda University. Its scale, scope, and level of excellence were impressive. Its faculty and alumni were famous. Its mission, values, culture, able self-governance, and generous support from kings, merchants, and the community explain how it sustained itself for over one thousand years.

Nalanda University: Ancient Indian and Buddhist Roots

Nalanda University Key Numbers

- Founded: around **100 CE**
- Students: **3,000–10,000**
- Teachers: **1,510–2,000**
- Number of lectures per day: **100**
- Endowment: land grant and revenues from **200 villages**
- Longevity: lasted for over **1,000 years** before being demolished around 1197 by invaders

Source: Various

Nalanda University's history can be traced back to Buddha and the empires of Magadha, Maurya, Gupta, and Harsha. According to Alexander Cunningham, founder of the Archaeological Survey of India, Nalanda, the ancient village, is the modern Baragaon, seven miles north of Rajgir in Bihar.

Gautama Buddha was born in sixth century BCE.[4] He renounced his royal privileges to find the meaning of life. Subsequently, he founded Buddhism and spent a number of years in Rajgir, where he is known to have given many important sermons.

The land where Nalanda University was established was initially a gift to the Buddha by five hundred merchants.[5]

Around the time of the Buddha, in Northern India, the Kashi, Koshala, Magadha, and Vajjan confederacies were important. After nearly a hundred years, Magadha emerged victorious and became the center of political activity in northern India. With its capital in Pataliputra, the Magadha Empire reigned supreme through 400 BCE. After Magadha came the Shishunaga and Nanda dynasties. Chandragupta Maurya became the founder of the Mauryan dynasty in 321 BCE. Kautilya, a Brahman also known as Chanakya, was his mentor and guide. Chandragupta was succeeded by Bindusara and then by Ashoka. Shortly after the Kalinga War in 260 BCE, Ashoka converted to Buddhism and stopped all of the wars. His encouragement fuelled the growth of Buddhism around the world.[6]

Ashoka gave significant gifts to promote Buddhism, including the first grant to establish a *vihara* or "monastery" in Nalanda.[7] However, not much is known about Nalanda University until the fourth century CE, when it most likely gained prominence as a university. R. K. Mookerji, historian and author of *Ancient Indian Education,* estimated that Nalanda was most likely established after the beginning of the Common Era and the advent of Mahayana Buddhism. This estimate is supported by Xuánzàng's account of his visit to India between 629–645 CE: "The priests dwelling here, are, as a body, naturally or spontaneously dignified and grave, so that during the 700 years since the foundation of the establishment, there has been no single case of guilty rebellion against the rules."[8]

In addition to the opportunity to learn Buddhist and Vedic philosophy, logic, grammar, practical sciences and arts, and public debating, there was an emphasis on physical health, moral development, and discipline.

After Ashoka's and the merchants' initial land grants, several merchants and kings provided lands and gifts to Nalanda University. Harsha is one of the last famous kings to have supported Buddhism. It is believed that the university at its high point received revenues from two hundred villages,[9] which along with the royal patronage enabled the monks and students to focus on their teaching and learning.

Scale: Grand

During the time when Buddhism was growing in popularity, Buddhist monasteries were the centers for higher education in the country. During Xuánzàng's time in India, there were five thousand monasteries and close to two hundred thousand monks.[10] The higher education system was connected to a well-developed elementary education system.[11]

Anywhere from three thousand to ten thousand students were enrolled at Nalanda. At ten thousand, it would be larger than most colleges or universities in today's India. It attracted students from all over the country and many parts of the world. Its preeminence was such that only 20 percent of those who took the entrance exam were admitted to the university. Only ordained students did not have to take the entrance examination.

By then in India, there were several sects of Buddhism and many schools of Vedic philosophy. Students included monks of different schools of Buddhist thoughts, and people of all creeds and faiths. These also included unordained students, including householders. Thus, there was a lot of diversity among students on the campus.

Thanks to generous endowments and gifts, Nalanda took care of all the clothing, food, supplies, residence, medicine, and related needs for its teachers and students. Non-Buddhist students had to take care of their tuition fees. Some received charitable contributions to study. Those who could not pay worked in the university-owned villages or the university itself. This suggests a well-developed financial model for sustaining excellence at the university and encouraging student enrollment.

Nalanda had about 1,500 teachers. According to one of the accounts, "There are 1,000 men who could explain twenty collections of Sutras and Shastras; 500 who can explain thirty collections, and perhaps 10 (including Xuánzàng) who could explain fifty collections."[12] The university offered over one hundred lectures per day.

It also had a well-equipped library. Yijing, the Chinese scholar who visited India in AD 672, collected 400 Sanskrit texts amounting to 5,000 *shlokas* or "verses." Based on archaeology and additional written commentary, there were three library buildings, one of which was nine stories tall.

Even measured by today's standards, Nalanda University's scale was grand and impressive.

Scope and Method:
Multidisciplinary, Holistic, and Demanding

Nalanda was a Buddhist monastery. Its official seal was the dharma wheel flanked by two gazelles. The dharma wheel has eight spokes representing the eightfold path of Buddhism, and gazelles are supposed to be the first witnesses to the Buddha's preaching. Yet, Nalanda University offered opportunities to learn in fields that were comprehensive at the time — Buddhist and Vedic philosophy, logic, grammar, practical sciences, and arts.[13]

At Nalanda, oral instruction and oral examinations were the norm. Reciting texts and understanding their meaning was the principal method of study. Sanskrit was the main language for literary expression. Meeting in assemblies and debating conflicting thoughts and philosophies was one of the high points of the Nalanda University experience. Thus, winning public debates was highly prized and rewarded.[14] Knowledge was tested periodically through oral examinations and also rewarded.

Education at Nalanda was holistic. In addition, there was an emphasis on physical health, moral development, and discipline. All monks were expected to do menial work. Walking to improve health and stamina was part of their daily ritual. All the distinguished teachers were renowned for their character as well as for their learning.[15]

Students' daily routines were disciplined. Time was measured by velachakras (time-wheels), a sundial, and clepsydra (a water clock.) Different points of time were noted by different strokes of a drum. Daily routine included doing basic chores for the teachers, saluting their seniors in nearby apartments, taking a bath, reading scriptures, attending lectures, reflecting on lessons old and new, and walking. The pace of learning and living was intense, and many students complained about not having enough hours in the day.

Excellence: World-renowned

The foundation of excellence for Nalanda University was its teachers. It also had a demanding culture that expected rigor and excellence from its students. Its student body represented diverse sects, creeds, and schools of thoughts.

"Thus all the priests submitted to their own laws without giving any trouble to the public court."

Nalanda had many famous teachers who were experts in their fields and wrote books. Several also helped establish *viharas* in India and around the world. For example, Shantarakshita, on invitation of the king of Tibet, established the first Buddhist monastery in Tibet in 749 CE.

According to Yijing, the rules and regulations governing life were stricter at Nalanda than anywhere else. The monks and students governed themselves. "Thus all the priests submitted to their own laws without giving any trouble to the public court."[16] Room assignments, which were an important distribution of privilege, were done by the great assembly of monks. Students administered the rules and regulations for themselves.

The excellence also manifested itself in Nalanda's buildings, which were massive and beautifully decorated. According to Cunningham, the sculptures found there were the finest in all of India. Also, known to be at very high levels of intellectual and moral standards, the students of Nalanda, according to Xuánzàng, "were looked up to as models by all of India."[17]

As a result, the highest academic degree or distinction of the times was a fellowship at Nalanda. Nalanda became a meeting ground in India for warring sects and creeds. According to Yijing:

> There eminent and accomplished men gathered in crowds, discussed possible and impossible doctrines, and after having been assured of the excellence of their opinions by wise men became far-famed for their wisdom.[18]

Kings from within the country and elsewhere frequently invited Nalanda teachers to share their wisdom and address disputes in understanding Buddhism or a particular school of thought. Xuánzàng and Yijing, both from China, were among the most famous scholars who visited Nalanda University.

Such was Nalanda University's impact and fame.

When the wave of Muslim invasion took place around 1197, it struck a lethal blow to Nalanda University. Buildings and libraries were destroyed, granaries and gifts were looted, and monks were killed. Survivors escaped and took their knowledge and wisdom to Nepal, Tibet, and eastward to Bengal.[19]

The high point of Nalanda University was during the Gupta

dynasty, considered by some to be India's Golden Age. That's almost sixteen hundred years ago. However, Nalanda's level of excellence, scope, and scale are relevant in today's India.

Lessons from Nalanda University: For Building a Golden India

We built the first few universities in the world. These were built over one thousand years before the first universities in the western world were built. Thus, a university is not a western concept. It has Indian roots. There are many lessons that we can draw from Nalanda University's excellence, reputation, and impact. Some of the key lessons include:

- **Scope and scale matters.** Nalanda had fifteen hundred teachers and three thousand to ten thousand students. The scale of the teachers to the students enabled the university to offer over a hundred lectures per day in several fields of study. The depth and breadth of fields attracted students of various interests and backgrounds to Nalanda. Thus, Nalanda became a hub of intellectual learning and growth for the best and the brightest teachers and students in India and around the world.

- **Excellence matters.** Outstanding teachers, moral standards, intellectual rigor, and mental discipline were foundations for excellence. Reputation and financial support followed.

- **Community engagement and impact matters.** Kings, merchants, and two hundred village communities supported Nalanda. The students and teachers were engaged with the villages. They also helped address disputes and build monasteries. Thus, their importance and impact was tangible and visible.

These lessons are as timely and relevant now as they were fourteen hundred years ago.

CHAPTER 6

The United States: Leading the World

The best way to predict the future is to create it.

— Abraham Lincoln,
sixteenth president of United States

New York City, 2014: Mayank Gupta, K. Venkat Raman, Lakshmi Reddy, Rajesh Sinha, and Kusum Thomas are a few of the many Indians who have just arrived at the JFK International Airport. These five are headed to various universities to pursue undergraduate and graduate studies. Like them, close to 900,000 students from over one hundred countries are enrolled in US colleges and universities.[1] US universities are magnets that attract the best and the brightest students from around the world.

Mayank, Venkat, Lakshmi, Rajesh, and Kusum are excited about their immediate future. They are joining some of the premier institutions in the world and are looking forward to promising careers and fulfilling lives. Mayank completed his IB diploma from the Doon School and received a full scholarship to pursue an undergraduate degree at Princeton University in math and music. Venkat, after doing a B.Tech. from IIT Madras, is headed to the Massachusetts Institute of Technology (MIT) to get a master's and PhD in material science on a research scholarship. Lakshmi is thrilled to be joining Bryn Mawr College. She is still unsure about her major, but the opportunity to get a liberal arts education at a women's college is exciting for her and comforting for her parents. Her father is an entrepreneur in India and is funding her education. Rajesh is going to New York

University (NYU) to get his MBA. Son of a prominent bureaucrat, he is being funded by the TLC Trust, the nonprofit arm of a prominent Indian corporation. Finally, Kusum is looking forward to completing her JD/MBA joint degree from Indiana University in Bloomington and being close to Joseph, her elder brother, who is a junior in the school of engineering at Purdue University. After graduation, she plans to join her family business in Mumbai.

These five, along with the other 900,000 foreign students in the United States, bring immense diversity to the learning experience of the students and faculty members. The United States and its communities also benefit from the tuition fees and money spent by these students and their families. Finally, after graduation, many of the students get attractive employment opportunities. They may fall in love with another person and the US lifestyle—never to return to their homelands, except for vacations, major family events, or business trips. This education-led immigration is driving tremendous research, innovation, and related wealth creation in the United States.

The US higher education system is the benchmark for the world. According to the 2014 ARWU rankings of global universities, 80 percent of the top 20 and 52 percent of the top 100 universities are in the United States.[2] With a gross enrollment ratio (GER) of 94 percent, the United States offers universal access to higher education.[3] Close to 20.7 million students are enrolled in 4,634 higher education colleges and universities. The student enrollments have been climbing, rising from just over 1.4 million in 1939 to 2.4 million in 1947 to 21 million by 2012.[4] US higher education system has evolved over the past four hundred years by taking the best aspects from various overseas models and innovating them further. The system has scale, excellence, and a diversity of students and faculty members. Students have many diverse choices and can enter and exit higher education at different ages and at multiple points. Global rankings, number of patents, citations of papers, Nobel Prizes, and global

Key Numbers

- Global Rankings: **8 of the top 10, 52 of the top 100** and **146 of the top 500** are US universities[1]

- Total number of higher education institutions: **4,634**[2]

- Total student enrollment: **20.7 million**[2]

- Gross Enrollment Ratio: **94%**[2]

Source:[1] www.shanghairanking.com, [2] 2010 Carnegie Classification; National Center for Educations Statistics, IPEDS Fall Enrollment (2009)

recognition of faculty members are just some of the key areas where the United States stands out. Excellence and impact are hallmarks of this system, and the individuals, industry, economy, society, and nation are its beneficiaries.

There are many factors that have contributed to making the US higher education system valuable for key stakeholders in the United States and around the world. The seeds of grand vision and thoughtful missions that were planted and nurtured by inspired and committed leadership have grown to be the envy of the world.

Early Years: Mission, Policy, and Leadership Matters

Led by visionary leaders, philanthropists, alumni, and those in academia, the US higher education system has evolved over the last four hundred years and continues to innovate. As early as the 1750s, Benjamin Franklin, one of the founding fathers of the United States, wanted the University of Pennsylvania to "serve mankind." His ideas were ahead of the times and were adopted later. This desire to rethink the role of the university and pursue continuous improvement and innovations are hallmarks of the US higher education system. It has drawn lessons from the Greek, English, and German higher education models, adapted them, and made them more relevant to the needs of society and the nation.[5]

US society has always valued education. In the beginning, religion, philanthropy, and economy were the primary drivers for investments in higher education. Various churches and religious groups were motivated to prepare "fine" men who were appropriately trained in religion and its associated virtues and values. Many of the first few universities were for men only. This created a demand for women's colleges and universities and later coeducational colleges and universities. Athletics and physical education were an important component of education. Thus, intercollegiate sports played a significant part in the development of these universities. The first seven colleges to be formed before American independence were in the "Ivy League" of intercollegiate sports.

The philanthropists that funded universities were spurred by their desire to establish institutions of excellence and provide young men and women opportunities to learn, grow, and prepare themselves for their lives and future professions. For many of these philanthropists, this is their surviving legacy. There are numerous examples of private institutions of the highest caliber that were funded by individuals, their families, or their estates. Some of these include:

- Cornell University: Ezra Cornell
- Harvard University: John Harvard
- Johns Hopkins University: Johns Hopkins
- Stanford University: Leland and Jane Stanford
- The University of Chicago: American Baptist Education Society and John D. Rockefeller
- Yale University: Elihu Yale

Economic interests stemming from rapid industrial and agricultural development gave birth to a movement that eventually led to the Land-Grant College Act, or the Morrill Act:[6]

Sponsored by Vermont Congressman Justin Morrill, the Morrill Act was signed into law by President Abraham Lincoln on July 2, 1862. Officially titled "An Act Donating Public Lands to the Several States and Territories which may provide Colleges for the Benefit of Agriculture and the Mechanic Arts," the Morrill Act provided each state with 30,000 acres of Federal land for each member in their Congressional delegation. The land was then sold by the states and the proceeds used to fund public colleges that focused on agriculture and the mechanical arts. Sixty-nine colleges were funded by these land grants, including Cornell University, the Massachusetts Institute of Technology, and the University of Wisconsin at Madison.[7]

The Land-Grant College Act transformed US higher education, providing land and funds to start new universities and add new schools to existing universities. It also democratized the higher education system by making it easy for sons and daughters of farmers and workers to attend universities. The second Morrill Act, passed in 1890, provided additional federal grants to the universities and forbade racial discrimination in admissions criteria.[8] The Hatch Act in 1887 and the Smith-Lever Act in 1914 established the agricultural experiment stations and created the agricultural extension service, respectively.[9]

In the late nineteenth century, various university leaders successfully experimented with the university model, its mission, and its curriculum. Daniel Coit Gilman, the founding president of Johns Hopkins University, is credited with creating important innovations in US universities. His mission for the university was, "To educate its students and cultivate their capacity for lifelong learning, to foster independent and original research, and to bring the benefits of discovery to the world."[10] According to Clark Kerr, author of *The Uses of the University*:

> The Hopkins idea brought with it the graduate school with exceptionally high academic standards in what was still a rather new and raw civilization; renovation of professional education, particularly in medicine; the establishment of the preeminent influence of the department; the creation of research institutes and centers, of university presses and learned journals, and the "academic ladder"; and also the great proliferation of courses.

Gilman's innovations were quickly adopted by leading institutions such as Harvard, Columbia, Cornell, Stanford, and the University of California. Wider adoption followed. Charles W. Eliot, president of Harvard University, added to these innovations by establishing the elective system, which enabled students to choose their own courses. Introduction of electives also offered faculty members additional freedom to offer courses of their interest.[11]

World War II and Beyond:
Scale, Scope, Federal Funding, and Impact Matters

World War II fundamentally changed the scale and scope of US universities. Several leading faculty members from universities and their research teams were engaged in military research. Their role in deciding the outcome of the war is well known from conducting research and developing methods, materials, and devices for the military such radar countermeasures and even the nuclear bomb.

After the war, two major forces came together: 1) millions of youth returned from the war front and 2) the US economy started to support the escalating Cold War. The youth returning from the war needed to be trained for jobs at an unprecedented scale. At the same time, the economy needed trained professionals on a larger scale. In 1944, the Servicemen's Readjustment Act, or the GI Bill, was passed. It gave the returning war veterans low-interest rate mortgages and stipends to cover tuition and expenses for attending college or university. From 1944 until the end of the first GI Bill in 1956, 7.8 million of 16 million World War II veterans participated in an educational program or a training program. At its peak in 1947, the war veterans accounted for 49 percent of college admissions.[12]

In 1945, Vannevar Bush published a report called *Science: The Endless Frontier* to President Roosevelt. Bush was an entrepreneur, a faculty member at MIT, and the head of the US Office of Scientific Research and Development (OSRD) during World War II. He is credited with playing an instrumental role in winning the war by applying scientific and technical knowledge to the war effort. Bush made a case for scientific research for the benefit of the society and national security. In this report, he said:

> Progress in the war against disease depends upon a flow of new scientific knowledge. New products, new industries, and more jobs require continuous addition to knowledge of the laws of nature, and application of that knowledge to practical purposes. Similarly, our defense against aggression demands new knowledge so that we can develop new and improved weapons. This essential, new knowledge can be obtained only through basic scientific research.

> Science can be effective in the national welfare only as a member of a team, whether the conditions be peace or war. But without scientific progress no amount of achievement in other directions can insure our health, prosperity, and security as a nation in the modern world...

> We shall have rapid or slow advance on any scientific frontier depending on the number of highly qualified and trained scientists exploring it.[13]

Vannevar Bush's report led to the creation of the National Science Foundation (NSF), which is one of the largest funders of scientific and engineering research in US universities. Much larger funds flowed from federal sources to the NSF and then to the universities. Established in 1950, the NSF has grown, and in 2015, it had an annual budget of US$7.3 billion. It funds approximately 24 percent of all federally supported basic research conducted by colleges and universities in the United States. Since 1951, 210 or 70 percent of all US Nobel laureates have received NSF funding.[14]

In addition to the NSF, the Department of Defense and the Department of Energy provide significant research funding. The National Institutes of Health (NIH), which started in 1887, provided US$30.3 billion in funding for medical research. Over 80 percent of this is awarded through competitive grants to universities, medical schools, and additional research institutions in the United States and around the world.[15]

In the late 1950s, the United States was shocked when the Soviet Union launched Sputnik I—the first artificial satellite in outer space. The US leadership and scientific community were taken aback by their rival's scientific and engineering capabilities. As a reaction to Sputnik I, the US government supercharged science and engineering research in universities and labs around the country and fueled another arms race—this time for the domination of outer space and the mind share of people around the world. The Defense Advanced Research Projects Agency (DARPA) was established in direct response to the Sputnik I surprise.[16] DARPA's budget is approximately US$3 billion per year.[17]

"Once a reputation has been established, once a set of policies and academic standards has been set in place, once a sense of pride takes over—they all tend to perpetuate themselves."

The GI Bill, an influx of federal funds to universities, and the significant growth in scientific and engineering research spurred the US economy. The economy benefited from advances in knowledge, its productivity grew, and society benefitted from an unprecedented prosperity from the late 1940s to the early 1970s. For over three decades, this economic boom further enabled the United States to strengthen its physical infrastructure, fund the research universities at significant levels, and fight the Cold War.

In 1980, the Patent and Trademark Law Amendments Act, more commonly known as the Bayh-Dole Act, was adopted. It gave universities the title to inventions from federally funded research.

It also allowed industry to license such inventions from universities on an exclusive basis. Finally, the universities could collect and keep the licensing revenues. They were expected to share some of the revenues with the inventors and use unused funds to spur education and research. This was a marked change from the pre-act situation where the government owned all IP rights and did not give any exclusive rights to anyone.[18] Thus, the Bayh-Dole Act cemented government, industry, and university collaborations. It also spurred the commercialization of IP for the benefit of the nation and society.

Past, Present, and Future: Governance Matters

University leadership throughout the course of history has nurtured these institutions in the face of growing demand, global competition, budget cuts, market swings, a changing funding environment, student movements, and geopolitical storms. Their leadership has made the institutions stronger and more relevant to the current and future needs of both students and society.

The university leadership typically includes a chancellor/ president, a provost, deans of various schools and colleges, vice-chancellors/vice presidents of various nonacademic departments, chairs of departments, and directors of research centers. At the university level, there is an external board of trustees that provides oversight and serves an advisory role. The board of trustees has a fiduciary responsibility. At the school or college level, there is a dean's advisory council or advisory board that plays a similar role, though it does not have any fiduciary responsibilities. The board of trustees includes stakeholders, such as alumni, corporate and foundation executives, thought leaders, venture capitalists, and investment bankers. Many friends or alumni who have made a significant gift to the university are also on the board. In the case of public universities, the governor or their representative(s) would also have a seat on the board. Thus, the board, in almost every case, consists of individuals with a vested interest in the success of the university.

The president is the head of the institution. However, some universities have a strong culture and tradition of "shared governance," where major decisions are discussed and debated at different levels. The president and provost consult with the deans, chairs, and appropriate vice presidents on key decisions. A faculty senate, consisting of tenured faculty members, discusses and debates ideas and policy changes. This is a wonderful example of "crowd-sourcing" ideas. The ideas that are vetted by a large and committed faculty ensure decisions are made that are in the best long-term interest of the university. Capable leadership has enabled these institutions to compete effectively within the United States and with universities around the world.

Jostling for Faculty, Students, Resources, and Prestige: Competition Matters

Competition has played an enormous part in the evolution of the US higher education system. Competition is both a self-propelling and a self-correcting engine. To survive and get ahead in a competitive global marketplace of talent, ideas, and innovation, universities are competing with one another for the best and the brightest faculty members and students. They are also competing for financial resources and prestige. Success in one area feeds the others and perpetuates the cycle. Clark Kerr wrote that "once a reputation has been established, once a set of policies and academic standards has been set in place, once a sense of pride takes over — they all tend to perpetuate themselves."[19] And it takes leadership, faculty members, students, alumni, and staff to perpetuate the cycle. Each position plays a vital role.

For the university leadership, attracting award-winning faculty members whose research and track records are likely to attract both research grants and students is critical. The competition for faculty members is reflected in offers from multiple universities and an attractive compensation package. The package, in addition to salary and benefits, may also include start-up funds, a research lab, and access to research infrastructure. Faculty salaries are competitive, market-based, and vary by discipline. For example, engineering, business, and economics faculty members are highly sought after by corporations. Thus, their salaries are typically higher than other fields.

Publishing papers and books, advancing frontiers of knowledge, and spurring innovation require original research. Conducting research requires resources, which by nature are finite. This has created competition among faculty members. Thus, faculty members are motivated and have a sense of urgency to advance the research, make an impact, and upgrade their research teams and infrastructure. The government and/or private funding organizations are more likely to fund faculty members who have demonstrated a strong track record in research and innovation.

For the faculty member, having bright and dedicated students in their research team becomes critical as well. This makes hiring the best and the brightest scholars from around the world one of the surest ways to ensure success. Competition for bright students takes the form of offering attractive scholarships and fellowships. Thus, competition for faculty members and students requires universities to have plenty of financial resources.

This competition spurs the university leadership, faculty members, and staff to do their best, have a compelling vision, a well-thought strategy, and excellent execution on all fronts. This also drives each university to find, create, or join a niche where they can stand out from the crowd, that is, establish a unique value proposition or a sustainable competitive advantage and create a brand around that positioning.

Globally, students and faculty members are attracted by diverse choices, the variety of learning opportunities, and a culture of excellence and making an impact in the US higher education system.

Many Options: Depth and Breadth of Choices Matters

There are over 4,600 higher education institutions in the United States, with a total enrollment of 21 million students. US higher education offers a diversity of choices for students to pursue their individual passions and interests. In addition, the universities offer multiple opportunities to enter and exit the system. Age, gender, sexual orientation or preference, ethnicity, religion, and country of origin are not barriers in admission.

There are various types of colleges and universities with unique positioning. According to *The Carnegie Classifications of Higher Education Institutions,*[20] these include:

1. Associate Colleges
2. Doctorate-Granting Universities
3. Master's Colleges and Universities
4. Baccalaureate Colleges
5. Special-Focus Institutions
6. Tribal Colleges

The classification is based on the highest degree granted. If the institution offers multiple degrees, then the scale of the degrees granted determines the final classification. Thus, college that offers associate degrees and less than 10 percent of bachelor's degrees are considered to be an Associate College. In the same vein, Baccalaureate colleges confer less than 50 master's degrees annually and more than 10 percent of bachelor's degrees. Master's colleges grant less than 20 PhDs and more than 50 master's degrees per year. Institutions granting more than 20 PhDs per year are classified as doctorate-granting universities. Special-focus institutions are ones where more than 75 percent of undergraduate and graduate degrees are focused on one field such as engineering or education. Tribal colleges belong to the American Indian Higher Education Consortium.

Table 6.1: US Higher Education Insitutions and Student Enrollments

	Institutions		Student Enrollment		Average Student Enrollment/ Institution
	#s	%	#s	%	
Associate's Colleges	1,920	42%	8,185,725	40%	4,263
Doctorate-granting Universities	297	6%	5,785,078	28%	19,478
Master's Colleges and Universities	724	16%	4,656,600	23%	6,432
Baccalaureate Colleges	810	18%	1,423,275	7%	1,757
Special-Focus Institutions	851	18%	657,296	3%	772
Tribal Colleges	32	1%	19,686	0%	615
Total	**4,634**	**100%**	**20,727,660**	**100%**	**4,473**

Sources: 2010 Carnegie Classification; National Center for Educations Statistics, IPEDS Fall Enrollment (2009).
Table created by Shail Kumar

In the United States, approximately 40 percent of students are enrolled in associate's colleges, 28 percent in doctorate-granting universities, 23 percent in master's colleges and universities, 7 percent in baccalaureate colleges, 3 percent in special-focus institutions, and 0.1 percent in tribal colleges. The Table 6.1 highlights enrollment and average enrollment by the type of institution.

As a result of all the factors discussed so far, students in US higher education system have many wonderful opportunities to learn, live, and grow.

Opportunities to Learn, Live, and Grow:
Learning Experiences Matters

Mayank Gupta, K. Venkat Raman, Lakshmi Reddy, Rajesh Sinha, and Kusum Thomas are going to different US universities each with unique positioning but similar in one important way. They all offer excellent opportunities to learn, live, and grow professionally and personally.

Mayank (who is headed to Princeton), Venkat (MIT), Rajesh (NYU), and Kusum (Indiana University) have chosen doctorate-granting universities. These comprehensive research universities offer undergraduate, graduate, and postdoctoral education in multiple fields. Most of these universities have professional colleges and a liberal arts college. Liberal arts typically includes: mathematical sciences (math and statistics), physical sciences (chemistry and physics), biological sciences, arts and humanities (languages and performing arts) and social sciences (economics and sociology). Professional programs include engineering, law, business, public health, education, architecture, and public policy. Some universities, such as Stanford, Johns Hopkins, University of Michigan, UCLA, and UC San Diego, also have medical hospitals and medical centers, which provide necessary preparation for doctors and medical and health researchers.

Lakshmi, on the other hand, is headed to Bryn Mawr College, a women's liberal arts college founded in 1885. According to the Carnegie Classification, it is a baccalaureate college. Liberal arts colleges are always small in size, from less than 1,000 to no more than 5,000 students. Their unique value proposition includes small class sizes, personalized attention, broad-based education, opportunities to conduct research, and more interactions with faculty members. Most of the liberal arts colleges are private and coeducational. There are several women's colleges such as Bryn Mawr.

Bryn Mawr, like many universities and liberal arts colleges, has established consortiums to provide additional value to the students. It is part of the Seven Sisters, a consortium of prestigious East Coast–based liberal arts colleges for women. The Seven Sisters was the female counterpart for the once-male-only Ivy League. This consortium originally included Bryn Mawr, Barnard, Mount Holyoke, Radcliffe, Smith, Vassar, and Wellesley. Bryn Mawr has 1,300 undergraduate women and more than 400 graduate women and men from forty-five states and sixty-two countries. The graduate school is coeducational. Bryn Mawr is in the Bi-College Consortium with Haverford College. It has a Tri-College Consortium with Haverford and Swarthmore, and is in the Quaker Consortium with Haverford, Swarthmore, and the University of Pennsylvania.[21] These relationships enable students to take classes in any of the consortium colleges without paying additional fees. Students can join clubs and eat in the dining halls of the consortium colleges with ease. There are frequent shuttle services between campuses to make it really convenient for the students. Thus, Bryn Mawr College students get all the benefits of a women's liberal arts college and all the resources of several liberal arts colleges and a large comprehensive research university.

Thus, Bryn Mawr College students get all the benefits of a women's liberal arts college and all the resources of several liberal arts colleges and a large comprehensive research university.

While there are differences in the mission, scope, and scale of US colleges and universities, there are many similarities. US universities offer a variety of learning opportunities—in the classrooms and outside, curricular and extracurricular. Students at a research university have thousands of classes to choose from. They also have access to libraries with millions of journals, books, publications, and databases. Students can also conduct research at the undergraduate level. At the same time, they can join or start student clubs and participate in athletic activities or intramural or intercollegiate sports and games. There are ample social and cultural opportunities, like attending an opera or a musical show, going to the movies, shopping, dining, visiting downtown or the city, or cheering on their university team. There are frequent guest lectures by entrepreneurs, corporate executives, researchers, dignitaries, Nobel laureates, and social activists. In short, the campus is a vibrant place to learn and live as well as grow intellectually, physically, and emotionally.

"Experiential learning and linkage are among the most powerful and enduring methods of creative understanding,"[22] notes Frank H. T. Rhodes, president emeritus of Cornell University. This takes many forms, like class projects and assignments and lab work or fieldwork. There are also opportunities for interdisciplinary research and ꞏllaboration. In a knowledge economy, increasingly new knowledge and IP are being created at the intersections of disciplines, such as engineering and medicine; math and biology; brain and cognitive science; and arts and engineering. The collaboration of faculty members in science, engineering, medicine, business, law, economics, public policy, and liberal arts is delivering more effective solutions to address problems involving energy, water, and health. The students have an opportunity to team up with faculty members and learn innovative ways to address issues of societal importance. In interdisciplinary research, faculty members and students learn valuable skills to collaborate with experts from various disciplines. They also learn how to communicate effectively with people outside their field of expertise.

Students are encouraged and expected to take the initiative and make the most of these opportunities. The value of rigor, hard work, initiative, punctuality, and integrity, which are needed in all walks of life, are reinforced in the class and in cocurricular and extracurricular activities.

Another similarity among the colleges and universities is their culture of excellence and making an impact. The culture of excellence manifests in processes such as the hiring and retention of faculty members and staff, admissions, financial aid, and scholarships. It also shows up in the design, construction, and maintenance of classrooms, research laboratories, academic buildings, residence and dining halls, arts and sports facilities, and landscaping. Most importantly, it is reflected in faculty members and professionals providing valuable mentoring and counseling for students' learning and success.

Faculty members and counselors also encourage students to explore additional learning opportunities by doing projects and internships with organizations outside of the university. These organizations can be nonprofit community-focused organizations, for-profit corporations, or government-related organizations. Internships, which can be from a few weeks to several months, are an excellent way for students to apply their knowledge and skills, learn from real experiences, and assess a profession and field.

Universities also offer opportunities to study or serve abroad. By establishing collaborations, mostly bilateral, with foreign universities and organizations, students have opportunities to spend a summer, a semester, or even a year overseas. The students in these cases learn valuable technical skills and knowledge and also get valuable exposure to a different culture and language.

The availability of funding, the attractiveness of the United States and its higher education, and favorable immigration policies have also attracted students and faculty members from over one hundred countries to US colleges and universities.

As a result of all these factors and perhaps a few others, during the period of 1940 and 2010 (see table below) the number of colleges and universities in the United States multiplied by 2.6 times, faculty grew by 9.8 times, and student enrollment shot up by 13.7 times. The degrees conferred follow the same remarkable growth with some interesting takeaways. The number of bachelor's degrees granted climbed by 8.8 times, master's degrees jumped by 26 times, and doctorate degrees shot up by 48 times.

Table 6.2: Growth of US Colleges and Universities: 1940-2010								
	1939-40	1949-50	1959-60	1969-70	1979-80	1989-90	1999-2000	2009-10
# of Insitutions	1,708	1,851	2,004	2,525	3,152	3,535	4,084	4,495
Total Faculty	146,929	246,722	380,554	450,000	675,000	824,220	1,027,830	1,439,144
Total Enrollment	1,494,203	2,444,900	3,639,847	8,004,660	11,569,899	13,538,560	14,791,224	20,427,711
Degrees Conferred								
Associate	---	---	---	206,023	400,910	455,102	564,933	849,452
Bachelors	186,500	432,058	392,440	792,316	929,417	1,051,344	1,237,875	1,650,014
Masters	26,731	58,183	74,435	213,589	305,196	330,152	463,185	693,025
Doctorate	3,290	6,420	9,829	59,486	95,631	103,508	118,736	158,558

Source: Digest of Education Statistics, National Center for Education Statistics (Table 301.20)

Table created by Shail Kumar

Challenges: Creeping Problems

Despite its successes, US higher education is facing a number of challenges as would be expected in a large system. One of the biggest issues is the increasing tuition and related costs for students and parents. Four-year costs have ballooned as a percentage of family income. This has led to monumental student debt, which now stands at over US$1 trillion.[23]

With the majority of states facing financial crisis, university budgets have been cut, and state universities' costs for the students have also mushroomed. As an example, University of California in the 1970s received over 30 percent of its annual budget from the state of California.[24] It is now down to less than 15 percent. As a result, tuition fees for in-state students at UC Berkeley have gone from a few thousand dollars per year to close to US$13,500 per year.[25] The percentage of in-state freshmen students at UC Berkeley and UCLA has also gone down to 70 percent from over 90 percent.[26]

A funding crisis at the federal level has resulted in shortfalls in funding for basic research. Agencies, such as NIH and NSF, are increasingly funding more applied research projects, which have higher chances of immediate payoff. It has reached such a level that Randy W. Schekman, Nobel laureate, took the opportunity at the Nobel banquet to make an impassioned appeal for increased funding for basic research.[27]

The four-year graduation rate, which is the percentage of students who complete the undergraduate program in four years, is yet another challenge. This ranges from 5 percent to over 90 percent. According to the US Department of Education, "The 2013 six-year graduation rate for first-time, full-time undergraduate students who began their pursuit of a bachelor's degree at a four-year degree-granting institution in fall 2007 was 59 percent. That is, 59 percent of first-time, full-time students who began seeking a bachelor's degree at a four-year institution in fall 2007 completed the degree at that institution by 2013."[28] Some take one semester or several years more to graduate. Others drop out of college altogether. Several factors play a role in students taking more than four years to graduate or dropping out. The most discussed reasons are the lack of availability of required classes at the university and student debt.

There is also an erosion of the popularity of a liberal arts education that has distinguished US universities for a long time. There are a growing numbers of students and families who think a professional education is more valuable than a liberal arts degree. There is also a group of people who believe higher education is not necessary at all. They frequently point to successful entrepreneurs like Steve Jobs, Bill Gates, and Mark Zuckerberg, who famously dropped out of college to start their respective companies and became billionaires. Some others believe that a few days or a few months of boot camp programs are sufficient for real-world jobs, especially in the fields of software programing and social media.

I expect that, just like in the past, the US colleges and universities will evolve and innovate and address the current and future challenges facing them.

Lessons from the United States: For Building a Golden India

There is much to be learned from the US success story.

- **Mission, policy, and leadership matters:** Leaders who have advocated a thoughtful mission and then supported policies that advance those objectives have left a legacy for the nation and its future generations.

- **Scale, scope, funding, and impact matters:** Like at Nalanda University, scale, scope, and impact matters. Funding is also important to conduct research, provide scholarships and fellowships, and build research and teaching infrastructure. Finally, it is also evident that scaling up student enrollments in a short period is achievable.

- **Governance matters:** Building and sustaining excellence depends on sound governance and committed and well-prepared talent in academia and nonacademia.

- **Competition matters:** Competing for faculty, students, and financial resources spurs institutions and faculty members to be creative, work hard, have a sense of urgency, and focus on problems and opportunities that matter to society.

- **Choices for students and faculty members matters:** Different people like different things, and learning and research interests frequently change and evolve. Thus, diversity of choices in colleges and universities and the flexibility to change paths or fields make the system more appealing for all.

- **Student learning experiences matters:** At the end of the day, student learning experiences and outcomes matter the most for the students, their society, and the future of the institutions and country.

The following chapters on the state of California, UC Berkeley, and Stanford University provide additional insights about the US success story and the unique and important role of universities in making an impact on the individuals, families, industry, economy, society, and nation.

CHAPTER 7

California: A Vibrant and Integrated System

Never doubt that a small group of thoughtful, committed citizens can change the world; indeed, it's the only thing that ever has.

— Margaret Mead, American
anthropologist

Los Angeles, 2014: Bill Chang, Mike Davis, Janaki Mitra, and Emily Vasquez, friends from their high school dance club, are seniors and discussing their college plans. Thanks to the California Master Plan and additional excellent choices of colleges and universities in the state, they are all planning to pursue undergraduate education in an institution that matches their aspirations, interests, and preferences. They are going to a community college, a state university, the University of California, and a private college — four distinct options available to California residents.

Emily, Janaki, and Bill are children of first-generation immigrants to the United States. Emily received a Regents Scholarship to attend the University of California at Los Angeles (UCLA). She will be the first in her family to attend college, and her family is overjoyed. Emily is looking forward to fulfilling her lifelong dream of becoming a doctor. Her parents immigrated to the United States from Mexico and have been toiling in low-paying jobs ever since. Janaki is going to nearby Claremont McKenna College (CMC), a private liberal arts college. Bill was accepted to San José State University's (SJSU) engineering program. Bill and his parents are excited about his future as an engineer. Mike is planning to attend Long Beach City College.

His mother, a single parent, hit a bump financially and is also recovering from cancer. Mike wanted to be with his mother during her recovery. It was also the least expensive option, one he could finance by working part-time. He plans to transfer to either an in-state public or private university after getting his associate's degree.

"Different strokes for different folks" rings true in California's higher education system. There are diverse choices that suit different aspirations, interests, and personal situations. Faced with challenging personal situation, Mike found a match in a conveniently located and inexpensive Long Beach City College. Janaki's interest in small class sizes and a liberal arts education and the proximity to her parents in LA led her to CMC. Access to scholarships and financial aid is enabling Emily to pursue her lifelong dream at UCLA. Finally, Bill was attracted by SJSU's engineering program, the Silicon Valley location, and a chance to be part of the area's innovation and entrepreneurial ecosystem. The fact that it was also less expensive than private universities or the UC system made it even more attractive to him.

California's investment in higher education is paying back rich dividends. California's Master Plan established and supported the University of California (UC), the California State University (CSU), and the California Community College (CCC) systems. Approximately 80 percent of the 2.6 million students in California are enrolled in the UC, CSU, and CCC systems.[1] In addition, California has some of the leading private universities and colleges such as the California Institute of Technology (Caltech), Stanford University, the University of Southern California (USC), and the Claremont University Consortium. These mostly private nonprofit institutions account for 20 percent of student enrollments. A few universities have medical centers and hospitals that are providing valuable health care and are researching better preventive care, drugs, vaccines, and diagnostics. Faculty members, students, and researchers are improving our understanding of the world and universe. They are extending the frontiers of knowledge in all fields. They are fueling an innovation and entrepreneurship engine and attracting funding from federal, state, and private resources. A well-prepared and hardworking talent pool has created a hub for industries and venture capitalists. Thus, the impact of these universities can be seen, felt, and measured in the economic vitality and prosperity in the local communities and the state. California, as a result of its vibrant higher education system, is home to many industries and a thriving entertainment, tourism, agriculture, and knowledge-based economy.

California's Master Plan for Higher Education: Access and Excellence for All

Passed in 1960, California's Master Plan guarantees universal access to higher education for every Californian. It was the first state in the United States to do so, and this model has been replicated around the nation. Clark Kerr, the architect of the Master Plan, wrote that it "guarantees that there would be a place in college for every high school graduate or person otherwise qualified who chose to attend." The Master Plan was initiated for a number of reasons. The biggest was the anticipated explosion in *"[The Master Plan] guarantees that there would be a place in college for every high school graduate or person otherwise qualified who chose to attend."*

student enrollments, or tidal wave, as Kerr calls it. There was a baby boom in the United States after World War II veterans returned home. There was also a movement toward providing universal access to higher education. And over 300,000 people per year were migrating to California from around the country. There was also a desire to provide skills and knowledge for the economy and society and ensure that the higher education system retained its autonomy from bureaucrats and politicians. It was under these circumstances that California's Master Plan was conceived and delivered.

The Master Plan created a three-model college and university system: junior colleges, now known as the California Community Colleges (CCC), the State College System (California State Universities, or CSU), and the University of California (UC). CCC is an open-access model, where any high school graduate or qualified person can enroll. They were to offer a two-year associate's degree or professional certification. CSU has master's colleges and universities offering bachelor's and master's degrees. UCs grant bachelor's, master's and doctorate degrees. This segmentation of roles and responsibilities ensured that finite state, federal, and private resources were allocated appropriately across the three models and each model performed a valuable and complementary role in the higher education system. Each segment was expected to strive for excellence.

The Senate bill that legislated the Master Plan declared that UC is the primary state-supported academic agency for research. It also gave UC exclusive responsibility, in public higher education, in the professions of law and graduate instruction in the professions of medicine, dentistry, veterinary science, and architecture. UC was also made the sole agency for awarding doctoral degrees in all the fields. Provisions were made for CSU to offer joint doctoral degrees with UCs.

According to the Master Plan, the CSU's primary responsibility is the education of undergraduate students and graduate students through the master's degree level in liberal arts and applied fields. This also includes the teaching profession. Offering two-year degree programs is restricted and requires formal approval. Research by faculty members is permitted as long it stays within its mission.

The community colleges' focus is to provide education until the fourteenth-grade level. According to the Master Plan, they can offer programs in three primary categories: 1) standard collegiate courses for transfer to higher institutions, such as UC and CSU, 2) vocational and technical fields leading to employment, and 3) general or liberal arts courses. The Master Plan also recommended that a CCC be established within commuting distance of all residents of the state, making higher education accessible on all accounts. Over 95 percent of Californians live within thirty minutes of a CCC campus.

In addition, the Master Plan set the admission policies for the three models. CCC would have 100 percent acceptance, CSU would guarantee admission to the top 33.3 percent of all graduates from the state's public high schools, and UC would guarantee admission to the top 12.5 percent. Applicants from out of state had to meet a higher threshold than in-state students. Furthermore, students would have opportunities to transfer within the system—the most popular options being transferring from a CCC to a CSU or a UC.

Finally, the Master Plan outlined the governance for the three models and coordination among them.[2] In short, the Master Plan laid out a blueprint for the state's public higher education and California's youth, society, and economy.

The University of California

Emily Vasquez is planning to attend UCLA as a Regents Scholar. She worked hard for it, spending time mastering her academic subjects, volunteering at a local hospital, taking leadership roles in high school clubs, and pursuing her personal passion for dance. At UCLA, Emily is looking forward to an amazing depth and breadth of curricular, cocurricular, and extracurricular learning opportunities. She is excited about the opportunities to gain hands-on research experience in faculty laboratories and about getting ready for medical training. She is also planning to be active in clubs and in her residence hall and make the most of open lectures, seminars, and cultural events at UCLA. UCLA's intercollegiate sports team is the Bruins, and she is also thrilled to be part of the UCLA school spirit and Bruins crosstown rivalry with USC Trojans.

Students across the UC system can expect experiences similar to what Emily is expecting. UC is now a ten-university system with campuses in Berkeley, Davis, Irvine, Los Angeles, Merced, Riverside, San Diego, San Francisco, Santa Barbara, and Santa Cruz. UC has five medical centers and hospitals at UC Davis, UC Irvine, UCLA, UC San Francisco (UCSF), and UC San Diego. UC also manages three national energy laboratories: Lawrence Berkeley National Laboratory, Los Alamos National Laboratory, and Lawrence Livermore National Laboratory (the last two with additional partners). It has 800 research centers, institutes, and programs and 39 natural reserve sites spread over 756,000 acres. UC also maintains over 5,800 buildings on 130 million square feet on approximately 30,000 acres.

Since the adoption of the Master Plan, the enrollment has quadrupled to over two hundred and forty-four thousand students across its ten campuses. It awards more than:

The University of California
- Campuses: 10
- Student Enrollment: 244,000
- Faculty and Staff: 138,390
- Alumni: 1.6 million
- Medical Centers: 5
- Research Centers: over 800
- Natural Reserve Sites: 39 and 756,000 acres
- National Energy Labs: 3
- Research Funding: US$4.1 billion

Source: www.universityofcalifornia.edu

- 30% of the state's bachelor's degrees
- 60% of doctoral degrees
- 60% of its medical and professional practice degrees

- UC's undergraduates include approximately 30 percent
  of transfer students from CCCs – a vital aspect of the
  Master Plan and its success.

The five UC medical centers manage more than 147,000 inpatient admissions, 290,000 emergency room visits, and 3.8 million outpatient visits annually. UC operates the largest health sciences education program in the United States with more than 14,000 students.

As a result of its scale, UC is one of the largest employers in the state with 138,390 faculty and staff. These include faculty members, doctors, nurses, and staff in research administration and laboratories, student services, food and auxiliary services, maintenance and physical plants, and management and clerical positions.[3]

UC is making a significant impact in California, the United States, and the world. It is preparing leaders, researchers, faculty members, entrepreneurs, doctors, innovators, and professionals for all walks of life. It is also preparing students for their lives and careers. Its faculty members are extending the frontiers of knowledge in all fields. Faculty members and alumni are starting companies that are making lives better and creating wealth. Its doctors and health care staff are providing valuable health care and developing more effective drugs, vaccines, and diagnostics.

California State University

Bill Chang is planning to attend San José State University. SJSU's engineering program is well "plugged-in" with Silicon Valley's high-tech firms. Bill wants to specialize in electrical engineering and become an engineer at a firm like Apple, Intel, Cisco, or Applied Materials.

Founded in 1857, San José State University is the oldest university in the UC and CSU system. CSU's twenty-three campuses are spread across California in eight regions. In 2008 and 2009, the CSU system enrolled 466,075 students and granted 74,643 bachelor's degrees, 19,011 master's degrees, and eighty-five joint doctorate degrees. It employed a total of 23,581 faculty members.

The CSU system is making an impact at a number of levels. Most importantly, it is preparing students for various professions and fields of study, which fuels public services and California's diverse knowledge-based economy. In addition, according to a study conducted for the CSU's Office of the Chancellor, in 2010, the economic impact totaled US$7.96 billion in 2008–09 and the impact based on the multiplier effect was estimated to be US$17 billion. Thus, every US$1 invested in CSU results in a US$5.43 impact on California's economy.

According to the same study, CSU granted 46 percent of all bachelor's degrees in California and 32 percent of master's degrees. In some areas, CSU's contribution was even higher. It conferred:

- 47% of degrees in California in electrical and communications engineering
- 52% in agricultural business and management
- 56% in civil engineering
- 62% in food, plant, and soil sciences
- 67% in animal sciences
- 94% in hospitality administration/ management
- 97% in dietetics and nutrition
- 100% in parks, recreation and leisure studies
- It also granted 52 percent of California's teaching credentials.

California State University

- Campuses: 23
- Student Enrollment: 446,075
- Degrees Granted: (CY 2008–2009)
- Bachelor's: 74,643
- Master's: 19,011
- Total Faculty: 23,581
- Full-time Faculty: 12,019
- Grants 46% of all bachelor's degrees, 32% of all master's degrees, and 52% of all teaching credentials in California.
- ROI: for every US$1 invested by the state, CSU generates US$5.43 for California's economy.

Source: www.calstate.edu

The second result of attending CSU is a higher median salary earned by its students upon graduation. CSU's 1.96 million alumni working in California earned an estimated US$122 billion in wages of which US$42 billion is attributable to their higher education degree earned at CSU. Thus, the total economic impact of CSU was valued at US$70 billion—a twenty-three-time return on US$3.12 billion invested by the state in CSU.[4]

California Community Colleges

Mike Davis is planning to attend Long Beach City College, which was established in 1927. Like Emily (UCLA) and Bill (SJSU), he is also looking forward to a rich educational experience. However, unlike Bill and Emily, he will be interacting with a more diverse student population—midlife professionals augmenting their skills and knowledge, veterans getting their associate's degrees, and students commuting from home.

California Community Colleges

- Campuses: 112

- Student enrollment: close to 2.1 million

- 20% of community college students in the United States attend a CCC.

- 31% of UC and 52% of CSU students started at a CCC.

- CCC trains 70% of California's nurses and 80% of firefighters, law enforcement personnel, and emergency medical technicians.

Source: www.cccco.edu

Long Beach City College is part of CCC, a 112-college system enrolling over 2.1 million students. CCC accounts for over 70 percent of California's students in higher education. According to the Master Plan, CCC prepares students to transfer to higher institutions such as UC and CSU and provides workforce training, certificate and degree programs, and remedial programs in English and math.

CCC's impact is primarily in preparing students for higher institutions and for professions that require some higher education but not a bachelor's degree.[5] In addition, 31 percent of UC students and 52 percent of CSU students started at one of California's community colleges.

Currently, California's community colleges offer short-term job training certificates in more than one hundred and seventy-five different fields. Approximately twenty-five thousand apprentices are educated each year in fields such as automotive technology, welding, and building trades. The CCC system trains:

- 70% of California's nurses
- 80% of firefighters, law enforcement personnel, and emergency medical technicians

The following table highlights the value of CCC. For the

individual, it helps in getting a higher paying job; for industry, it provides a capable and profession-ready workforce; and for the state, it spurs economic activity and makes the state more attractive for corporations to open or expand their businesses.

Table 7.1: Impact of Community College on Employability and Median Salaries			
Program Title	Total Number of Degrees and Certificates Awarded (2007-2008)	Related Occupation	Median Earnings in US$ (2008)
Nursing	8,262	Registered Nurse	$84,635
Automotive Technology	2,157	Auto Mechanic	$42,702
Office Technology Computer Applications	1,747	Computer Specialist	$52,291
Construction Crafts Technology	1,155	Solar Roofer	$45,115
Paralegal	911	Paralegal	$57,470
Electronics and Electrical Technology	888	Electrician	$56,077
Dental Occupations	802	Dental Hygienist	$86,652
Manufacturing and Industrial Technology	774	Wind Turbine Installer	$52,603
Radiologic Technology	621	Radiological	$63,022
Source: CCC Preparing Students For The Jobs Of Tomorrow (report), The Employment Development Department, California Community Colleges Chancellor's Office			

Dreams of a better life and future are taking Bill Chang, Mike Davis, Janaki Mitra, and Emily Vasquez to California's vast public and private college and university system. California's Master Plan was a masterstroke for public education. Together, the UC, CSU, and CCC systems enroll close to 80 percent of California's students.

In addition, there are private non-profit and for-profit institutions that account for the remaining 20 percent of student enrollments.

Private Colleges and Universities:
Synergistic with the Public System

Claremont McKenna College (CMC), which Janaki is planning to attend, is a private nonprofit college and part of the Claremont University Consortium. This consortium includes Claremont Graduate University, CMC, Harvey Mudd College, Keck Graduate Institute, Pitzer College, Pomona College, and Scripps College. Each of the consortium colleges has a unique focus and small class sizes. They are consistently ranked among the top colleges in their respective segments. Much like Lakshmi, who is headed to Bryn

Mawr College, Janaki can expect all the benefits of a small liberal arts education and all the resources of a large research university. But Janaki can walk to all the consortium colleges — they are co-located. Janaki's parents are also excited that she is planning to attend CMC because it is a mere thirty-minute drive away from home.

Claremont University Consortium's seven institutions are one of 141 private nonprofit institutions in California.[6] Caltech, Stanford, and USC are universities with very high research activity. There are additional private research universities such as Pepperdine University and the University of San Diego; master's colleges and universities such as Santa Clara University and Chapman University; and associate's colleges such as Marymount College.

In addition, California has 167 private for-profit higher education institutions.[7] Most of these are associate's degree, vocational, or technical certificate–granting institutions. Many are regional or local campuses of organizations like the University of Phoenix, WyoTech, and ITT Technical Institute, which have a multistate, national, or global presence.

All of the public and private colleges and universities constitute California's vibrant and integrated higher education system.

A Vibrant Higher Education System: And a Vibrant Economy

Due in large measure to its higher education system, California is home to a thriving economy and diverse industries such as agriculture, entertainment, financial and business services, manufacturing, tourism, life sciences and health care, trade, and high-technology. If it were a nation, California would be the eighth largest in the world with a gross state product of US$2.2 trillion. It would be behind only the United States, China, Japan, Germany, France, the United Kingdom, and Brazil.[8]

Lessons from California: For Building a Golden India

California's Master Plan offers a compelling way forward for India and its states and union territories. It also provides evidence that:

1. Public and private colleges and universities can coexist for the benefit of all the stakeholders.

2. Universal access and excellent education is not just a dream; it is an achievable goal.

3. The impact of a vibrant higher education system can be seen in better skills and jobs for people, a thriving economy, and a better environment and health care system for all its citizens.

In addition, the California Master Plan led to the establishment of many new colleges and universities. There are pertinent lessons for India from one such new university — UC San Diego.

UC San Diego: From Founding to Preeminence in a Few Decades

UC San Diego (UCSD) is an outstanding example of how to build a world-class research university quickly. UCSD was founded in 1960 and was inducted to the prestigious Association of American Universities (AAU) in 1982 — making it the youngest university to do so in recent times. The seeds of the university were sown with the establishment of the Scripps Institution of Oceanography in the early 1900s. However, UCSD came to its current form through inspired leadership and efforts on the part of Roger Revelle, a successful researcher and faculty member. The San Diego community also played an instrumental role in the founding of a UC campus in San Diego by securing land and providing seed capital. After World War II, the community leaders recognized that San Diego's economy would change. Government spending on the military and nuclear science was expected to go down. They came to the conclusion that a research university would make the city more attractive for the best and the brightest researchers to relocate there.[9] Richard Atkinson, president emeritus of the University of California, was its chancellor from 1980 to 1995. Prior to joining UCSD, he was a faculty member at Stanford University and was influenced by its legendary leader Frederick Terman (more on Terman in the chapter on Stanford). Atkinson adopted many of the lessons from Stanford University to make UCSD more industry-focused and entrepreneurial.[10]

UCSD is a comprehensive university with over 25,000 students and was recently ranked number fourteen in the world.[11] It attracts over US$1 billion in research funding annually, making it one of the top ten among US universities.[12] Several start-ups that have originated from UCSD have become multibillion-dollar companies. One such company is Qualcomm, a leader in wireless telecommunication business. San Diego has become a hub for biotechnology, wireless, tourism, and medical science industries. The San Diego community's past and ongoing investments in UCSD are paying a rich dividend to the city, region, state, nation, and global society.

It is intriguing to note that UCSD's current chancellor and executive vice chancellor are both of Indian heritage and IITians. Pradeep Khosla, alumnus of IIT Kharagpur and CMU, is the chancellor, and Suresh Subramani, alumnus of IIT Kanpur and UC Berkeley, is the executive vice chancellor. (I briefly worked with Subramani at UCSD and Khosla at UCSD and IIT Foundation.)

So far, in addition to Nalanda University, we have reviewed higher education systems at the national level (the United States) and at the state level (California) and learned many important lessons for building a Golden India. In the next two chapters, we will review in depth two world-class research universities—UC Berkeley and Stanford University.

CHAPTER 8

UC Berkeley: The DNA of
Excellence and Impact

We are what we repeatedly do. Excellence,
then, is not an act, but a habit.

— Aristotle, Greek philosopher

Berkeley: Bob, a valedictorian at his high school in Philadelphia, was a highly sought after student. He received scholarships from a number of Ivy League schools, but he found UC Berkeley and the west coast's unique culture appealing. Like Bob, tens of thousands of talented students from California, the rest of the United States, and around the world are attracted to study at UC Berkeley every year.

Driving to Berkeley from the airport for the first time, Bob felt that he was coming home. His family expected him to pay his way through college. Thus, he joined a student cooperative that provided low-cost housing. In that co-op, he mingled with students from the United States and the rest of the world. It took him ten minutes to realize that UC Berkeley attracted exceptional talent. Being his high school's valedictorian, he prided himself in his grasp of subjects such as math, physics, and biology. In fact, he had planned to major in mathematics. He found he was not even close in math to some of the whiz kids within his co-op. When Vijay, his friend from India, scored a near perfect 149 out of 150 on a physics test when the class average was seventy-five, it was apparent to Bob that he had to find a field where he would stand out. At the same time, he recognized that he belonged at UC Berkeley.

He found his passion for biology and chemistry while reading James Watson's work. In his sophomore year, he conducted research in Dan Koshland's biochemical lab. Koshland was a legendary Berkeley faculty member and leader. And the rest, as many would say, is history. Bob completed his BA in biochemistry from UC Berkeley and then received a PhD in biochemistry and molecular biology from Harvard University. Then UC Berkeley won again: Bob joined as a faculty member. Bob's colleagues and friends call him Tij.[1] He is Dr. Robert Tjian.

Tjian is currently the president of Howard Hughes Medical Institute (HHMI). He was an HHMI investigator at UC Berkeley from 1987 to 2009 before becoming president of HHMI—an organization that funds biomedical research and science education for the benefit of humanity. In 2013, HHMI invested US$727 million in US research and provided US$80 million in grants and other support for science education.[2]

As a researcher, Tjian continues his efforts on the biochemistry of gene regulation at HHMI's Janelia Research Campus and at UC Berkeley. As the head of a highly respected organization, he brings thought and organizational leadership to research and education. He has made, and continues to make, a significant impact in the fields of biomedical sciences and health.

UC Berkeley was recently ranked #4 in the ARWU world rankings.[3] Its faculty and alumni have won twenty-two and twenty-nine Nobel Prizes respectively.[4] Since 1868, it has been contributing to the city of Berkeley, the state of California, the regional and national economy, and the global society. It attracts some of the best and the brightest students and faculty members from around the world. The faculty members are drawn to the university because of its talented students, and the students are attracted to its faculty. For over 150 years, UC Berkeley, or Cal as alumni fondly call it, has been able to sustain this seemingly simple yet powerful recipe for success.

A comprehensive research university, UC Berkeley offers a rich and diverse experience to its students at the undergraduate, graduate, and postgraduate levels. Interdisciplinary research and education are increasingly the norm. Excellence, making an impact, and collaborating with industry, government, and overseas partners are part of the institution's DNA. This DNA comes from its outstanding faculty members. It also comes from its unflinching commitment, vision, leadership, rigorous process, and thoughtful incentives to recruit and retain outstanding faculty members.

Across-the-Board Excellence: —150 Years and Counting

UC Berkeley is a university with a public mission. Founded in 1868, it is the first campus and the flagship campus of the University of California. It has grown to include 130 academic departments and 34 interdisciplinary graduate groups that offer degrees. Student enrollment is over 35,000. It has 1,620 full-time and 616 part-time faculty members and offers almost 8,000 courses in approximately 276 degree programs. The university is divided into fourteen colleges and schools: business, chemistry, education, engineering, environmental design, information, journalism, law, letters and science, natural resources, optometry, public health, public policy, and social welfare. The College of Letters and

Key Numbers

- Founded in 1868
- Living alumni: 464,000
- Faculty: 1620 full-time, 616 part-time
- Enrolled students: 36,204 as of fall 2013
  - Undergraduates: 25,951
  - Graduates: 10,253
- Degrees awarded (2012–13)
  - Bachelor's: 7,774
  - Master's: 2,198
  - Doctoral: 1,304
- Nobel Prizes
  - Faculty: 22
  - Alumni: 29

Source: www.berkeley.edu

Science, where I worked for just over five years, encompasses over sixty departments in the arts and humanities, biological sciences, physical and mathematical sciences, and social sciences. It has more than half of the campus's faculty, three-quarters of its undergraduate students, and half of its PhD candidates.

One of the school's measures of excellence is its award-winning faculty members. The current faculty includes 3 Turing Awards in computing, 3 Fields Medals in Mathematics, 4 Pulitzer Prizes, 7 Nobel Prize winners, 1 National Poet Laureate, and 32 MacArthur Fellows. It also includes faculty members who have been inducted to prestigious memberships: 15 in the Institute of Medicine, 40 in the American Philosophical Society, 95 in the National Academy of Engineering, 144 in the National Academy of Sciences, and 235 in the American Association of Arts and Sciences, to name a few.[5]

Another measure of its excellence is found in national and global rankings. In various rankings of universities in the world, Berkeley consistently ranks in the top five. In the 2014 ARWU rankings, Cal was ranked number one in natural science, mathematics, physics, and chemistry. It was in the top ten in all of these fields: engineering/ technology and computer science (number three), social sciences (number four), life and agricultural science (number eight). It was the only public university in the United States to be in the top ten in the overall ranking.[6]

The National Research Council's most recent rankings of doctoral programs at American universities were published in 2010. They collected and analyzed data on more than 5,000 doctoral programs in 62 fields at 212 colleges and universities. According to the NRC analysis, forty-eight UC Berkeley programs (out of fifty-two ranked) were in the top ten in the nation.[7]

The faculty awards and the rankings indicate amazing, across-the-board excellence. How has Berkeley sustained its virtuous cycle and excellence over one hundred and fifty years?

The answer, simply and powerfully, lies in its unrelenting focus on recruiting and retaining outstanding faculty members and attracting the best and the brightest students.

The Best Faculty and Students: A Virtuous Cycle

What attracts the most talented faculty members to UC Berkeley? The answer for most faculty members is the amazing pool of students at the undergraduate and graduate levels. Having smart students is intellectually stimulating. They ask thought-provoking questions, push the envelope in research and education, and bring immense curiosity and passion to the classrooms and labs. As members of the research team, these talented students provide passionate and tireless efforts to probe a question, test a hypothesis, learn from the results, and continue the research cycle.

Tsu-Jae King Liu is the chair of the department of electrical engineering and computer sciences (EECS) at UC Berkeley. Previously, she was the associate dean for research in the College of Engineering. (Liu and I co-led Berkeley's efforts to advance relationships with Lam Research and successfully secured a multimillion-dollar gift.) She completed her bachelor's, master's, and PhD from Stanford

University. For Liu and many faculty members, the university, college, and department vision and mission statements and what they mean and how they are translated into actions are deeply important and attractive.[8] Here are two examples:

The **College of Engineering's** mission statement[9] is:

- To prepare our students for careers of leadership and innovation in engineering and related fields.
- To deepen and broaden current knowledge through original research and to serve society with technology and science.
- To benefit the public through service to industry, government, and the engineering professions.

At **Berkeley Law,** we are committed to excellence in education and scholarship, as well as equality of opportunity. We believe we have a responsibility to use our substantial intellectual capital to help solve real-world problems and to create a more just society through clinics, research, and policy engagement. We believe that a Berkeley Law degree is a tool for change, both locally and globally, and that we should be educating the leaders of tomorrow. We maintain an environment that nurtures academic and personal growth, respects a diversity of ideas, and stimulates independent thought and critical reasoning.[10]

In the university, college, and department mission statements, the importance of education, conducting research, serving society, solving important problems, making an impact at the local, regional, national, and global scale stand out. The vision and mission statements are noble, aspirational, relevant, and inspiring. They set Berkeley apart from all of its private university peers. They attract exceptional faculty members who are inspired by the school's public mission.

Faculty members are also attracted by the opportunity to work with outstanding colleagues. The ability to interact and collaborate with exceptional, like-minded, and like-valued individuals is incredibly attractive. Buildings are being designed to foster interactions that lead to interdisciplinary research and spontaneous creativity. In these buildings, a leading biologist could expect to have an office next to a leading engineer, chemist, mathematician, or computer scientist.

So what attracts the best and the brightest students to UC Berkeley? The answer for most of the students is its award-winning faculty, an exceptional group of students, and Berkeley's culture of excellence and making an impact.

Thus, it is no surprise that some of the best and the brightest minds from India attend UC Berkeley and call it their home. Sreeta Gorripaty recently graduated from IIT Bombay with a bachelor's in civil engineering and is now pursuing a PhD at Berkeley. She chose Berkeley since it has one of the top programs in transportation systems, her field of interest. Alok Goel, faculty member at IIT Bombay and a Berkeley alumnus, also encouraged her to pursue graduate studies at UC Berkeley. Gorripaty finds Berkeley culture welcoming. "Wacky ideas are always welcome," she noted. She has a lot of freedom in pursuing her research interests and loves the school's strong focus on ethics. Everyone collaborates and is happy to help. She also finds interdisciplinary research and industry-university collaborations valuable and a welcome change from her experiences in India.[11]

Raj Shekhar Singh participated in the UC Berkeley–IIT Kharagpur collaboration. As part of the program, he spent eight weeks in Berkeley conducting research and fell in love with the research culture. Singh said, "Research can be fun and impactful at the same time. It also gave me confidence in my ability to do world-class research." He then decided to pursue a PhD at Berkeley. "My life was completely transformed. I had never thought I would go for higher studies, but I did and got a PhD. I got married to a Chinese girl [who] I met in I-House and that has completely changed my life. I never thought about a lot of issues in India in a very critical way as I can now because of my experience outside India and talking to people from around the world."[12]

Anindya De (in theoretical computer science), Avinash Nayak (in seismology), and Aamod Shanker (in electrical engineering and computer science), all from IITs, were all attracted to Berkeley for similar reasons.[13]

Some of India's brightest have joined Berkeley as faculty members in diverse fields such as engineering, sciences, social sciences, and arts and humanities. For example, Ramamoorthy Ramesh, one of the most highly cited researchers in the world, has a joint appointment in physics and material science and engineering.[14] Pranab Bardhan is a faculty member in economics,

Raka Ray in sociology, Ananya Roy in city and regional planning, and Irfan Siddiqi in physics. Several of these faculty members have joint appointments with Lawrence Berkeley National Laboratory (LBNL). For example, Ashok Gadgil, who has found inexpensive ways to remove arsenic to make safe drinking water and developed fuel-efficient stoves, is the director of the Energy and Environmental Technologies Division at LBNL and a professor in UC Berkeley's civil engineering department. A few are in senior leadership roles. Jitendra Malik was the former chair of the EECS department, and Shankar Sastry is the current dean of the College of Engineering. The list of faculty members who grew up in India and are now at Berkeley is much longer.

What a virtuous cycle! Exceptional students attract exceptional faculty members, and exceptional faculty members attract exceptional students.

Academic-Personnel Committee: Exceptional Process, Effort, and Leadership

UC Berkeley's academic senate, consisting of its faculty members, is empowered by the board of regents, the top governing body, to "determine academic policy; set conditions for admission and the granting of degrees; authorize and supervise courses and curricula; and advise the administration on faculty appointments, promotions, and budgets." Thus, the academic senate plays a leadership role in maintaining and sustaining Berkeley's excellence.[15] The senate has many committees that provide leadership for various important university matters. The budget and interdepartmental relations committee,[16] better known in Berkeley as the budget committee, is responsible for faculty hiring, merit-based pay increases, promotions, tenure, and retention-related decisions.

"It is prestigious and an honor to be a faculty member [at UC Berkeley]."

The founding principle for the budget committee was that faculty members should be reviewed primarily by their peers and not just by the administration. The Committee on Committees (COMS) is responsible for appointing all committees. COMS in consultation with current budget committee members, reviews new candidates. COMS recommends the names, which then have to be reviewed

135

and approved by the divisional council of the academic senate. This extensive process to select, nominate, and approve budget committee members to "safeguard the academic distinction" is taken seriously by all concerned. A lot of thought and care is given to ensure that the committee represents the academic diversity of the campus. This is to enable the second mandate of the committee to: "promote equal treatment of similarly situated faculty across the campus."[17]

Joining the budget committee is considered prestigious and is a three-year commitment. Appointment to the committee is staggered, such that every year one-third of its members are new. Having outstanding, well-respected, and thoughtful faculty members on the budget committee is the first step toward maintaining and sustaining excellence.

Once selected, the nine-member budget committee works tirelessly to promote and maintain excellence. In the last few years, the budget committee has reviewed over 900 cases annually. Barring exceptions, they meet once a week throughout the year. The faculty members are reviewed every two to four years, assistant professors are reviewed every two years, and senior professors every four years. The committee gets the

"He was concise, organized, entertaining, and perhaps most important, friendly." Others call his research seminars 'Rinestone' lectures because they're "gems."

case after the department committee, the department chair, and the dean have reviewed the case and made their recommendations. The budget committee then reviews the entire file, which typically includes all the accomplishments since the last review on three dimensions: research, teaching, and service. External recognition, peer reviews, publications, conference lectures, and grants are considered and deliberated on before making a recommendation. The budget committee results are then forwarded to the campus administration. The cases for promotions conclude with the chancellor, who can alter the decision if necessary. Such differences with the administration occur in just a handful of cases. Such is the rigor and respect for the process and commitment to excellence.

David Patterson is a great example of a faculty member hired through the extensive recruiting process who was later selected to be on the budget committee. A highly sought after faculty member and mentor, Patterson agreed to meet me for this book.

I was impressed by his humility, openness, and commitment to all of the things that matter—research, teaching, and service to society. Patterson completed his bachelor's and PhD in computer science at UCLA. He likes to call himself an "accidental computer scientist, PhD, and professor." Yet there is no accident to his winning ways. A hardworking and committed teacher, mentor, and researcher, he lives by the motto "There are no losers on the winning team, and no winners on a losing team." Patterson wins by building the best research teams of faculty and students, fostering interdisciplinary research, and creating an open and collaborative research environment. He also engages the industry, seeks thoughtful external inputs, and works on critical problems and high-impact solutions. He also likes to use baseball analogies to communicate his thoughts and approaches, such as swinging for the fences, increasing his at-bats, and hitting home runs. He has hit many home runs.

Patterson is best known for his pioneering work on reduced instruction set computers (RISC), redundant array of inexpensive disks (RAID), and networks of workstations (NOW). All of these helped spawn several billion-dollar industries. He is a recipient of many awards and accolades, such as the Institute of Electrical and Electronics Engineers (IEEE) John von Neumann Medal, and was elected to the National Academy of Engineering (NAE) and the National Academy of Sciences (NAS). He has authored six books, including two with John Hennessy, president of Stanford University. "It is prestigious and an honor to be a faculty member [at UC Berkeley]," he said.[18] He has earned that honor.

Jasper Rine is another exceptional faculty member who served in the budget committee. He is an HHMI professor and a professor of genetics, genomics, and development. He is a member of the prestigious NAS and the American Academy of Arts and Sciences. He is also a fellow at the American Association for the Advancement of Science. By 2014, he had mentored thirty-seven PhDs, thirty-five postdoctoral scholars, and tens of thousands of students and participated in fifteen faculty search committees and over one hundred PhD thesis committees.

As a child, Rine, a self-made man, grew up farming in upstate New York. After paying his way through the State University of New York (SUNY), he got his PhD at the University of Oregon and completed postdoctoral studies at Stanford. He thrives on research and loves teaching.[19] When he received a Distinguished Teaching Award from UC Berkeley in 1997, one student said, "He was concise, organized, entertaining, and perhaps most important, friendly."

> *"If we do not find a candidate who meets our standards, we declare the search a failure, close the process, and restart the following year."*

Others call his research seminars 'Rinestone' lectures because they're "gems."[20] He loves Berkeley since it is a place where "talented students with no backwind can succeed, and where first-generation college students can come to the top of the heap."[21]

These rigorous and transparent processes led by exceptional faculty members such as Patterson and Rine have an added benefit. They provide confidence to the faculty members that they will be treated fairly and to the administration that decisions are thoughtful, fair, and in the best interests of the institution.

Faculty Excellence: A Habit and a Culture

Commitment to faculty excellence as a foundation for academic and institutional excellence is pervasive. This manifests in many ways.

Randy Schekman, Nobel laureate, HHMI investigator, and UC Berkeley faculty member, joined Berkeley after completing postdoctoral training at UC San Diego, a PhD from Stanford, and a bachelor's from UCLA. (I enjoyed working with him during my time at UC Berkeley.) According to him, he was touched by excellence throughout his education. At UCLA, he sought and got an opportunity to work in a lab and was forever hooked on research. He went on to conduct research under two Nobel laureates, one at Stanford and the next at UC San Diego. These Nobel laureates were outstanding researchers and extremely demanding. At Berkeley, Koshland, a highly respected senior faculty member, mentored him. He learned to "never settle for second best." Despite early setbacks in research, Schekman, with Koshland's support and encouragement, pursued his research direction. In 1979, his seminal work was published in *Proceedings of the National Academy of Sciences* (PNAS) and was communicated by Koshland.[22] This research became the foundation for his winning the 2013 Nobel Prize in Physiology and Medicine. According to Berkeley's press statement:

He won the Nobel Prize for his role in revealing the machinery that regulates the transport and secretion of proteins in our cells. He shares the prize with James E. Rothman of Yale University and Thomas C. Südhof of Stanford University. Discoveries by Schekman about how yeast secrete proteins led directly to the success of the biotechnology industry, which was able to coax yeast to release useful protein drugs, such as insulin and human growth hormone. The three scientists' research on protein transport in cells, and how cells control this trafficking to secrete hormones and enzymes, illuminated the workings of a fundamental process in cell physiology.[23]

On faculty recruitment, Schekman, who also heads the chancellor's advisory board for biology, likes to say, "If we do not find a candidate who meets our standards, we declare the search a failure, close the process, and restart the following year." Tough decisions are made all the time well before the case gets to the budget committee.[24]

"The university administration, academic senate, and the budget committee do everything to protect the faculty-related salary and merit budget."

Commitment to excellence is unflinching, and everyone in the university is committed to it. Incentives matter, especially in a global competition for top-notch faculty members. While Berkeley benefits from being located in vibrant and sunny California and from its proximity to Silicon Valley, the faculty salaries, benefits, merit increases, start-up research grants, and research infrastructure play a critical role in recruitment and retention. According to Bardhan, who has also served on the budget committee, "The university administration, academic senate, and the budget committee do everything to protect the faculty-related salary and merit budget." Despite California's budget woes, UC Berkeley has been able to ensure that it continues to attract and retain the best and the brightest minds as faculty members.

In addition, significant university resources are invested to ensure that Berkeley has the necessary financial resources to be competitive with private research universities such as Harvard and Stanford, which have significantly larger endowments. Chairs, fellowships, scholarships, discretionary research funds, and research equipment funding are important. These private resources could be given to retain a faculty member or to attract a rising star. Frequently, these private resources are leveraged to attract larger research funding from US government agencies or additional sources. University leadership members, including the chancellor, deans, vice chancellors, department chairs, and faculty members, are actively engaged in stewarding philanthropists, corporate executives, and foundation leaders around the world, all the time. University Relations, a staff organization, is dedicated to reaching out and engaging with and raising funds from alumni, friends, parents, corporations, and foundations. Several colleges also have an additional industry liaison arm that strengthens the colleges' and faculty members' existing relationships with corporate executives and researchers.

Private and public resources are also deployed to improve teaching and research infrastructure. These resources give the Berkeley leaders necessary discretionary funding flexibility to make the difference at the margins. Discretionary funds and outstanding infrastructure may sometimes be the difference in hiring the next Bardhan, Liu, Patterson, Rine, or Schekman or losing them to Stanford, Caltech, or Harvard and starting the search process all over in another year.

The vision is realized and the mission is accomplished by doing many things right all the time, none more important than hiring and retaining outstanding faculty members who are inspired and committed to the mission. And, just like it takes a village to raise a child, it takes a team to ensure excellence. Results are rich dividends for all.

Rich Dividends: For California and Its People, the United States, and the World

Berkeley's DNA of excellence, its culture of making an impact, and its recipe for success have been paying rich dividends to all its stakeholders. Its faculty members are advancing frontiers of research and innovation, starting companies, and training the next generation of leaders, entrepreneurs, researchers, and faculty members in all fields. The faculty members have contributed to our improved understanding of our past, and the world and the universe around us. These advances make the world safer, more sustainable, healthier, and more productive.

Health

They have improved our understanding of the positive dietary role of vitamins, minerals, and proteins, and the negative role of cholesterol and fats. They discovered vitamins E and K. They also created nuclear medicine and pioneered the use of radioisotopes to control disease. They crystallized the virus for polio and founded the first biotechnology company. These and many more discoveries led by Berkeley faculty members have resulted in improved drugs, diagnostics, and vaccines that have improved the health and lives of Californians, Americans, and people globally.

Natural Resources

Berkeley faculty members were the first to demonstrate the successful use of an insect pathogen to control insects in the field. Today, these bacteria are used worldwide to fight crop diseases. They are improving our understanding of seeds, crops, forests, ecosystems, and the impact of climate change. Several were members of the Intergovernmental Panel on Climate Change, which won the Nobel Prize in 2007.

The Universe

In 1980, Luis Alvarez and Walter Alvarez, father and son, were the first to offer evidence that an asteroid or comet struck our planet sixty-five million years ago, causing the extinction of the dinosaurs and profoundly altering Earth's environment. In 1992, a team led by Berkeley cosmologist George Smoot revealed the early beginnings of the universe. These findings confirm the predictions of the Big Bang theory, and in 2006, George Smoot was awarded the Nobel Prize in Physics. In 2011, Saul Perlmutter won the Nobel Prize in Physics for discovering that the universe was expanding faster than it was billions of years ago.

Science and Engineering

Basic discoveries and key technology advances have made our lives better. Ernest O. Lawrence designed the first cyclotron. In 1939, he was the first of the twenty-two Berkeley faculty members to win the Nobel Prize for this invention. The cyclotron made a major impact on the treatment and diagnostics of diseases and led to the discovery of many new elements, such as plutonium.

More recently, UNIX and open source software could be traced back to UC Berkeley faculty members. Integrated circuits are pervasive in everything we do from computers to mobile phones and sensors. All integrated circuits are designed using the Simulation Program with Integrated Circuit Emphasis (SPICE) tool or one of its derivatives. Donald O. Pederson, professor in EECS at UC Berkeley, and his team developed SPICE.

Defense

Our world was suffering during World War II. More than sixty million people were killed during the war. The war spurred the development of technologies for military applications, and the universities were actively engaged in winning the war. UC directed the operation of the US government laboratory in Los Alamos, New Mexico. Berkeley physics professor J. Robert Oppenheimer led the efforts, and the work of several Berkeley faculty members was incorporated in the making of the atomic bomb. Thus, UC Berkeley faculty members played a key role in bringing an end to World War II.

Arts and Humanities

The humanists and artists have created deeper understanding and appreciation of different languages, cultures, ethnicities, races, and nations. They have also improved our understanding of various cultures and history.

As an example, UC Berkeley has been teaching Sanskrit since 1906. Robert Goldman, a professor of Sanskrit, is the general editor and a principal translator of the critical edition of the *Valmiki Ramayana*. In 2013, the president of India recognized Goldman for his contributions to Sanskrit. Thousands of students, including international students from India and those with Indian heritage, have learned Sanskrit and Vedic texts by taking his classes. I took one of his classes, learned a lot, and wondered why these subjects are not taught in IITs or educational institutions in India. The Center for South Asia Studies, of which he was one of the early directors, frequently invites speakers from India and India experts from around the world. They host conferences and public talks to disseminate knowledge, exchange ideas, and engage students, faculty members, and the local community about India and related topics.

Social Sciences and Policy

Berkeley faculty members have improved our understanding on how markets, companies, and nations work, compete, and collaborate. Economics faculty members have won five Nobel prizes for their contributions. Many of the faculty members from across the university have and continue to serve in important US and state government policy-making committees and think tanks. They are influencing policies in fields such as agricultural, climate change, economics, education, energy, health, international relations, law, and trade. For example, Arthur Rosenfeld, UC Berkeley faculty member and researcher at LBNL, is credited for influencing California's energy policies and standards. His research and findings have influenced energy-efficient refrigerators, lightbulbs, windows, heaters, and air conditioners. As a result, California consumes 30 percent less electricity per capita than the rest of the nation. His work is also credited for saving US$100 billion annually.[25]

Education

Since its inception, one of Berkeley's goals has also been ensuring that students could attend the university regardless of means. The school has the proud distinction of educating more Pell Grant recipients, whose family incomes are generally less than US$45,000 per year, than all the Ivy League universities combined. UC Berkeley produces more PhDs annually than any other US university, and a significant percentage join academia. Preparing the next generation of faculty members ensures that the cycle of learning, teaching, experimenting, and pushing frontiers of knowledge continues into the future.[26]

Source: UC Berkeley, http://www.berkeley.edu/about/history-discoveries

UC Berkeley's vibrant research, education, and service engine powers the local, regional, and national economy. The results of a study conducted on behalf of UC Berkeley by CB Richard Ellis

Consulting were released in 2007.[27] It was based on 2005 to 2006 fiscal year data. Some of the highlights included: that Berkeley had revenues of US$1.4 billion, of which 71 percent came from outside the Bay Area. It spent approximately US$144 million on capital projects and US$401 million on goods and services and US$808 million in payroll. A large percentage was spent in the local community. With 24,700 employees, it is one of the largest employers in the region. In addition, students spent US$395 million in the Bay Area and visitors to Berkeley spent another US$30 million in the city of Berkeley. According to the study, this spending has a multiplier effect of approximately 1.5. Thus, the total impact of UC Berkeley was more than US$1.5 billion, generating an additional 9,200 indirect jobs in the Bay Area.

Many famous corporations such as Apple, Intel, Gap, Chiron (now Novartis), and Sun Microsystems have been founded by faculty members or alumni, or because of university-based research. These large corporations and numerous start-ups create jobs, bring in revenues and tax windfalls, and benefit the local and regional economy significantly with the multiplier effect.

UC Berkeley's excellence and impact can be seen, felt, and measured by its outstanding faculty members, vibrant economy, thoughtful policies, engaged community and in the transformed lives of its students and alumni. Berkeley's impact also manifests in the improved understanding of ourselves and the world around us, extending frontiers of knowledge, enabling innovations and new industries, and shedding light where none existed. UC Berkeley lives by its motto *fiat lux,* or "let there be light."

Lessons from UC Berkeley: For Building a Golden India

Colleges and universities in India can learn a number of lessons about how to build and sustain excellence. Central and state government leaders, bureaucrats, and philanthropists can also learn what it really takes to build and sustain world-class institutions. Finally, everyone can learn about the value of a world-class institution for the local community, state, society, and nation.

- **Attracting and retaining the best and the brightest faculty members matters.** Great institutions like UC Berkeley are established on the shoulders of faculty members who are experts in their respective fields and who are deeply committed to the mission of the university.

- **Attracting the best and the brightest students matters.** The virtuous cycle, where exceptional faculty attracts exceptional students and exceptional students attract exceptional faculty members, is a recipe for success.

- **A culture of excellence and making an impact matters.** Excellence and making an impact are deeply ingrained in the culture. They are habits. They are parts of the DNA. The processes and incentives are aligned to sustain this culture.

When one assembles outstanding faculty members and students in an environment where there is a culture of excellence and making an impact, and where the processes, infrastructure, and incentives are all aligned to foster that culture then great things happen—basic and applied research, innovation, start-ups, and engagement with the community. Thus, a world-class research university makes significant contributions to students and enables social and income mobility. It contributes directly and indirectly to the vibrancy of the local, state, and national economy. It also makes a tangible impact in all fields that matter to the society, such as health care, the environment, natural resources, science and engineering, defense applications, arts and humanities, and social science and policy.

In this chapter, we learned about UC Berkeley, a public university. In the next, we will review Stanford, a private university. Are they more similar or different? What could we learn from Stanford that is uniquely different from UC Berkeley?

CHAPTER 9

Stanford University:
An Innovation Powerhouse

The credit belongs to the man who is actually in the arena...

— Theodore Roosevelt, president of
United States (1901–09), Nobel laureate

Palo Alto, 2014: Arogyaswami Paulraj, professor emeritus at Stanford University, was awarded the prestigious Marconi Prize. It is considered to be the Nobel Prize in the field of information technology. According to the Marconi Society's press release, "[Paulraj's] idea for using multiple antennas at both the transmitting and receiving stations—which is at the heart of the current high-speed Wi-Fi and 4G mobile systems—has revolutionized high-speed wireless delivery of multimedia services for billions of people."[1] Multiple Inputs, Multiple Outputs (MIMO) technology pioneered by Paulraj is now being used in every Wi-Fi router and 4G phone. Paulraj is one of many award-winning Stanford faculty members who are advancing the frontiers of knowledge, creating wealth, and making an impact on humanity.

Paulraj's route to Stanford was unlike many of his peers. Until 1991, he had served for over thirty years in the Indian Navy. After joining India's National Defense Academy (NDA) Khadakvasla, as a young person he graduated at the top of his class and won the prestigious President of India Gold Medal. Subsequently, he completed his bachelor's in electrical engineering from the Naval College of Engineering (NCE) in Lonavala. He impressed his superiors with his dedication, creativity, and technical competence. Despite early objections, he completed his PhD from IIT

Delhi with the help from some of his mentors. Shortly thereafter, the 1971 war with Pakistan exposed several technical limitations of the Indian Navy. Due to import restrictions for military-use technology, India was forced to undertake indigenous development. He led a project to develop several important electronics-based systems for which he was awarded the Vishisht Seva Medal (VSM) by the government of India. Soon, he was made project leader for the development of the advanced panoramic sonar hull (APSOH), a state-of-the-art sonar system. He was awarded the Ati Vishisht Seva Medal (AVSM) for this accomplishment. Later, he was the founding director of three research labs in India. In those leadership roles, he had to periodically interact with IAS officials. Unfortunately for India, he felt compelled by the Indian bureaucracy to leave India.[2] His track record of excellence and making an impact brought him to Stanford.

Since joining Stanford, Paulraj has charged forward with the same zeal he exhibited in NDA, NCE, IIT, the Indian Navy, and various Indian research labs. He has mentored over fifty PhDs, founded several start-ups, advised many corporations, and has had the distinct honor of being one of the few who have won *both* the prestigious IEEE Alexander Graham Bell and the Marconi Society awards.[3]

Ranked in the top five in various world rankings, Stanford has raised the bar for universities around the world. Fred Terman, referred to as the "father of Silicon Valley," is widely credited for Stanford's remarkable rise from a regional university up until the World War II to a premier research university in the world by the 1960s. The "Terman Model," as the formula for success is referred to, has taken the successful models in universities such as Harvard, UC Berkeley, and Cambridge several notches higher. Not only is Stanford attracting outstanding and award-winning faculty like Paulraj from around the world, its faculty and students are also fueling the innovation and entrepreneurial engine. Global brands such as Google, Yahoo, and Cisco originated from research conducted at Stanford. In yet another mark of across-the-board excellence, Stanford is the proud winner of the Directors' Cup, awarded to a university for their cumulative performance in Division I men's and women's sports. Stanford has won the cup twenty-one years in a row. Last year, the university raised close to US$1 billion in private resources from alumni, grateful patients, friends, corporations, and foundations. Stanford is an innovation powerhouse and getting stronger every year.

Rise to Preeminence: Remarkable

Leland Stanford, railroad president, land baron, and US senator, and his wife Jane founded Stanford University in 1885 in memory of their son. Their vision was to create a different type of university — tuition free, coeducational, nondenominational, and practical. This was in great contrast to what was popular then. According to the founding grant, the university's objective was (and is) "to qualify its students for personal success, and direct usefulness in life" and its purpose was "to promote the public welfare by exercising an influence in behalf of humanity and civilization."

In 1891, David Starr Jordan, president of Indiana University, was appointed as the founding president of Stanford. Stanford opened with 555 students and fifteen faculty members. It has grown in size, scope, and prestige since then. In 2014, it had an enrollment of over 7,000 undergraduate students and over 9,000 graduate students for a total of over 16,000. It had over 2,100 faculty members in its seven schools and colleges: the Graduate School of Business, School of Earth Sciences, Graduate School of Education, School of Engineering, School of Humanities and Sciences, School of Law, and School of Medicine.[4]

Key Numbers

- Founded in 1885
- Physical Size: 8,180 acres
- Faculty: 2,118
- Enrolled students: 16,137 as of fall 2014
  - Undergraduates: 7,018
  - Graduates: 9,119
- Degrees awarded (2014)
  - Bachelor's: 1,651
  - Master's: 2,563
  - Doctoral: 729
- Nobel Prizes
  - Faculty (Overall): 31
  - Faculty (Current): 21

Source: www.stanford.edu

The seeds of excellence and success were sowed at Stanford's inception and nurtured throughout the early years. Jordan recruited outstanding faculty members, primarily his friends and colleagues at Indiana, universities in the Midwest, and Cornell, his alma mater. Ray Lyman Wilbur, Stanford's president after Jordan, transformed its academic organization, upgraded facilities and faculty salaries, jump-started fund-raising, expanded graduate study and professional education, promoted faculty research and consulting, and stressed scholarship over extracurricular activities. During Wilbur's time, the medical school was firmly attached to the university, and the Hoover Institution, Food Research Institute, and the schools of business, engineering, and education were founded. The culture of industry-academia collaboration was fostered. For example, the Federal Telegraph Company, then a leading radio communications company in the world, had active collaborations with Stanford. In 1916, power companies began contributing equipment to Stanford. Research conducted by Stanford faculty members, in turn, helped these companies. Faculty members and students were also actively engaged in local and global affairs, prominently so during World War I. In 1922, Wilbur initiated the first development campaign in Stanford's history with a "First Million for Stanford" campaign to raise endowment funds for faculty salaries. In 1925, Stanford's graduate programs were ranked fourteenth in the United States.[5]

Stanford's rise to preeminence is especially remarkable after World War II. Since then, it has been climbing steadily toward the upward echelons of universities and now is firmly placed at the very top of global rankings. Some of this rise can be observed in the growth in students and faculty members. In 1940, Stanford had just over 3,400 undergraduate students, 1,700 graduate students, and 300 faculty members. By 1980, that shot up to over 6,600 undergraduate students, 6,200 graduate students, and 1,200 faculty members. The growth from 1940 to 2014 is even more striking — the undergraduate enrollment has doubled, graduate student enrollment has gone up 5.1 times, and academic faculty members 5.3 times.[6]

Stanford is also consistently ranked in the top 5 universities in the world. The 2014 ARWU ranking placed it as the #2 university in the world. In all the fields ranked by ARWU, it was placed in the top 10.[7] The current faculty includes 21 Nobel Prize and 5 Pulitzer Prize winners, 2 Fields Medalists in mathematics, and 27 MacArthur Fellows. It also includes faculty members who have been inducted to prestigious memberships: 50 in the American Philosophical Society, 66 in the Institute of Medicine, 105 in the National Academy of Engineering, 154 in the National Academy of Sciences, and 276 in the American Association of Arts and Sciences, to name a few.[8]

What has driven Stanford's spectacular transformation since World War II?

Stanford and the "Terman Model": Building Steeples of Excellence

In the success of a large and complex organization such as Stanford, there are always many contributing factors — the unifying vision and mission; capable and dedicated leadership, faculty members, and staff; an engaged community and friends; and successful, generous, and committed alumni and families. California's culture and its sunny weather are also said to have contributed to its success. The leadership of Wallace Sterling and Richard Lyman, president of the university from 1949–68 and 1970–80 respectively, are widely accepted as being pivotal to Stanford's success. However, Fred Terman, also known as the "academic architect of Silicon Valley" and the "father of Silicon Valley" is credited for the amazing rise of Stanford from a regional university in the United States in the 1940s to a premier research university in the world by the 1960s. "Fred Terman set a standard of excellence for the Stanford campus that has endured to this day,"[9] noted Richard C. Atkinson, president emeritus of the University of California, who was a faculty member at Stanford during Terman's tenure as the provost.

Frederick Emmons Terman was a brilliant student, an avid ham radio hobbyist, an outstanding researcher, and a dedicated leader. He was an award-winning faculty member, president of the Institute of Radio Engineers (IRE, a precursor to IEEE), and the author of highly regarded books on radio engineering. He received his bachelor's in chemistry and master's in electrical engineering from Stanford and a doctorate degree in electrical engineering from MIT, where he was the first doctoral student of Vannevar Bush. Terman joined Stanford's faculty in the department of electrical engineering. During World War II, he led the government's secret efforts to develop radar countermeasures at the Radio Research Laboratory (RRL) at Harvard (1942–45). He held increasing leadership roles at Stanford: executive head of the Electrical Engineering Department (1937–41), dean of the School of Engineering (1946–59), and provost of the university (1955–65).[10]

Terman's formula for personal and professional success was straightforward: hard work, persistence, dedication to clearly articulated goals, ambition, accountability, and expecting excellence from himself and everyone around him.[11] His devotion to Stanford's success is legendary.

After his stint at RRL concluded with the end of the war, Fred Terman returned to Stanford as the dean of the School of Engineering. Terman's ambition was to make the school "the most attractive and leading School of Engineering west of Mississippi River, with the possible exception of California Institute of Technology."[12] His ambition for making Stanford top-notch was not just restricted to electrical engineering or the School of Engineering. He was driven to make Stanford the Harvard of the west.

"Terman Model"

- Building steeples of excellence in targeted areas by recruiting outstanding faculty members.

- Having close links to industry and government.

- Promoting the talents of faculty and students.

- Providing the best research and teaching facilities.

- Actively involving alumni and benefactors.

- Having large numbers of outstanding students.

- Enabling entrepreneurial, corporate, and academic cultures.

To realize these goals, Terman steadfastly followed a philosophy that he advocated and implemented at Stanford as a professor, chair, dean, and provost. Referred to by some as the "Terman Model," it can be summarized as: building steeples of excellence in targeted areas by recruiting outstanding faculty members; having close links to industry and government; promoting the talents of faculty and students; providing the best research and teaching facilities; actively involving alumni and benefactors; having large numbers of outstanding students; and enabling entrepreneurial, corporate, and academic cultures.[13]

Much like UC Berkeley and other leading universities, Terman viewed faculty hiring as critical. He explained, "If we are to build up a department of the greatest possible strength, the appointments to the lower ranks must be guarded just as carefully and given just as much consideration as appointments to the higher positions."[14] The faculty recruitment process, which he led or oversaw, typically included a well-rounded search committee. In addition, he solicited input from his friends and colleagues in academia and industry. In some cases, he wanted suggestions for new candidates and in others he wanted to get valuable insights on the short-listed ones. In a few instances, when the candidate was well known and it was important to make a decision quickly, he ensured that it was made. To make Stanford more attractive for exceptional faculty members, he helped increase faculty salaries and raised funds for fellowships, chair endowments, and research facilities. He also used the vast land gifted to Stanford by its founders as a magnet to attract them. By offering an opportunity to own a house on the university-owned land, he made Stanford even more attractive for faculty members who were typically weighing offers from multiple universities.[15] Thus, Terman himself was a magnet for students and he also made it attractive for outstanding faculty to join Stanford, as was the case with Tom Kailath and Krishna Saraswat.

"If we are to build up a department of the greatest possible strength, the appointments to the lower ranks must be guarded just as carefully and given just as much consideration as appointments to the higher positions."

Tom Kailath is a distinguished and highly acclaimed faculty member at Stanford. Recently, he was awarded the prestigious US National Medal of Science by President Obama. An alumnus of Fergusson College and the College of Engineering in Pune, Kailath completed his PhD from MIT. After MIT, he applied to IIT for a faculty position and never heard back. He also mentioned how Fred Terman played an important role in his joining Stanford as a young associate professor in the early 1960s.[16] One good act follows another, and decades later, Kailath was instrumental in recruiting Paulraj to Stanford.[17]

Krishna Saraswat completed his bachelor's in engineering from BITS Pilani and was inspired to be a scientist. He chose Stanford for his graduate studies because he wanted to learn from Terman and his colleagues.[18] Saraswat completed his PhD from Stanford and now is an award-winning professor in Stanford's School of Engineering.

Terman also encouraged his students to start companies. David Packard and William Hewlett were Terman's students. He mentored and brought them together.[19] Soon, Hewlett-Packard (HP) was formed, and the rest, as they say, is history. He also encouraged start-ups and large corporations to locate their businesses in the newly established Industrial Park (later renamed Stanford Research Park.) Varian Associates, a company started by Stanford alumni and mentored by Terman, was the first company to lease space at the park.[20] He was also pivotal in William Shockley's return to Silicon Valley. Shockley's co-invention of transistors spawned a whole new semiconductor industry. Terman believed that the proximity of corporations and new ventures would spur interactions with Stanford. He believed that it would also lead to meaningful research interactions, and Stanford students would receive valuable experience and employment. Faculty members also received valuable consulting engagements. The Honors Cooperative Program that enabled engineers from local companies to get their master's degrees was another innovation that helped Stanford enormously. It fostered closer ties with the local companies and gave the university higher tuition revenues. Finally, these corporate relationships also benefitted the fund-raising efforts.[21] Stanford Research Park and companies located in it further attracted additional companies to move their businesses to the area. Terman and Stanford nurtured Research Park and the ecosystem has evolved into today's Silicon Valley.[22]

After World War II, Terman, in large measure due to his prominent role in RRL and his connections, brought Stanford to the forefront of federal research contracts. Prior to the war, the big research projects usually went to Harvard, MIT, Caltech, the University of Chicago, and UC Berkeley.[23] Terman ensured that Stanford benefited from the postwar research. The increased research funding provided much-needed resources to increase faculty salaries, hire more graduate students, and improve research facilities. Winning big projects also gave Stanford's prestige a welcome boost.

By 1959, Stanford had made rapid progress, and according to Wallace Sterling, president of Stanford University from 1949 to 1968, "With the exception of Harvard, we are catching up fast with California [UC Berkeley], Princeton, and others. Our problem is to stay caught up."[24]

William Miller, former president of the Stanford Research Institute (SRI) and former provost at Stanford University, was one of the last faculty members Terman recruited. I first met Miller in 2004 and was struck by his love for Stanford and youthful energy. Past his prime in most cultures, he was actively advising start-ups and governments. In 2005, when I was the president of the IIT Foundation, we invited him to share his insights with IIT Kharagpur's academic and alumni leaders. Miller gave a wonderful presentation about Stanford's success. He reiterated the impact of the "Terman Model" and its role in decision-making. As an example, he mentioned that the nursing school was deemed unlikely to be a steeple of excellence even though it was serving an important purpose. They made the tough decision of closing the program down. Stanford has figured out where to invest its time, intellectual power, and financial resources, and where not to invest—both are equally important and hallmarks of a great institution.

Great institutions like Stanford attract exceptional students. Some of the best and the brightest students from India attend Stanford. Raghu Mahajan, who topped IIT JEE in 2006, came to Stanford and took a very different path than most IITians. He joined IIT Delhi's computer science program, as was expected by everyone and also encouraged by his parents. His heart however was in physics, and it would not stop tugging at him. After spending a year at IIT, he came to the conclusion that the physics faculty at IIT was bad. After his second year, he left IIT Delhi and joined MIT. He is currently pursuing a PhD at Stanford after completing a bachelor's at MIT and a master's from the University of Cambridge, all in physics. Answering to the question, "What makes Stanford special?" Mahajan noted that "Everyone likes what they are doing and everyone is working on the next big thing, the next big idea." "[There] is an irresistible urge to make and create things," he added.[25]

Stanford Faculty and Alumni Entrepreneurs
(Since the 1930s)

- Started 39,900 companies
- Created 5.4 million jobs
- Generated $2.7 trillion in annual revenues

Source: www.stanford.edu

Arpit Goel is currently pursuing a PhD in computer science. An IIT Delhi alumnus, he likes the freedom of choosing topics and molding his research direction at Stanford. Like Mahajan, Goel is struck by the focus on doing and building. "The stress on exams is not as much. There is a lot of doing as opposed to solving problems," he notes.[26]

In addition, Bharath Bhat found that "Faculty cares and puts a lot of thought and effort in lectures, assignments, and curriculum." In one of his computer programming classes, Mark Zuckerberg was invited to speak. Bhat was also pleasantly surprised by the emphasis on ethics and the honor code. He believes that Stanford is the hottest place for start-ups. Every day there is some event for start-ups. Bhat, an IIT

155

Kharagpur alumnus, recently completed his master's from Stanford and joined a start-up, whose founder he met at one of these events.[27]

No surprise then that Stanford's impact is most visible in its research, innovations, and start-ups.

Start-Ups and Innovations: US$2.7 Trillion and Counting

Stanford's breadth and depth of research are driving significant wealth creation, economic prosperity, and an impact on humanity. Currently, there are more than 5,300 externally funded sponsored projects across Stanford. In 2014, Stanford received US$1.33 billion in research funding, with 82 percent from federal sources. This includes funding for the SLAC National Accelerator Laboratory, originally called the Stanford Linear Accelerator Center. In 2013–14, the university received approximately US$108 million in gross royalty revenues from licensing 655 of its technologies.[28]

Massive open online courses (MOOCs) have shaken up traditional universities and how students learn. MOOCs are transforming how students learn, test, and receive credentials globally. This has huge implications for the entire learning stages from kindergarten to twelfth grade to university and continuing education. Further, innovations in adaptive learning are likely to merge with MOOCs to deliver an even higher impact. Stanford is again at the forefront of this revolution. Several of its faculty members are engaged in this, and three faculty members have cofounded two of the leading MOOCs companies: Udacity by Sebastian Thrun and Coursera by Andrew Ng and Daphne Koller.

According to a 2012 study, since the 1930s Stanford entrepreneurs (faculty and alumni) have started 39,900 companies, which in turn have created 5.4 million jobs and generate US$2.7 trillion in revenues annually. Some of these were started in the 1930s and are iconic names:

> **Hewlett-Packard Company:** Founded in 1939 in a garage by Bill Hewlett and Dave Packard—both Stanford graduates. The garage was recently dedicated as a "birthplace of Silicon Valley." In 1999, HP's test and measurement business unit was spun off and is now Agilent Technologies. HP designs, manufactures, and markets personal and enterprise computing, storage, and networking hardware, software,

printers, and additional imaging products and related services. Annual revenues of approximately US$106 billion.

Varian: Started in 1937, Varian split into three businesses in the late 1990s. Varian Semiconductors was acquired by Applied Materials in 2011. Varian Inc. was acquired by Agilent Technologies in 2010. The third unit, Varian Medical Systems, designs, manufactures, and markets medical imaging and cancer therapy devices and X-ray machines for inspection and cargo screening. Annual revenues of approximately US$3 billion.

Some companies were started more recently and have become global brands:

Charles Schwab & Company: Brokerage, banking, money management, and financial advisory services company. Annual revenues of approximately US$6.1 billion.

Cisco Systems: Designs, manufactures, and sells Internet Protocol-based networking products and services. Annual revenues of approximately US$49.2 billion.

eBay: Online marketplace to buy and sell and provider of payment and settlement services. Annual revenues of approximately US$18.4 billion.

Electronic Arts: Developer, marketer, publisher, and distributor of video games, content, and services. Annual revenues of approximately US$4.5 billion.

Gap: Retailer offering clothing, accessories, and personal care products under Gap, Banana Republic, Old Navy, Athleta, and Intermix brands. Annual revenues of approximately US$16.2 billion.

Google: Search, advertising, cloud-computing, information, and software company. Annual revenues of approximately US$70 billion.

LinkedIn: Social networking service for professionals. Annual revenues of approximately US$2.6 billion.

Nike: Designs, manufactures, and markets athletic footwear, apparel, equipment, accessories, and services. Annual revenues of approximately US$30.6 billion.

Yahoo: Internet technology company that provides services such as e-mail, news, and photo sharing. Annual revenues of approximately US$4.8 billion.

Several companies were acquired by others:

Instagram: Photo and video sharing service. Acquired by Facebook in 2012 for US$1 billion.

Odwalla: Maker of juices, bars, smoothies, and protein drinks. Acquired by Coca-Cola in 2001 for approximately US$181 million.

Sun Microsystems: Designed, manufactured, and marketed computers, related components and software. Acquired by Oracle in 2010 for US$7.4 billion.

One start-up—**MIPS Technologies,** a fabless semiconductor company—was cofounded in 1984 by John Hennessey, president of Stanford University.

Some have created new industries and some are disrupting existing ones. These and the following companies represent an impressive diversity of fields. They range from networking and semiconductors, to e-commerce and the Internet, to retailing and financial services. In all cases, they have pushed the frontiers of innovation in products, services, delivery, and business models.

Dolby Labs: Creates audio, imaging, and communications technologies for cinemas, home theaters, PCs, mobile devices, and games. Annual revenues of approximately US$964.8 million.

IDEO: Design and innovation consulting firm with over six hundred employees.

Intuit: Provider of financial and tax preparation software and services. Annual revenues of approximately US$4.2 billion.

Intuitive Surgical: Designs, manufactures, and markets surgical systems for minimally invasive robotic-assisted surgery. Annual revenues of approximately US$2.3 billion.

Kiva: Nonprofit organization that connects people through lending to alleviate poverty. Enabled approximately US$749 million in microloans in over eighty-five countries.

Logitech: Provider of personal computer and tablet peripherals and videoconferencing products and services. Annual revenues of approximately US$2.1 billion.

Netflix: Provider of movies and TV shows on demand via the Internet and by mail. Annual revenues of approximately US$6.1 billion.

NVIDIA: Designs, manufactures, and markets visual computing processors. Annual revenues of approximately US$4.8 billion.

Orbitz: Online travel company where customers can search, plan, and book airline tickets, hotels, car rentals, cruises, and vacation packages. Annual revenues of approximately US$933.5 million.

SunPower Corporation: Designs, manufactures, and delivers solar cell systems. Annual revenues of approximately US$2.6 billion.

Tesla Motors: Designs, manufactures, and markets electric cars and electric vehicle power train components. Annual revenues of approximately US$3.7 billion.

Theranos: Designs, manufactures, and markets blood testing technology and services. Estimated to be valued at US$9 billion.

Trader Joe's: Specialty grocery retailer. Annual revenues of approximately US$11.3 billion.

VMware: Designs, develops, and markets virtualization software. Annual revenues of approximately US$6.3 billion.

Zillow: Home and real estate marketplace to find and share information about homes, real estate, mortgages, and home improvements. Annual revenues of approximately US$197 million.

(Sources: a) Stanford start-ups: *Stanford Facts 2015;* b) Business information and most recent revenues: *Stanford Facts 2015,* respective company websites, and Yahoo Finance; c) Valuations: respective company press releases or news stories)

Many companies have failed as well. In Silicon Valley, failure is considered integral to achieving success. An extension of this culture is "fail fast, learn fast." This culture has enabled entrepreneurs to take risks. For every business plan that gets funded, a venture capitalist may reject 100 to 1,000 plans. For every new venture that becomes big and successful, 10 to 20 new ventures are likely to fail. So the odds of being big and successful could be one in 1,000 to one in 20,000.

> ### Unofficial Motto
>
> ***"Die Luft der Freiheit weht."***
>
> Translated, it means, "The wind of freedom blows."
>
> Source: www.stanford.edu

Considering these odds of success, it is remarkable what the Stanford faculty and alumni are achieving. They are designing, manufacturing, and marketing products and services that are making our lives better. They are creating jobs and wealth. And they are making the world a better place to live, learn, and grow.

"Die Luft der Freiheit weht" is a quote attributed to Ulrich von Hutten, a sixteenth-century German humanist. It is a German translation of Latin text and means "The wind of freedom blows."

It is Stanford's unofficial motto and is part of the university seal. The winds of freedom (innovation and impact) are blowing through Stanford and across the world thanks to its leaders, faculty, staff, and alumni, past and present.

Lessons from Stanford University: For Building Golden India

There are many takeaways from Stanford. These few are the most relevant for India:

- **Existing institutions can transform themselves.** Stanford's transformation from a regional university to the top of the world rankings is inspirational. It provides evidence that existing colleges and universities in India, with the right vision, mission, leaders, model, and hard work, can transform themselves to a premier status in the country and the world.

- **The Terman Model.** The demonstrated success of this well-thought-through and executed approach could transform existing institutions as well as provide a blueprint for building new ones.

- **Innovation and start-ups matters.** The ultimate testament for basic and applied research and innovation is building new products or services that make our lives more productive, improve our health and environment, and make the world a better place. Despite the odds of success, start-ups generate tremendous wealth and collectively create millions of jobs. Stanford provides compelling evidence that an innovation and start-up culture in a university pays dividends for all the stakeholders.

What does all this learning mean for India? What are the next steps? Where do we go from here? In the next section and last two chapters, I answer those questions.

SECTION 4

Solutions:
For Building a Golden India

CHAPTER 10

Next Steps: A Gray Revolution

Above all, embrace high aspirations.
Aspirations energize us to overcome the limitations posed by context.

—N. R. Narayana Murthy, co-founder of Infosys
and author of *A Better India: A Better World*

Mumbai, 2014: "Check out the 'broken window' syndrome," suggested Gopal. "It will explain why everything in India is in a crisis mode—land, air, water, education, you name it." Thanks to him, I now understand the concept and its relevance to India.[1]

R. Gopalakrishnan—Gopal or RG to his friends—is one of the most fascinating people I have ever met. An IIT Kharagpur alumnus, Gopalakrishnan is a director at Tata Sons, an author of several best sellers, and a member of the board of directors of many corporations and educational institutions. I first met him in the early 2000s when we wanted his advice on improving IIT Kharagpur's brand. I was then a member of the IIT Foundation's board of directors. He was the natural choice. He had led major brands in India and overseas with Tata and Hindustan Lever. Since then, our paths have crossed a number of times, most recently in establishing the Tata–UC Berkeley collaboration. When you walk out after a meeting with him, you will have laughed at one of his jokes and been inspired by his insightful stories and wit. You would also come away with lots of new ideas and a clear action plan. He is a great thinker and strategist, masterful manager, and remarkable person. Gopalakrishnan's family story is equally riveting and captured in the book *A Comma in a Sentence*, which is written by him.

The "broken window" theory suggests that if a window is broken and is not repaired, people in the building or neighborhood will conclude that no one cares or that no one is in charge. This could motivate someone to damage one or more windows. This cycle then continues until the building is in disrepair. This is similar to a situation in which there is garbage on the street, people put more, and soon the place is a garbage dump.[2] The theory suggests that when minor problems are left unattended, they can become big problems. In India's case, they could escalate to become a crisis.

India does well in crisis, Gopalakrishnan pointed out to me. He cited numerous examples where India emerged stronger once a crisis was followed by a revolution. The green revolution followed a severe food shortage, and the white revolution transformed milk production and distribution. The 1991 economic liberalization was also done at gunpoint. India had no foreign exchange reserves left and had just

[India's higher education system] is not just in crisis — it is sinking."

pawned its gold deposits to keep its promises. India's economy has been on a more rapidly growing track since then.[3]

We have a crisis in higher education. Just to recap, from details in Chapters 2 to 4, India's higher education system is broken on all fronts that matter and is disconnected from the needs and aspirations of its people, society, industry, and nation. India's few tiny islands of excellence serve a small fraction of the population. The student enrollments are meager, the breadth and depth of curriculum is limited, and most of the institutions are focused on one field. A culture of excellence and making an impact to local, regional, and national problems is mostly missing. There is an extreme shortage of well-prepared faculty members. Furthermore, there is not one comprehensive world-class research university in the country. The nation, the society, and its individuals are paying a huge price for the dysfunctional state. There is hyper-competition among students to join one of the premier institutions. An increasing number of students are going overseas for higher education. The majority of the students who have received their degrees in India are considered unemployable. As a result, there is hyper-competition among corporations to recruit and retain employable graduates. India's mega challenges are unsolved. Finally, the economy is heavily dependent on imports, and the new venture creation engine is tiny and weak.

The view that higher education is in crisis is widely shared. According to the National Knowledge Commission in its *Report to the Nation (2006-2009)*, "There is a quiet crisis in higher education in India which runs deep."[4] Boston College's Altbach and TISS's Jayaram note "Just pumping money and resources into a fundamentally broken university system is a mistake."[5] Everyone I interviewed—CEOs, corporate executives, entrepreneurs, investors, university leaders, and faculty members in India and the United States, all of whom care about India—were deeply concerned about India's higher education system. Many were blunt in their assessment. Here is what they said:

"[India's higher education system] is in shambles."

"There is a deep malaise in higher education."

"There is tree rot."

"GER is woefully low."

"Urgent reforms are required. Unfortunately the pace is regressive."

"Most [higher education institutions] are money-making factories."

"Situation is rather grim."

"Too much corruption."

"Higher education has failed India."

"[We are] serving great food and variety but the kitchen is full of bacteria. We have to remove bacteria from the entire kitchen."

"[India's higher education system] is not just in crisis—it is sinking."

"Sick system, which is not worried that it is sick."

"India has wasted 30-40 years in higher education."

"Quality at best is mediocre and the average is somewhere between shoddy and mediocre."

"[We are] too complacent by comparing with each other."

While researching the "broken window" syndrome, I also learned about the "bystander effect." The "bystander effect", a term coined by social psychologists John Darley and Bibb Latane, explains why bystanders do not come to help someone in trouble. There are many reasons, but one that stands out, and is relevant to India, is that the bystander's engagement is inversely proportional to number of bystanders.[6] If there are more bystanders then there is less of a chance of someone coming to help the person in trouble. In India's context, hundreds of millions of people are bystanders while the higher education system is in crisis.

Every crisis needs a revolution. We need a Gray Revolution for gray matter: knowledge, skills, and wisdom. The goal of the Gray Revolution is building a Golden India. It must transform India's higher education system, urgently and sustainably. It must unleash the potential, power, and passion of 1.3 billion Indians. The unleashed potential will address India's mega challenges and make its economy vibrant, more robust, and sustainable. People will be more fulfilled and have better lives. Students, families, their society, and the nation will have a bright and shining (golden!) future.

"A vision without a plan is just a dream. A plan without a vision is just drudgery. But a vision with a plan can change the world."

Every successful revolution needs a compelling road map. Such a road map must have a vision, shared values, and a plan with clear goals. It must also have measures of success, a time line, ownership, and accountability. All these components are very important. As an old proverb said, "A vision without a plan is just a dream. A plan without a vision is just drudgery. But a vision with a plan can change the world." The rest of the chapter outlines this five-step road map.

Figure 10.1: The 5-Step Road Map for Gray Revolution

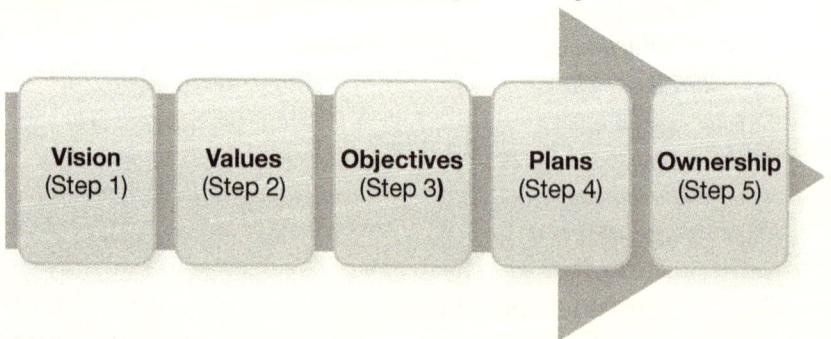

Vision (Step 1) — Values (Step 2) — Objectives (Step 3) — Plans (Step 4) — Ownership (Step 5)

Figure prepared by Shail Kumar

STEP 1:
Vision: An Excellent Education for All

Revolutions must have a bold vision. We must have an excellent education for all.

According to the census in 2011, India's population was estimated to be 1.2 billion with approximately 900 million people forty years of age and below, 630 million people twenty-five years of age and below, and 470 million people eighteen years of age and below. In addition, it estimated that close to 70 percent of India's population is rural. As outlined in Chapter 1 in the section on India's mega challenges, 60 to 70 percent of India's population is poor. Thus, India's population is large, mostly young, poor, and living in the villages.

An excellent education must be accessible to all including the poor and those in rural India. It must also be for professionals regardless of their age. It must be available for people to reeducate or retrain themselves to pursue a second or third career. Thus, it should be possible for a thirty-five-year-old women who did not get a chance earlier to enroll in a community college or research university to pursue her dreams of a better life and career. It should also be possible

Vision

*An excellent
education for all*

for a sixty-five-year-old person with a physical disability to avail of education. This implies an excellent education being available to all regardless of their age, class, caste, gender, religious affiliation, or sexual orientation.

It has to be excellent in all fields and professions. Students aspiring to become doctors, engineers, lawyers, teachers, and those interested in becoming mechanics, welders, drivers, or nurses must all have access to an excellent education. In all cases, the teacher quality, curriculum, pedagogy, research and practice infrastructure, cocurricular and extracurricular programs, and institutional culture must enable successful learning outcomes for the students.

An excellent education must also mean more than credentialing or specializing in a narrow field. It must prepare the person for a career and life. The five-week boot camp for incoming first-year students initiated by IIT Gandhinagar's Jain, which I shared in detail in Chapter 3, is a wonderful innovation. Jain also expects IIT undergraduate students to take at least eight social sciences and humanities courses, get international experience, and be socially engaged. He wants them to learn from project-based curriculum and extracurricular activities and participate in at least two industry visits per semester. He has established a "Tinkerers' Lab" and is encouraging students to start new ventures.[7] These efforts fill an important void in today's higher education and are steps in the right direction. We need similar commitment to students' preparation for their careers and lives.

Realizing this vision is the surest way to ensure a vibrant and sustainable economy and provide all Indians opportunities for a fulfilling life and career. A vibrant economy and well-educated individuals would further provide the necessary financial and human capital to address India's mega challenges. We would then have a virtuous cycle that propels us toward a Golden India.

STEP 2:
Values: Excellence, Making an Impact, Honesty and Integrity, a Sense of Urgency, and Meritocracy

Increasingly values and value-based leadership are gaining traction in organizations. Values are a set of principles and moral codes of conduct that define the organization, the team, or a person. Values are critical to ensuring that anyone in the organization, even in the absence of supervision or direction, behaves or makes decisions that are in the best interest of the organization. It's the *Lakshman Rekha,* the line in the sand, the red line that one does not cross. One is safe when operating within the preset boundary and exposed once they step out. To achieve the vision, we must agree on certain values and have an uncompromising commitment to them. Following these values must be recognized and rewarded, and those who do not must be appropriately penalized.

Values

1. Excellence
2. Making an impact
3. Honesty and integrity
4. A sense of urgency
5. Meritocracy

Higher education institutions are where the country's youth, our next generation, are learning important knowledge, skills, and values. The students will be the future armed forces personnel, artists, bureaucrats, businesspeople, doctors, engineers, farmers, humanists, lawyers, politicians, police force, researchers, scientists, service and manufacturing industry workers, and teachers. Thus, values ingrained in higher education institutions will flow through to professions and society. To build a Golden India, the higher education institutions must adopt these as core values—*excellence, making an impact, honesty and integrity, a sense of urgency, and meritocracy.*

Excellence

Excellence is about establishing and executing to the highest standards. Since we live in an interconnected world, we must aim for and excel at global standards. A software program developed by engineers sitting in Pune or Bengaluru could be used by a New York– or London-based financial company. The guests from Switzerland in Taj Hubli expect room, food, and guest services at levels they are accustomed to receiving in Europe and across the world. For the *Make in India* initiative launched by Prime Minister Modi to succeed in attracting foreign investments and work orders, the manufacturing plants must consistently operate at world-class efficiency and productivity. Various states will compete for these plants, so states like Bihar, West Bengal, and Uttar Pradesh have to be competitive with more advanced states such as Gujarat and Maharashtra. Winning in a competitive marketplace locally and globally demands excellence. Thus, excellence must be one of the core values.

Making an Impact

Solving problems that matter to us is making an impact. Creating ventures that open new opportunities is also making an impact. Higher education institutions must focus on making an impact in their local communities, the state, the region, and the nation. Deshpande's Hubli Sandbox model of engaging students with problems of the local community is exemplary. This focus is critical in all walks of life and at all levels, especially in our colleges and universities.

Our own mega challenges are complex and interdisciplinary. I have outlined these mega challenges in Chapter 1 and they include: poverty; economy and global competitiveness; urban migration; interrelated challenges of food, energy, environment, health, and water; climate change; gender inequality and women's security; law and order; corruption; and education. All our potential, power, and passion must be directed to solving these mega challenges. The only way to address them quickly and cost-effectively is to establish, encourage, and reward efforts and outcomes that make an impact.

Honesty and Integrity

The credentials of the higher education institutions must have the highest standing in the country and the world. The new knowledge that is being produced in colleges and universities must be able to pass the scrutiny of peers and experts in the nation and around the world. Knowledge that is being passed from one generation to another must be accurate. Cheating on examinations, projects, or research papers has to be unacceptable and grounds for appropriate penalties. All of this requires that honesty and integrity must be a core value in higher education institutions and for its faculty, students, and staff.

A Sense of Urgency

In India's context, where delivering on the demographic dividend potential is time sensitive, the scale of mega challenges enormous, and global competition for financial and human capital fierce, a sense of urgency must also be a core value. GER growth from 20 percent to 40 percent and ultimately to 80–90 percent must be accomplished in the next few decades. We must also build and sustain hundreds of world-class research universities and thousands of top-notch teaching and community colleges in a similar timescale. We must address our mega challenges again in the near future. We do not have unlimited time. We must proceed with urgency in our thinking, planning, and execution across all levels and in all fields.

National and State Objectives

- Increase GER to 40 to 50%
- Establish 40-100 world-class universities
- Develop a master plan for every state and union territory

Meritocracy

To realize the vision and achieve the goals in a timely manner, colleges and universities must attract and retain the best and the brightest people. One of the surest ways is to recognize and reward excellence, hard work, honesty, integrity, and impact. It is well known that A-grade talent attracts A-grade talent. It is also well known that a B-grade person is more likely to hire and promote a C-grade or a D-grade person, which starts the slippery race to the bottom. It is also known that once you hire or promote a person for nonmeritorious reasons, the institutional culture and character quickly degenerates. On the other hand, hiring and retaining the best faculty members attracts the best students and having the best students attracts the best faculty members. We have seen ample evidence of this in Chapters 5 through 9, where I have outlined the successes of Nalanda University, the United States, the state of California, UC Berkeley, and Stanford University. This means that meritocracy has to be one of the fundamental values of the higher education system.

STEP 3:
Objectives: Goals and Metrics

We must unleash India's vast potential and be well positioned for future generations. Thus, there is a need for a massive transformation in scale, structure, scope, and excellence.

1. **GER:** Increase the GER from 20 percent to 40 to 50 percent.

2. **World-Class Research Universities:** Establish forty to one hundred world-class research universities and propel five to ten of these to be in the top one hundred of global rankings.

3. **Master Plan:** Establish a master plan for higher education for every state and union territory. Build and transform a thousand institutions to be top-notch master's and bachelor's degree-granting colleges and community colleges.

We must achieve all of these in the next ten to fifteen years.

In addition, colleges and universities must achieve the following objectives:

A. **Students:** Significantly improve the learning outcomes for the students. Ensure that all students have an equal opportunity to higher education and that the students are prepared for their lives and careers.

B. **Faculty Members:** Prepare, attract, and retain faculty members in colleges and universities who are global experts in their respective fields and are passionate about research, education, and making an impact.

C. **Research, Innovation, and Entrepreneurship:** Establish and enable a culture of conducting research, fostering innovation, and spurring entrepreneurship. Every student and faculty member must work on at least one local problem and at least one mega challenge facing the nation. Achieve a critical mass of tens of thousands of start-ups per year from IP developed in these universities.

Bold visions require ambitious and audacious goals. These must be our goals and some of the metrics.

STEP 4:
Plans: How to Realize the Vision and Achieve the Objectives

The recommended plans I–XIV are grouped in five categories and collectively can help achieve our objectives:

1. World-Class Research Universities

2. A Master Plan for Every State and Union Territory

3. Leveraging MOOCs, Technologies, and Innovations

4. Removing Hurdles and Cleaning Up

5. Attracting and Nurturing Talent

World-Class Research Universities

Plan I: Establish 20–50 new world-class comprehensive research universities in the next 10 years.

Currently, there is no comprehensive world-class research university in India. Establishing twenty to fifty new National Universities of India (NUIs) will build critical scale and excellence at the highest levels. NUI alumni who become faculty members and teachers will raise the quality of teaching and research in colleges and universities around the country and quality of teaching in primary and secondary schools. As I outlined in Chapters 5 through 9, Nalanda University, UC Berkeley, and Stanford offer compelling evidence of the learning opportunities for students in a comprehensive university. The impact to the local community, society, and nation is also compelling.

NUIs could be public universities such as UC Berkeley or private like Stanford University. The government-funded universities could be called "NUI" followed by the city name. For example, the one in Gandhinagar would then be called NUI Gandhinagar.

NUIs must be comprehensive and include all fields — arts and humanities, architecture and city planning, biological sciences, business, education, engineering, law, mathematical sciences, medical sciences, nursing, physical sciences, public health, public policy, and social sciences — all co-located in one campus. Further, NUIs must excel in research, innovation, and education. They must make an impact on the local community, state, region, and nation. They must also foster interdisciplinary thinking, dialogue, and research. As the primary doctorate-granting institutions, they would be expected to prepare the next generation of faculty members for colleges and universities. Finally, these NUIs must have a capacity of thirty to fifty thousand students per campus.

Spread across the country, the NUIs must also serve as state and regional hubs for excellence in research and innovation, education,

NUIs: World-Class Research Universities (New and Transformed)

Key Numbers

- Numbers: 40–100

- Student enrollments per campus: 30,000–50,000

- Faculty per campus: 1,500–3,000

- Total student enrollments: 1.2 million to 5 million

- Total faculty members: 60,000 to 300,000

and entrepreneurship. NUIs would be expected to set the standard for excellence in the country and be in the top echelons of global rankings within ten to fifteen years of their founding.

Plan II: Transform 20–50 existing institutions of excellence, such as IITs, IIMs, and AIIMS, to NUI status.

For India's scale and growing aspirations of its youth, we need over one hundred world-class research universities. Some of the existing colleges and universities must transform and could become comprehensive and world-class. However, the NUI status must be earned based on demonstrated excellence in research, education, innovation, and entrepreneurship. All existing institutions, whether government or private, must be allowed to compete for research funding. Research funding must be awarded based on excellence in research and education of its faculty members and the merits and relevance of the research proposal. These institutions would also be expected to have the same standards of excellence, structure, scope, and impact as the new NUIs.

Plan III: Immediately stop establishing new single field institutions, such as IIT, IIM, AIIMS, IISER, NIT, IIIT, NISER, IIPH, ISI, NIFT, NID, and Nursing and Teacher Training Institutes.

Single field institutions are ineffective and inefficient. They cannot compete in today's world, and they do not have the economies of scale or scope. This model may have worked well for the imperial British with its "divide and conquer" strategy or in our early postindependent years. However, they make *no* sense in the new knowledge-based society that favors holistic and interdisciplinary learning. Thus, India's single discipline model is ineffective in today's world and for the future.

They are also an inefficient use of human, financial, and land resources. Each institution needs a seasoned academic and administrative leadership team. They also need land, buildings, and research infrastructure. Currently, these precious resources are being spread across hundreds of institutions. The current crisis of leadership in IITs and various universities are a glaring example of the lack of adequate academic and administrative leaders that is plaguing the country. By establishing new NUIs, transforming some of the existing institutions into NUIs, and putting a stop on further growth of balkanized institutions, we have a good chance of having outstanding leadership across all levels in our colleges and universities.

Most of current single field focused institutions hire faculty in noncore fields. For example, each IIT has a small group of faculty who teach economics, psychology, business, English, and some foreign languages. IIMs recruit faculty members that have expertise in manufacturing, information technology, and additional technical areas. The single field specialization causes two key issues. One, faculty resources are being duplicated. Two, with no critical mass of faculty members in noncore fields, the institutions are unable to recruit and retain the best in that field.

For example, arts, humanities, and social sciences faculty may prefer to teach at a more traditional university or liberal arts–focused institution such as St. Stephen's College or SRCC rather than at an IIT or IIM. Similarly, a faculty member in business would prefer to teach at IIM or XLRI rather than at IIT, SRCC, or St. Stephen's. And a math or science faculty would rather join IISc, IISER, or IIT rather than any other institution. At an NUI, these precious faculty resources would be better deployed and there would be a critical mass of outstanding faculty members in all the disciplines in one co-located campus. And faculty member in every field and discipline would be a core faculty member of the university.

Many fields need research infrastructure, which currently cannot be shared by faculty members from other fields. Thus, human, financial, and physical resources again have to be duplicated. For example, IITs, AIIMS, and the DBT and CSIR labs may be purchasing the same expensive biomedical research equipment. Each of these labs will need competent technical staff, lab space, maintenance, and supplies. At an NUI, science, engineering, and medical faculty members could use shared resources, not just the equipment but also trained scientific staff. With large-scale projects, the NUI may be able to purchase more equipment and supplies more frequently and have more negotiating leverage with the suppliers and get a better price. Thus, NUIs will have economies of scale and increased opportunities for interdisciplinary research

Master Plan for States and Union Territories

Plan IV: Establish an integrated higher education master plan in all the states and union territories.

Similar to the state of California (as discussed in Chapter 7), each state must establish an integrated higher education master plan to provide an excellent education for all its residents. The mix of institutions could include comprehensive research universities, master's and bachelor's degree granting colleges, and community colleges. The community colleges would be responsible for vocational education, remedial training, and preparing students to transfer to research universities and master's and bachelor's degree granting colleges. The research universities and master's and bachelor's colleges would also be expected to prepare the next generation of teachers for primary and secondary schools. The community colleges must be widely dispersed to ensure easy access to rural, town, and smaller city-based communities.

Done well, the master plan will help build and transform thousands of institutions in every state and union territory into top-notch doctorate, master's and bachelor's degree granting universities, and community colleges.

The Gray Revolution would require actions on multiple fronts at the same time. New world-class research universities have to be established at the same time as some existing institutions are transformed to world-class levels. At the same time, the master plan for each state and union territory has to be developed and executed. By nature of the process, this would take some time. Thus, we must also leverage MOOCs, blended learning, adaptive learning, and all available technologies and innovations to provide an excellent education to all now.

Leveraging MOOCs, Technologies, and Innovations

Plan V: Rapid adoption of MOOCs, blended learning, and new technologies and innovations to provide an excellent education to all now.

We must adopt existing platforms, courses, and technologies to offer world-class education to our students now. MOOCs, especially blended MOOCs—where students get the basic instruction online and then discuss their questions and clarify their doubts in the classroom—offer an opportunity to address the severe faculty shortages and difficulties in reaching remote locations. Combined with smart phones, mobile technology, gaming, and adaptive learning technologies, MOOCs can help address India's need for large scale, rapid speed, low cost, and high quality education now. This will also provide a compelling alternative for female students, who currently drop out of the education system due to many factors. Swayam, a MOOCs platform launched in India in 2014,[8] and the 10,000 Teachers Training are timely initiatives for the nation that must be scaled in depth and breadth quickly. We must also learn from others and take advantage of opportunities.

Companies such as edX, Coursera, and Udacity are some of the leading MOOCs companies in the world. Anant Agarwal is the CEO of edX, a not-for-profit MOOCs company jointly founded by MIT and Harvard University. An alumnus of IIT Madras and Stanford University, Agarwal is also a professor at MIT. According to him, edX currently offers over 600 classes taught by some of the best faculty members in the world for free. Soon edX will offer close to 3,000 classes, which is equal to most universities' total academic offering. IIM Bangalore, IIT Bombay, and BITS Pilani are actively contributing to the edX platform. In addition, edX is making blended learning modules even more effective. Soon faculty members locally would get access to their students' performances and have the ability to add local content. It also offers open edX—an open source software platform that companies or countries can adopt and then offer their own indigenous courses. All classes on edX are free, and there is no cost to adopting open edX.

Recently, edX launched a Global Freshmen Academy (GFA) with Arizona State University (ASU). In the GFA, students can enroll and complete their first-year undergraduate courses on edX. For a small fee, currently forty-five dollars per course, they can get official credit for the course after taking a virtually proctored exam. If they pass the course and want to also receive ASU credit, then they can pay just half of ASU's tuition fees, currently six hundred dollars per course. Thus, any student in the world has the opportunity to complete a first-year of a degree program for six thousand dollars. In the future, it will be possible to imagine completing a four-year undergraduate degree program online, perhaps called Global Academy.[9] These new models have the potential of transforming the higher education model. They will make higher education accessible to everyone in the country, especially students in remote locations, women who feel unsafe or have limited commuting options, and working professionals; increase education quality; reduce costs to the students and families; and improve learning outcomes.

The plans I–V, taken together, can address India's scale, structure, scope, and excellence needs in the short term and for future generations. In addition, we must also change and stop some practices that are currently damaging the system.

Removing Hurdles and Cleaning Up

Plan VI: Eliminate the affiliated college system.

The affiliated college system was adopted from the British. It may have been relevant in our early years. Now it fosters all the worst attributes in a higher education institution—a lack of ownership and accountability in leadership and faculty members, a lack of transparency, poor governance, corruption, politicization, and degrees without learning.

We must eliminate the affiliated college system now. Each college must stand on its credentials. Existing affiliated colleges could be given one to two years to disengage from their affiliated university and stand on their own two feet. If valuable and agreed by the parties, some of the affiliated colleges may merge. Existing affiliating universities, which have faculty and physical infrastructure, must strive to become a research university with undergraduate students. Affiliating universities that are merely serving as corporate headquarters and collection agencies must find a more valuable purpose.

Plan VII: Scrap the requirement of public sector jobs being open only to AICTE-UGC-regulatory agency-approved institutions.

The central and state government jobs must be open for all qualified individuals. Those who get such jobs must be selected on their abilities and merit and not on the basis of having a degree from a "UGC approved" university or a "deemed university."

Under British rule, jobs were available for Indian students who passed the British-approved matriculation examinations or graduated from colleges recognized by the British government.[10] UGC, AICTE, and regulatory bodies have perpetuated this discriminatory practice that has only led to rampant corruption to get approvals and licenses. The students, our society, and the nation are paying a heavy price for this imperial-era practice and it must be immediately stopped.

Plan VIII: Eliminate the requirement to get approvals and licenses to establish a new university from UGC, AICTE, and additional central and state government agencies.

The regulatory bodies must *not* be involved in either licensing or inspecting roles. Also, they must *not* be involved in directing curriculum, the number of seats, or fees. These decisions belong to each college and university.

Thus, the role and existence of regulatory bodies such as UGC, AICTE, MCI, and the Bar Council must also be reexamined. Any future role on their part must also be conducted in a single-window mode for those who may still need their services.

Plan IX: Stop government labs from offering doctoral degrees and consolidate laboratories with NUIs.

The government of India, like the US government, must channel a large percentage of its research funding through colleges and universities. Government labs, such as DST, DBT, and CSIR Labs, could be merged with NUIs. It is critical that research and teaching are kept together and are the sole focus of universities. Thus, the labs *must not* be in the business of awarding PhD degrees. Instead, research funding must be directed to universities on a competitive basis. Increased competition for research funding by university faculty members has the added benefit of reinforcing a culture of research and innovation, sense of urgency and making an impact. In addition, a large number of students at universities would benefit from an increased exposure to vital research and innovation projects.

Plan X: Spruce up accreditation by independent third parties.

The state or central government must not have any direct or indirect influence on the assessment methodology, process, or reports. The focus of the assessment must be on research, innovation, and education outcomes, not on the square footage of buildings or number of chairs, desks, and rooms.

Plan XI: Change the funding model.

Institutions that receive government funding get almost all of their capital and all operating expenses directly from the government, via UGC, central or state ministries, or some combination of these entities. There is an overreliance on GOI and states for funding. This has created a situation where a vice chancellor or director of an institute has either become subservient to the central and state IAS officials, or is unable to take a bold stand on any issue lest the institution does not get the needed funds. In addition, the funding is given to the institution to cover its operating deficits. This overreliance on government and this deficit-financing model have removed all incentives for the institutions to engage corporations or the community in any meaningful manner. The new funding model must ensure that IAS officials or politicians cannot hold the VC, the director, or the institution as hostage. The model must spur the institutions to raise private resources from corporations, foundations, alumni, friends, and community.

Plan XII: Change the governance model.

The governing body must include people of eminence who have the best long-term interests of the institution. The governing body, such as the board of directors or the board of governors, must be responsible for all financial and legal matters and appoint the VC or director of the institution. The government or regulatory bodies cannot have any role in this matter. In government-funded institutions, such as NUIs, IITs, and IIMs, it is important to have government representatives but with more limited powers than they currently have. We must also eliminate layers of bureaucracy that have emerged over time, such as the IIT Council. Such councils could be useful for sharing best practices and ideas but not for institution-level decision-making, where the council could cause delays or corrupt the processes.

Attracting and Nurturing Talent

Plan XIII: Prepare, attract, and retain the best and the brightest minds as faculty members.

In Chapter 1, I discussed how the starting sample, the seed corn, or the seed crystal defines the quality of the yogurt, crop, or semiconductor wafer respectively. For colleges and universities, the starting sample is its faculty. Thus, the success of the Gray Revolution rests entirely on the shoulders and gray matter of India's faculty members. Criticality of faculty quality is outlined in great detail in the chapters on Nalanda University (Chapter 5), the United States (Chapter 6), California (Chapter 7), UC Berkeley (Chapter 8), and Stanford University (Chapter 9). Three more voices, below, add valuable perspective on the importance of well-prepared and passionate faculty to universities and colleges.

"Great educational institutions are not built by money, but by talented and dedicated teachers," wrote P. V. Indiresan, award-winning IIT faculty member and former director of IIT Madras.[11] A fearless and tireless campaigner for excellence in higher education, Indiresan inspired many students and researchers. Paulraj, award-winning faculty member at Stanford University, counts Indiresan as his mentor. I, too, was touched by his passion and energy for India's higher education system.

Donald Kennedy, former president of Stanford University noted, "Surely the composition and quality of the faculty is the single most important determinant of the character and prestige of the university."[12]

"All of these schools [two-thirds of the best US universities] correctly assume that the quality of the faculty is the most important factor in maintaining their reputation and position,"[13] wrote Henry Rosovsky, former dean of the Faculty of Arts and Sciences and briefly acting president of Harvard University.

One of the fundamental changes we must institutionalize is a radically new compensation and incentive structure for the faculty members. Their total compensation and incentive structure has to be benchmarked with the local industry and global faculty compensation and not pegged to IAS or any other government category pay scales. A flexibility to pay differential salaries based on market forces and merit must be part of this transformation.

We must also make colleges and universities great places to work. The physical environment does matter. Nalanda University in 400 CE had majestic buildings, inspiring architecture and design, and large libraries. Stanford and UC Berkeley have beautiful campuses and are among the most attractive places to work. The facilities are well maintained, and everything appears to work seamlessly.

The processes and work culture must also be attractive. Self-driven and talented people thrive in a work environment with people who share similar values and are like-minded. They also thrive when the processes and support infrastructure enable their commitment to research, education, and making an impact.

Institutional, state, and national awards and recognition must be aligned with rewarding the core values: excellence, making an impact, honesty and integrity, a sense of urgency, and meritocracy. The National Impact Award, which Gautama Raju, Arjun Das, Meera Gupta, Ziya Khan, Pooja Shah, and Amarjit Singh won in 2047 in Chapter 1, could be made the most prestigious government of India award. This could be given for making an impact at a national scale and for addressing one of India's mega challenges. The award would be given only after the impact has been measured over at least five to ten years. This award would not only have national and international repute but would also come with a sizeable financial benefit to the individuals and the institution.

Along with the transformed compensation structure, culture, and rewards and recognition, we must also ensure that the processes to train, select, and retain faculty members are of the highest standards. The tenure system in the United States has several supporters and critics. However, it does one thing well—it filters and selects the best. At times, it is also known to reject a few good people. But, by and large, those who join the ranks of tenured track faculty have demonstrated talent, hard work, passion, and determination, and also delivered results in research, education, and made an impact. To become tenured takes around twenty-two to twenty-four years of education and an additional six to eight years of work as a postdoctoral researcher and assistant professor. This is in stark contrast to the current situation in India, where a faculty member is confirmed to a life-long faculty position after just one year of joining a college or university.

Plan XIV: Provide great learning experiences for students.

When universities are powered by talented faculty members who are experts in their respective fields and who enjoy teaching, mentoring, conducting research, and making an impact, positive outcomes from higher education institutions can be expected. However, no plans can be complete without a reassertion of the importance of students. If faculty members are the foundation of the higher education system, students are its most important stakeholders. "The guiding principle simply has to be the interest of the student," commented Stanford's Kennedy.[14] Cornell's Rhodes also notes, "Like it or not, the campus of today is the larger society of tomorrow."[15] By the sheer scale of numbers, students are the largest percentage of any university campus.

Thus, it is critical that students learning experiences be transformed. Curriculum must have the necessary depth and breadth, and be relevant and up-to-date. Key life skills such as communication, project management, problem solving, time management, critical thinking, and leadership must be nurtured. Holistic development that also considers physical and spiritual growth must be encouraged. The universities must prepare students for their lives and respective careers, which means also providing opportunities for meaningful cocurricular and extracurricular activities.

Student interests often change or evolve over time. Colleges and universities must accept this reality. Thus, the ability to change fields of study or pursue additional fields must be integral to the system. Flexibility must also be built in to accommodate students of all ages, working professionals, and students who want to transfer from one college to another.

Experiential learning for students, or learning by doing, in clinics, labs, and the field must be part and parcel of the transformed education system. Engaging students in public service, conducting research, and on projects that make an impact on the local community and nation must be part of the institution's DNA.

Taken together, these plans would unleash the passion, power, and potential of students, faculty members, professionals, philanthropists, and businesses in India.

STEP 5: Plan: Ownership and Accountability

The Gray Revolution is about a sweeping transformation to India's higher education system. It is a much-needed jolt. It is difficult to suggest who would lead such a transformation, considering that the past and current political leadership, bureaucracy, and regulatory bodies are likely to have vested interest in the status quo and had varying degrees of roles in bringing about the current crisis in higher education. Nonetheless, at the cabinet level, the entire education system must be under one portfolio. Currently, vocational education is under the Ministry of Labor, and many ministries, such as agriculture, health, industry, mines, and railways oversee higher education institutions. There are tremendous synergies in having education under one portfolio.

Sam Pitroda, former chairman of the National Knowledge Commission and chief architect of the telecom revolution, told me, "India is a country with a nineteenth-century mind-set, twentieth-century processes, and twenty-first-century needs." He also made an interesting observation that all of the past successful revolutions have been led by a technocrat with the backing of a political leader – Atomic Energy: Homi Bhabha and Jawaharlal Nehru; Space: Vikram Sarabhai and Jawaharlal Nehru; Green: M. S. Swaminathan and Lal Bahadur Shastri/Indira Gandhi; Milk: Verghese Kurien and many political leaders; Telecom: Sam Pitroda and Rajiv Gandhi.[16]

These revolutions succeeded due to the political and technical leadership and on the shoulders of many talented, hardworking, and dedicated people. In some revolutions, there was more than one leader. For example, in the Green Revolution, Lal Bahadur Shastri appointed C. Subramaniam to the head of the ministry of food and agriculture. Subramaniam's top aides included B. Sivaraman, secretary of agriculture, and M. S. Swaminathan, who was directing the research teams to adapt Mexican wheat to Indian conditions.[17] Their collective leadership was literally and figuratively instrumental in sowing the seeds around the country for bumper crops that followed.

Gopalakrishnan was correct; the "broken window" theory does explain a lot. I am also hoping that he is right about India doing well in a crisis—because India's higher education system is in a crisis. Like in the Green Revolution or the Milk Revolution, the government enabled talented people such as C. Subramaniam, B. Sivaraman, M. S. Swaminathan, and V. Kurien to take charge. During the early post-independence years, GOI attracted the best and the brightest to join the newly established IITs, IIMs, and AIIMS as leaders and faculty members and also to lead the atomic energy and space efforts. There was a critical mass of talented people, freedom to pursue their goals, and resources to achieve their objectives.

We need a similar drive and energy for the Gray Revolution. To spearhead the Gray Revolution, we need a leader and a dream team consisting of stakeholders from all walks of life at the state and central level. The leader and dream team members must be passionate about the vision, committed to the core values, and bring relevant and complementary knowledge and expertise to fuel the Gray Revolution.

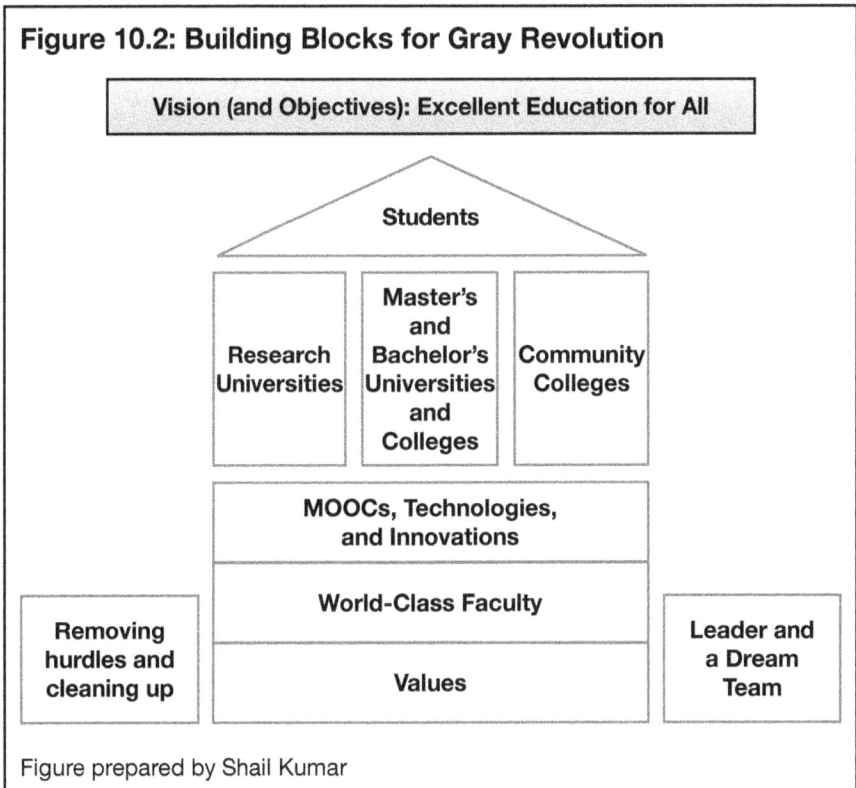

Figure 10.2: Building Blocks for Gray Revolution

Vision (and Objectives): Excellent Education for All

Students

Research Universities | Master's and Bachelor's Universities and Colleges | Community Colleges

MOOCs, Technologies, and Innovations

World-Class Faculty

Removing hurdles and cleaning up | Values | Leader and a Dream Team

Figure prepared by Shail Kumar

The figure above is a pictorial summary of five-step road map and plans I-XIV. Before one builds a new building, one needs to have a clear idea of what to build (vision–Step 1, and objectives–Step 2), select an architect (leader and a dream team–Step 5), clear the area (removing the hurdles and cleaning up–Step 4, plans VI–XII), build a strong foundation (values–Step 2, world-class faculty–Step 4, plan XIII, leverage MOOCs, technologies and innovation–plan V), mount the pillars (research universities, master's and bachelor's colleges and universities, and community colleges–Step 4, plans I–IV), and then build the roof (students–Step 4, plan XIV).

The Indian economy is in a much better place than it was in the early 1950s and 1960s, when it was mired with poverty and stagnant growth. In today's India, there is no resource shortage. The mega corruption scandals in lakhs of crores of rupees, the fact that only a fraction of the government's allocated funds reach their intended target, and the tens of billions in black money suggest that there is no shortage of resources. Thus, the ambitious and much-needed Gray Revolution can be delivered with the central and state governments' existing resources.

Gopalakrishnan also told me that everyone knows what to do, but the key is who will do it and by when. Ultimately, the buck stops with the prime minister of India and the state chief ministers (CM) who must make tough decisions, back a technocrat, and provide the necessary political backing and financial resources to implement all plans. Transforming India's higher education is not just about human resource development; it is also about economy, defense, energy, environment, geopolitics, global competitiveness, health, and water. It is about fulfilling the aspirations of the youth and their families. It is also about a more prosperous and peaceful society. It is about our individual and collective golden future.

Thus, in the scheme of revolutions, the Gray Revolution would be the largest and most impactful. Who will make a Gray Revolution their legacy at the state and central level?

The buck also stops with the industry titans, ultrarich individuals, and popular figures who have the power or the influence to advocate these changes or simply build top-notch colleges and Stanford-like comprehensive world-class research universities.

The ownership and accountability also stops with the educated youth, professionals, activists, and community leaders and the 1.3 billion Indians who must raise their voices and demand a world-class higher education system. India's and our collective future depends on it.

CHAPTER 11

The Journey: Must Start Now!

Be the change that you wish to see in the world.

—Mohandas Karamchand Gandhi,
Mahatma and Father of the Nation

Silicon Valley, 2015: As I was approaching the last stages of writing this book, I felt it was important to hear from my friends, family, and countrymen and -women about India's new Golden Age. So I started a survey and made it available on my Facebook page. I also sent e-mails to over a thousand contacts and called some of them. I was pleasantly surprised by the responses, which came from India, Australia, Canada, France, the Netherlands, New Zealand, Thailand, Singapore, Sweden, the United Kingdom, and the United States. They represented all ages from eighteen to those over seventy-five.

Many responded to the question, "India was once called a Golden Bird. Could we build a new golden era again?" Approximately 92 percent felt that we could. Most of the responses to the question "What would India's new Golden Age look like to you?" were thoughtful and hopeful. I am sharing some of those quotes here and more of them are available on my Facebook page (www.facebook.com/ShailendraIIT87) and my Twitter account (twitter.com/ShailendraIIT87):

"Time where birth does not decide future."

—Akshay Kumar Anugu

"Where Indians no longer struggle to survive but thrive."

— Himanshu Baral

"When we are free to dream and pursue our passions. When a person is judged by his talents and not by his possessions. When sparks are recognized and developed into a full-blown flame. When ideas are fostered and creativity is appreciated. When people don't confirm and strive to be different. When technology is used to make India greener, safer, and cleaner. When girls can freely walk on streets. When the underprivileged get an opportunity to grow. When everyone can voice opinions without any fears. Then India would be liberated. It would be the true golden age."

— Monalisa Gupta

"An India where: Everyone is treated equally and has equal opportunity to achieve their dreams.

1. *Intellectual honesty is considered a virtue and corruption is completely eliminated from all walks of life.*
2. *Dignity of labor holds across the entire spectrum of jobs/careers.*
3. *Everyone is held accountable, and justice is consistent no matter where you are in the pecking order/hierarchy.*
4. *There is no religion higher than truth!"*

— Narayanan K.

"India's new golden age will entail the following, when: The person born in the lowest strata of society will have the confidence that he/ she can climb up the ladder by merit and hard work alone.

- *The rule of law applies equally for all sections of the society.*
- *Citizens are not discriminated against on the basis of gender, caste, language, religion, or ethnicity.*
- *Meritocracy rules all public appointments.*
- *The electorate becomes conscious of their responsibility and seeks accountability of its elected representatives."*

— Bodhibrata Nag

"It would be a time when to access the 'best,' Indians will not have to leave India. Be that the best education, health care, research, technology, or business opportunity. It will be an era of self-belief and self-reliance for achieving our goals."

—Suman Bikash Mondal

Three wrote poems that captured their thoughts and emotions:

मेरा देश
जहाँ सबके तन पर कपड़ा हो,
पेट में खाना हो,
चारों और हरियाली और खुशहाली हो,
जहाँ पड़ौसी, पड़ौसी की जान हो, शान हो,
यही मेरे देश की पहचान हो।

— Madhu Aggarwal

वो देखो अब आसमान में इसरो ने झंडा गाड़ा है।
यमन में कर शांति काम बन रहा एक ध्रुवतारा है।
गर घर के आँगन से अब हम हर विषधर मार भगा पाएं।
फिर स्वर्ण युग के शुभारम्भ का शंखनाद हमारा है।

— Abhishek Mandal

पूर्व सम्राट कब तक, माँगता रहेगा भिक्षा ?
आध्यात्मज्ञ कब तक, माँगता रहेगा शिक्षा ?
स्वर्णयुग विलुप्त नहीं, सुषुप्त - यही है समीक्षा !
स्वर्णिम भारत पुनर्निमाण - यही है परीक्षा !!

Translated:
The pauper you see, was an emperor in the ages olden,
To its spirituality and wisdom, the world was beholden
Lost, definitely it is not
Asleep, yes and she is in rot
The hour of our redemption: let's awaken India Golden

— Pradeep Prasad, a friend from IIT Kharagpur, wrote this poem after he learned about my book title and subtitle, and captured the spirit.

However, some felt that we must address some basics first.

"Unless we make real strides to provide people basic necessities, education, and rights, no growth would look golden."

— Divya Bohra

"[The] biggest problem in India is corruption. Once you solve that, everything else will fall in line."

— Arvind Chhabra

"We really need to kill our satisfaction with substandard stuff and attain the average world standard."

— Ahmed Faraz

"Roti, Kapda, and makaan for one and all!"

— Bhaskar Sengupta

A few were not optimistic at all.

"India's new golden age — a pipe dream! Certainly not in my lifetime. Till we are able to incorporate integrity into our national character any aim is corruptible and no goal is achievable. It is however important to have the dialogue and spread awareness with the hope that in some distant future — if ever — it may happen!"

— Shailaja Srinivasan

"The caste system and inequality of women in Indian society will always hinder India achieving a Golden [age] once again. Bribery and corruption [have] become part of the Indian psyche and [the] majority of Indians practice it to survive."

— Ram D. Pathak

For another question, "What would make such an era a golden one?" I listed thirteen factors and asked them to be rated by the degree of importance. Respondents could rate them one—not important, two—somewhat important, and three—very important.

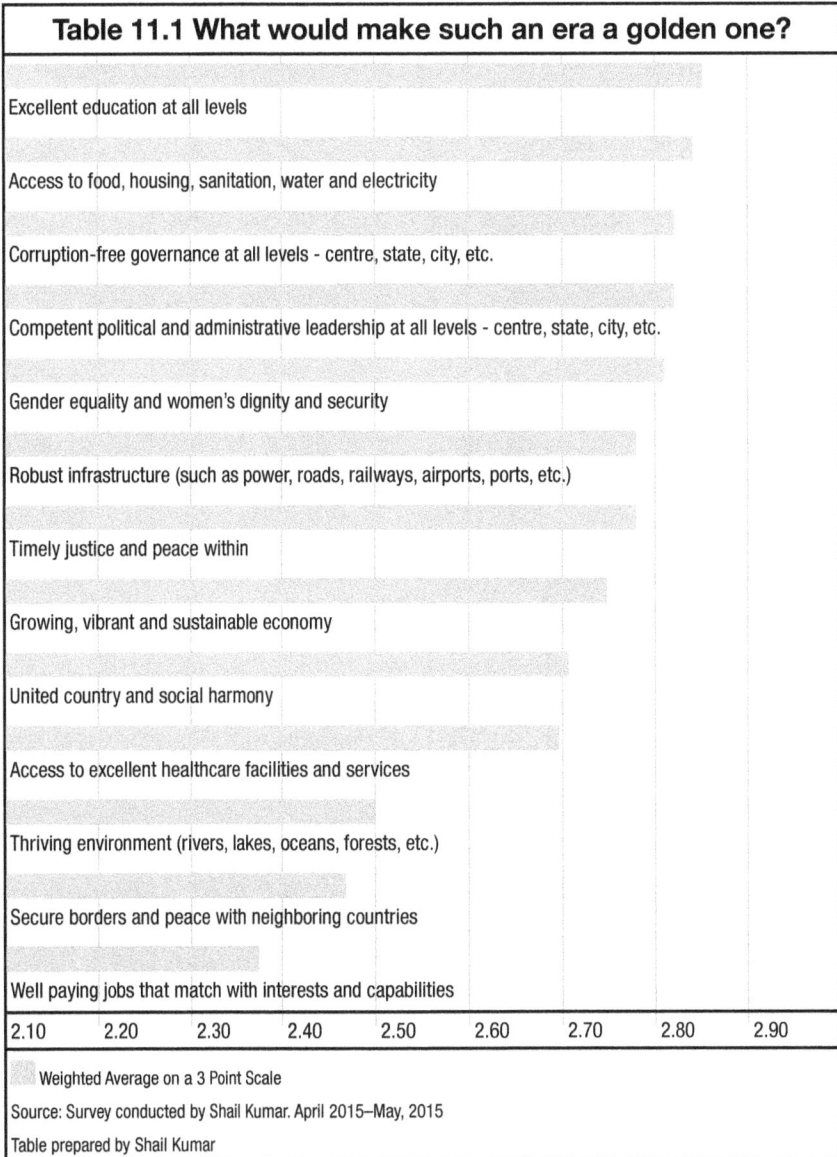

Table 11.1 What would make such an era a golden one?								
Excellent education at all levels								
Access to food, housing, sanitation, water and electricity								
Corruption-free governance at all levels - centre, state, city, etc.								
Competent political and administrative leadership at all levels - centre, state, city, etc.								
Gender equality and women's dignity and security								
Robust infrastructure (such as power, roads, railways, airports, ports, etc.)								
Timely justice and peace within								
Growing, vibrant and sustainable economy								
United country and social harmony								
Access to excellent healthcare facilities and services								
Thriving environment (rivers, lakes, oceans, forests, etc.)								
Secure borders and peace with neighboring countries								
Well paying jobs that match with interests and capabilities								
2.10	2.20	2.30	2.40	2.50	2.60	2.70	2.80	2.90

Weighted Average on a 3 Point Scale
Source: Survey conducted by Shail Kumar. April 2015–May, 2015
Table prepared by Shail Kumar

The weighted scores once again emphasize the importance of an excellent education. It also underscores the importance of basic needs, capable leadership, removing corruption, and addressing many of the mega challenges that I discussed in Chapter 1. I was somewhat surprised by the relative lower scores for the "thriving environment (rivers, lakes, oceans, forests, etc.)," "secure borders and peace with neighboring countries," and "well-paying jobs that match with interests and capabilities." Since there is so much to be done in the top ten, I can understand and rationalize the scores.

One comment brought me to my next point:

> *"If we could achieve something in the 4th century,*
> *why can't we do that in 21st?"*

> — Arijit Chakraborty

Fortunately, our history shows us that we once had a golden past. India was called the Golden Bird. Perhaps it is in our DNA to build one again. We can most definitely be informed and inspired by our glorious past.

India's Previous Golden Age: 1700 Years Ago

Several historians place India's previous Golden Age to be during the reign of the Gupta Empire starting with Chandra Gupta II who ruled from 376–415 CE.[1] According to A. L. Basham, the peace, prosperity, and unity observed during the times of Chandra Gupta II marked "the high watermark of ancient Indian culture." In *The Wonder That Was India,* he notes, "Soon harsher and more primitive elements were to remerge, but in the best days of the Gupta Empire Indian culture reached a perfection, which it was never to attain."[2]

Chandra Gupta I founded the Gupta Empire in 319 CE and was followed by Samudra Gupta, Rama Gupta, Chandra Gupta II, Kumara Gupta, and Skanda Gupta. The Gupta Empire collapsed after the death of Skanda Gupta in 467 CE. During the Gupta Empire, India witnessed remarkable peace and prosperity. Arts, literature, music, science, philosophy, and education flourished with royal patronage and support from merchants and common people. Sanskrit became the primary means of literary expression. The decimal system was created. Aryabhatta proclaimed that the

Earth revolved around the sun and gave pi its value to six decimal places. Kalidasa, the Sanskrit poet and dramatist, thrived during this time. The largest amounts of new materials were introduced into the Puranas and Mahabharata.[3]

Faxian, a Chinese scholar, visited India from 399 to 414 CE. One account, attributed to him, shed valuable perspective on India's situation during those times:[4]

> The inhabitants (of the Gupta Empire) are rich and prosperous and vie with one another in the practice of benevolence and righteousness. The heads of the Vaishya families establish in the cities ('in all the other kingdoms as well') houses of dispensing charity and medicines. All the poor and destitute in the country, orphans, widowers, and childless men, maimed people and cripples, and all who are diseased, go to those houses, and are provided with every kind of help, and doctors examine their diseases.

Donations from kings, merchants, and householders supported various educational institutions. Land and revenues from two hundred villages supported Nalanda University—the premier center of higher learning in those times, which I have outlined in more detail in Chapter 5.

During the survey, I received several comments stating that the Golden Age during the Gupta Empire was north India centric. Clearly there were pockets of unity and prosperity around the country under several kings. Some kings are still worshipped. Some of the respondents think of the Chola dynasty, the Mughal's during Akbar, and the Maratha's during Shivaji as Golden Ages.

There are also views that suggest that the Golden Age was not so golden and not golden for everyone. Romila Thapar, historian and author *The Penguin History of Early India: From the Origins to AD 1300,* notes that the lifestyle of the majority was not as golden as it was made out to be. D. N. Jha, another historian and author of *Ancient India,* states that during the Gupta dynasty, serfdom appeared, women became items of property, and caste distinction and rigidity became sharper than ever before. According to him, "For the upper classes all periods of history have been golden; for the masses none. The truly golden age of the people does not lie in the past, but in the future."[5]

I concur with Jha's comments — India's new Golden Age has to be golden for *all* of its 1.3 billion people. Can India do it at a massive scale and in limited time? There are various examples from around the world that suggest that it can be done. While there are distinct differences between India and the cited countries, there are also many similarities. The important message is that it can be done.

Transformations Around the World: At Scale and Speed

The United States is an excellent example of a nation that has added significant capacity quickly while sustaining excellence in its higher education system. It is the oldest democracy and the largest economy. I have written in detail about the United States, the state of California, UC Berkeley, and Stanford University in Chapters 6 through 9. The United States has seen a steady higher education enrollment growth since the 1930s and gone from over 1 million enrolled students in the 1930s to 20 million by 2009-2010. From the 1930s to the 1960s, the enrollments almost doubled every decade to reach 8 million by 1969-1970. The enrollment growth did not come at the expense of excellence or the impact the universities made in their respective communities, state, or nation. In fact, universities such as Stanford and Berkeley grew in scale, excellence, and reputation at the same time. California adopted a higher education master plan in the 1960s and grew in scale, excellence, and reputation at the same time as well. As a result, it has become the benchmark for its higher education system.

In addition to the United States, China, South Korea, Finland, and Singapore offer compelling evidence that transformation with scale *and* excellence is achievable quickly and simultaneously.

China: The Dragon's Charge

"Work hard. Don't waste time. Don't waste money. For the nation and for yourself." – a banner in Shanghai Jiao Tong University[6] captures the Chinese spirit towards higher education.

China is the second largest economy and its ambition, national interests, and military capabilities are influencing geopolitics around the world. Building on its manufacturing prowess, market size, and modern infrastructure, China is aggressively preparing for success in our knowledge-based society. Its investments in higher education, IP creation, and entrepreneurship are strategic. In 1993, the government adopted the *Guidelines of China's Educational Reform and Development,* which became the basis for transformation of its higher education system.[7] In 1995, China launched Project 211, an ambitious initiative to strengthen at least one hundred out of its 1,700 higher education institutions. Accounting for only 6 percent of the total institutions, Project 211 universities are responsible for training 80 percent of doctoral students, 67 percent of graduate students, 50 percent of overseas students, and 33 percent of undergraduates.[8]

"The Chinese government has chosen Peking University and Tsinghua University to become MIT in the next five years."

In 1998, China launched Project 985 that was aimed at establishing world-class research universities. Within Project 985, a total of forty universities are currently being funded and an alliance of the top nine universities (called the C9 League) is leading the pack in the efforts to break into the top echelons of world rankings. The C9 League includes Fudan University, Harbin Institute of Technology, Nanjing University, Peking University, Shanghai Jiao Tong University, Tsinghua University, the University of Science and Technology of China, Xi'an Jiaotong University, and Zhejiang University. These nine universities have 3 percent of the nation's research and development personnel and receive about 10 percent of country's research and development expenditures. C9 researchers generate more than 20 percent of the nation's output of journal articles indexed by Thomson Reuters, and these papers have attracted some 30 percent of China's total citations.[9]

"The Chinese government has chosen Peking University and Tsinghua University to become MIT in the next five years," mentioned Pranab Bardhan, UC Berkeley professor and author of *Awakening Giants, Feet of Clay: Assessing the Economic Rise of China and India.*[10] It is evident that the Chinese government understands the strategic value of higher education and has embarked on ambitious projects that are not just well funded but also well thought through and well executed. The overarching goal of both the initiatives appears to be making its economy more robust, competitive, and less dependent on foreign technology, and providing world-class opportunities for its people to learn and develop.

Anil Kakodkar, former chairman of the Atomic Energy Commission and former chairman of the board of governors of IIT Bombay, is a respected researcher and thought leader in India. He chaired a committee that published a report in 2011 called *"Taking IITs to Excellence and Greater Relevance: Report of Dr. Anil Kakodkar Committee."* As part of the assessment, some of the committee members visited China to learn about their practices. The report mentioned Projects 985, 211, and C9. It also noted that faculty salaries could vary by a factor of ten, depending on faculty performance on various dimensions.[11] In contrast, India's sixth pay commission has set up a salary differential of a mere 50 percent, or a factor of 1.5, between assistant professor and professor. China is investing heavily in attracting bright scholars from around the world to join its universities. The government, universities, and philanthropists are working collaboratively and offering financial incentives such as augmented salaries, funds to establish labs, and bonuses to bring overseas-based faculty members and researchers to Chinese universities.[12]

The outcomes of the transformation started in 1993 are promising. Between 1999 and 2005 the total number of undergraduates and graduates quadrupled.[13] It has now one of the largest share of peer-reviewed scientific research articles. By 2007, China was ranked sixth in the world in its enrollment of foreign students.[14] Forty-four Chinese universities are in the top 500 in the world university rankings.[15]

India and China have a long and complex history and relationship. "In 1991, there was not much [of a technological] gap between China and India. Now we cannot compete," noted B. K. Syngal, former chairman and MD of Videsh Sanchar Nigam Limited (VSNL) and one of earliest graduates of IIT Kharagpur. He believes that the Indian government, industry, and universities are not working well together in research efforts. Syngal also feels that poor government policies and incentives are hurting India.[16]

In addition to sharing a large border, India and China share key challenges of providing food, water, and jobs for over 1 billion people. China's charge into higher education, IP creation, and entrepreneurship must be understood and must motivate thoughtful and urgent actions in India.

South Korea: Rising from the Ashes

South Korea, which was devastated by the Korean War in the early 1950s, has transformed itself in the past fifty years. South Korean students' scores on the Program for International Student Assessment (PISA) are among the top five.[17] It has achieved a 100 percent literacy rate and has ten universities in the top 500 of worldwide rankings.[18] It is spending 2.6 percent of its GDP on higher education, among the highest and second only to the United States. In 2008, it launched its World Class Universities program. For this program, it budgeted US$800 million over five-years to import foreign professors on part-time basis to teach and conduct research.[19] Fueled by a well-prepared, educated professionals and an export-oriented economy, it is now one of the wealthiest nations.

Finland: Transformation in Fifty Years

Finland also has transformed itself in the last fifty years. Following a different educational philosophy than South Korea, it has also achieved a 100 percent literacy rate. It is ranked number four in the World Economic Forum's Global Competitiveness Index. In the same report, it is ranked number one for its higher education, training, and innovation.[20]

Singapore: From Poor Port City to Wealthy Island Nation

Singapore became an independent country in 1965. Before that, it was part of Malaysia, which was under British imperial rule until 1959. Lee Kuan Yew, the founding father and first prime minister of Singapore, is credited for Singapore's transformation from a port city to one of the wealthiest nations in the world. Singapore has done many things well, including making its education system one of the best in the world. Its students score among the top on the PISA, and it is ranked number two on the Global Competitiveness Index.[21] Singapore, a nation with less than six million people, attracts over 90,000 foreign students from over 120 countries to its higher education system.[22] It also has two universities in the top two hundred.[23] One of them is the National University of Singapore (NUS).

NUS: Transformation to a Research University in Less Than Two Decades

In less than two decades, NUS has also successfully transformed from a teaching institute to a research university. The Singaporean government, its research agencies like the Agency for Science, Technology and Research (A*STAR), and NUS have collaborated to make Singapore an attractive location for research and manufacturing, and also the regional headquarters for multinational corporations. NUS has also established many high-profile research and teaching collaborations with world-class universities such as MIT, Duke, UC Berkeley, and Stanford. Its students have opportunities to study overseas through collaborations with various universities around the world. It is attracting faculty from around the world to relocate to Singapore and teach and conduct research at NUS.

NUS's transformation has been noted widely. Ben Wildavsky, author of *The Great Brain Race: How Global Universities Are Reshaping the World*, notes "By contrast, NUS seems to have done everything right. ...One final distinguishing feature of NUS's rise to excellence is that it has cultivated a meritocratic culture, backed by resources and freed from bureaucratic hiring constraints..."[24] This point was reinforced by many faculty members who I met at NUS.

Hang Chang Chieh is currently a professor and an executive director of the Institute for Engineering Leadership at NUS. For a number of years, he served in the Singapore government's various research–university–industry initiatives, notably as the executive deputy chairman of A*STAR. When speaking with him, it was evident that he deeply cares about Singapore's national agenda of building industry. He understands the role institutions such as NUS and A*STAR play in making this happen. It was also evident from his narrative that he and his colleagues at NUS and A*STAR were open to ideas and willing to experiment and make decisions in the best interest of the country. He was emphatic about attracting the best faculty members to NUS from around the world. "Singapore pays the highest compensation to faculty members second only to the United States," noted Hang. Their compensation is three to four times higher than Chinese and Indian institutions.[25] Singapore's attractiveness as a country to live in and the availability of research funding, along with this competitive compensation, has helped NUS attract faculty members such as Paul Matsudaira and John Thong.

In Paul Matsudaira's case it was MIT's loss and NUS's gain. Matsudaira is a professor and head of the department of biological sciences at NUS. Prior to that, he was a faculty member at MIT. A distinguished researcher, he got his PhD from Dartmouth College and conducted postdoctoral research at the Laboratory of Molecular Biology (LMB) at Cambridge. A self-made man, he was the first in his family to go to college. Through dogged perseverance and hard work, he has made a name for himself. By his own admission, he works twelve to fourteen hours a day, seven days a week. He was working with the MIT-NUS collaboration when he spent some time at NUS. He was impressed by NUS's "can-do" attitude and access to research funding. At NUS, he could focus a lot more on research than in the United States. Thus, it was a relatively easy decision for him to relocate to Singapore and NUS.[26]

Born and raised in Malaysia, John Thong is currently a professor and the head of the Electrical & Computer Engineering Department at NUS. He spent ten years at the University of Cambridge, where he received his BA (honors) in electrical sciences and a PhD in electrical engineering. He then spent two years as a research fellow at King's College. Joining NUS was a good decision for him. Singapore is a great place to bring up children, he is close to his family in Malaysia, and at NUS, he is doing what he enjoys most—teaching and conducting research. Thong is impressed by the university leadership, which shows a lot of foresight and has the best interests of the country at heart.[27]

Thus, not surprisingly, NUS is ranked among the top 200 universities in the world. In some global rankings, NUS is adjudged to be in the top 30.

Start Building a Golden India: Now!

Unleashing the passion, power, and the potential of 1.3 billion Indians is a powerful incentive to initiate India's next revolution—the Gray Revolution—one that transforms the higher education system.

Govind Swarup, professor at TIFR, wrote, "Most important is to increase [the] educational level and talent of millions of young persons in India. Without that, we cannot achieve *Make in India*." Narendra Modi, India's PM, and his government launched the *Make in India* initiative to boost the manufacturing sector and generate

"Most important is to increase [the] educational level and talent of millions of young persons in India. Without that, we cannot achieve Make in India."

more manufacturing jobs in India. *Make in India* would indeed receive a huge momentum from higher education reforms. Initiatives such as Skills India,[28] the economy, and our society would also benefit. For ruling parties at the center and states, it will also improve the chances of winning the next elections. It is a win-win for all—politicians who would make the tough decisions and win elections, businesses who would hire well-prepared professionals and make more profits, and people who would get an excellent education and move up in their careers and lives. It will truly usher in *Acche Din* (good days, a slogan popularized by the Bharatiya Janata Party (BJP) during the Lok Sabha elections in 2014) and also sow the seeds for India's new Golden Age.

India's PM and various state CMs would have to make tough decisions. The political ripple effects will be many and widespread. The powerful Member of Parliament (MP) and Member of Legislative Assembly (MLA) lobbies consisting of legislators who are running colleges directly or indirectly would be stomping for the status quo. They are making boatloads of money from the current broken and disconnected higher education system. Any change that dramatically increases quality, transparency, and competition would be unwelcome for this group. Most of the political party leaders would also be nervous about raising education levels for India's youth. It could be a game changer in electoral politics. Divisions based on caste, class, religion, reservation, language, gender, and color of skin could become irrelevant. They would have to work harder to get votes, and the easy money would dry up.

The politicians and businesspeople with vested interests in keeping the education system broken and disconnected are likely to lobby for ideas that could delay, confuse, or kill any reform initiatives. Sharu Rangnekar in his book *In the Wonderland of Indian Managers,* with illustrations by R. K. Laxman, outlined all the ways decisions are delayed or not made in India. One such way is to establish a committee. The group with vested interests may suggest a national committee to review the situation. They would then fill the committees with people they could control to delay the process and influence the outcomes. The more powerful politicians with vested interests could ensure that an education transformation bill would never pass just like many others have not passed in the past.

On the other hand, the opportunity to build India's new Golden Age is historic! By transforming the higher education system and unleashing the passion, power, and potential of 1.3 billion, it would truly place the PM, CMs, political leaders, and party in the same league as legendary leaders such as Chandragupta Maurya, Ashoka, Chandra Gupta II, Rajaraja Chola I, Akbar, and Shivaji. They would correct the many missteps in Indian history. As the leaders of a united and independent India, they indeed could change the course for the nation and its people for the next thousand years.

However, they must act now. The demographic dividend is a time-sensitive phenomenon. And it takes time to establish new world-class institutions and transform the entire higher education system.

We had a golden past marked with unity, peace, prosperity, flourishing world trade, world-class universities, and a community engaged and vested in the education system. In recent times, many countries have transformed their education systems and brought extraordinary prosperity for their people. All the past and present evidence from India and around the world suggests that India can create a golden era for its 1.3 billion people.

We must transform our higher education system now so it can transform the overall education system, unleash the potential of all Indians, make the economy more robust and sustainable, and address our mega challenges. It makes sense for its 1.3 billion people. It makes economic sense. It also makes sense from a perspective of building competitive and comparative advantage, strengthening national security, and enhancing peace, and improving the health and the environment. With over nine hundred million people below the age of forty, this is the time to do it. The upside from the transformation is delivering a demographic dividend and India's new Golden Era. The downside, from not making the necessary changes, could well be an unmitigated disaster. The stakes are high, and so are the payoffs.

Before I close, I have a few questions and some suggestions for you. What will you do now? How will you address the broken window? Will you be a bystander? Or will you take actions? Could you ask at least three friends to read this book and then think of ways of making an impact?

If you are a student, parent, professional, or concerned citizen, could you:

- Join the social media campaign #IAmForGoldenIndia on Twitter or Facebook, be part of the movement, and demand transformation of India's and your state's higher education system?

- Ask tough questions of your MP or MLA?

- Demand a Gray Revolution from your state's CM or country's PM?

If you are a faculty member or a university leader, could you:

- Take actions to make your class, lab, department, college, or university world class?

- Provide your students opportunities to solve problems that matter for the local community and the nation?

- Foster a culture of excellence, conduct research, spur innovation, encourage start-ups, and make an impact?

If you are a high-net-worth individual or a senior corporate executive, could you:

- Start a world-class community college, a bachelor's and master's college, or a comprehensive research university in India on your own or with your friends?

- Engage students in colleges and universities on problems that your company is facing?

- Influence the transformation of India's higher education system?

If you are an influential leader or a decision-maker in the central or state government, could you:

- Make changes to the structure, scale, scope, and excellence in the higher education system at the national or state levels?

I conclude with one of my favorite quotes, a Chinese proverb: "The best time to plant a tree was twenty years back. The next best time is now."

Mahatma Gandhi, Subhas Chandra Bose, Sarojini Naidu, Jawaharlal Nehru, Bal Gangadhar Tilak, and all the freedom fighters gave us independence from Britain. Let's use this freedom to build a brighter future. There are over one billion good people in India. Let's break our silence, demand our new golden era, and build it together. The future of India's education, its economy, and all the mega challenges are inexorably linked with the higher education system. The future depends on what you do about it. The current and future generations of Indians will thank you for transforming the broken system. You could also reap the benefits in this lifetime.

The earlier we start on this journey, the faster we will reach our destination. Let's sow the seeds for our new Golden Age now. Let's make the stories of Gautama Raju, Arjun Das, Meera Gupta, Ziya Khan, Pooja Shah, and Amarjit Singh a reality. Let's unleash the potential, power, and passion of 1.3 billion Indians. Let's start building a Golden India. Now.

Join the conversation. Be part of the movement. #IAmForGoldenIndia

Notes

Chapter 1: Destination: India's New Golden Age

1   Will Durant, *The Case for India* (Mumbai: Strand Book Stall, 2011), 4.

2   Jean Dreze and Amartya Sen, *An Uncertain Glory. India and Its Contradictions* (London: 2013. Penguin Books, 2014), 21.

3   A. L. Basham, *The Wonder That Was India* (London: Pan Macmillan Ltd, 2004), 71.

4   Ibid., 73–75.

5   Durant, *The Case for India* (Mumbai: Strand Book Stall, 2011), 5.

6   Ibid., 91.

7   Ibid., 31.

8   Ibid., 1–39.

9   http://www.ggdc.net/maddison/oriindex.htm

10 Dreze and Sen, *An Uncertain Glory. India and Its Contradictions* (London: 2013. Penguin Books, 2014), Table A5.

11 Ibid., 262.

12 http://www.internetlivestats.com/internet-users-by-country/

13 http://www.forbes.com/sites/singularity/2012/10/15/how-indians-defied-gravity-and-achieved-success-in-silicon-valley/

14 http://www.forbes.com/sites/naazneenkarmali/2015/03/03/a-record-90-indians-on-forbes-billionaires-list-2015/

15 Arjun Malhotra (co-founder, HCL and Techspan), in discussion with the author, September 2014.

16 http://timesofindia.indiatimes.com/india/New-poverty-line-Rs-32-in-villages-Rs-47-in-cities/articleshow/37920441.cms

17 McKinsey Global Institute, "The 'Bird of Gold': The Rise of India's Consumer Market," May 2007.

18 https://ruralindiaonline.org/pages/about/

19 PRS Legislative Research, *Swaminathan Committee on Farmers* (October 2006) http://www.prsindia.org/administrator/uploads/general/1242360972~~final%20summary_pdf.pdf

20 Dreze and Sen, *An Uncertain Glory. India and Its Contradictions* (London: 2013. Penguin Books, 2014), Table A5.

21 Dow Jones VentureSource 2014 and EY *Global Venture Capital Insights and Trends 2014.*

22 http://scroll.in/article/720463/rafael-deal-how-make-in-india-becomes-made-in-france

23 McKinsey & Company, ed., *Reimagining India: Unlocking the Potential of Asia's Next Superpower* (New York: Simon & Schuster, 2013).

24 World Economic Forum, *Global Competitive Index 2014–15.* http://reports.weforum.org/global-competitiveness-report-2014-2015/view/methodology/.

25 Ibid., http://reports.weforum.org/global-competitiveness-report-2014-2015/rankings/.

26 https://www.allianz.com/en/about_us/open-knowledge/topics/demography/articles/111018-indias-urban-migration-crisis.html/

27 Ibid. http://www.un.org/en/development/desa/news/population/world-urbanization-prospects-2014.html

28 http://envirocenter.yale.edu/news/237/56/India-s-Air-the-World-s-Unhealthiest-Study-Says/d,newsDetail

29 Dreze and Sen, *An Uncertain Glory. India and Its Contradictions* (London: 2013. Penguin Books, 2014), 148–177.

30 McKinsey & Company, ed., Reimagining India: Unlocking the Potential of Asia's Next Superpower (New York: Simon & Schuster, 2013), 183.

31 http://www.arlingtoninstitute.org/wbp/global-water-crisis/606

32 http://documents.worldbank.org/curated/en/2008/06/16784682/indias-water-economy-bracing-turbulent-future

33 http://thewaterproject.org/water-in-crisis-india

34 http://asiancenturyinstitute.com/environment/525-infrastructure-of-water-security-in-india

35 http://iomenvis.nic.in/index2.aspx?slid=758&sublinkid=119&langid=1&mid=1

36 Dreze and Sen, *An Uncertain Glory. India and Its Contradictions* (London: 2013. Penguin Books, 2014), 253.

37 http://www.bbc.com/news/world-asia-india-31865477

38 http://www.hindustantimes.com/india-news/justice-has-a-mountain-to-climb-of-31-3-million-pending-cases/article1-1259920.aspx

39 McKinsey & Company, ed., *Reimagining India: Unlocking the Potential of Asia's Next Superpower* (New York: Simon & Schuster, 2013), 228.

40 http://www.ibnlive.com/news/india/pending-cases-cji-hl-dattu-says-trial-to-end-within-five-years-979269.html

41 McKinsey & Company, ed., *Reimagining India: Unlocking the Potential of Asia's Next Superpower* (New York: Simon & Schuster, 2013), 229.

42 http://www.huffingtonpost.com/2015/05/06/salman-khan-guilty-fatal-hit-and-run_n_7219522.html

43 https://www.transparency.org/cpi2014/infographic/compare

44 https://groups.google.com/forum/?hl=en#!topic/national-election-watch/agzkzylozgw

45 Gurcharan Das, *India Grows at Night: A Liberal Case for a Strong State* (New Delhi: Penguin Books, 2012), 196 –200.

46 http://www.censusindia.gov.in/2011census/population_enumeration.aspx

47 Dreze and Sen, *An Uncertain Glory. India and Its Contradictions* (London: 2013. Penguin Books, 2014), 120–126.

48 http://data.uis.unesco.org/index.aspx?queryid=142&lang=en

49 http://www.dnaindia.com/analysis/main-article-the-unemployable-literates-of-india-1532691

50 Center for World-Class Universities of Shanghai Jiao Tong University, *Academic Ranking of World Universities 2014,* http://www.shanghairanking.com/ARWU2014.html

51 Krishna Kumar, *Politics of Education in Colonial India* (New Delhi: Routledge, 2014), 24.

52 Ibid., 13–66.

53 Dreze and Sen, *An Uncertain Glory. India and Its Contradictions* (London: 2013. Penguin Books, 2014), 107.

54 N. S. Rajan (chief human resources officer, Tata Group), in discussion with the author, November 2014.

55 N. R. Narayana Murthy, *A Better India: A Better World.* (New Delhi: Penguin Books, 2009), 9.

56 Sanjay Lalbhai (chairman and MD, Arvind Limited), in discussion with the author, November 2014.

57 Raghu Mahajan (graduate student at Stanford University), in discussion with the author, July 2015.

58 Rajiv Ratn Shah (graduate student at National University of Singapore), in discussion with the author, July 2015.

59 Suma Jaini (Boston University and IIT alumna), in discussion with the author, July 2015.

Chapter 2: The Current System: Broken and Disconnected

1   http://www.mhrd.gov.in/university-and-higher-education

2   Department of Higher Education, Ministry of Human Resources Development, government of India, *All India Survey of Higher Education (2010–2011)*. 2013.

3   http://data.uis.unesco.org/index.aspx?queryid=142&lang=en

4   Ministry of Human Resources Development, government of India, *Taking IITs to Excellence and Greater Relevance: Report of Dr. Anil Kakodkar Committee* (April 2011), 35.

5   http://www.thehindu.com/features/education/college-and-university/an-indian-education/article4683622.ece

6   Jagori Saha (PhD student at Washington University, and alumna, Presidency College and University College London), in discussion with the author, July 2015. 14 (which was a second interview) Patralekha Ukil (PhD student at the University of Connecticut and alumna of Presidency College and the University of Warwick), in discussion with the author, July 2015.

7   *Nature*, May 14, 2015, http://www.nature.com/news/a-nation-with-ambition-1.17520.

8   N. R. Narayana Murthy, *A Better India: A Better World.* (New Delhi: Penguin Books, 2009), 136.; Department of Higher Education, Ministry of Human Resources Development, government of India, *All India Survey of Higher Education (2010–2011)*, 2013.

9   P. Balaram (former director of IISc Bangalore), in discussion with the author, November 2014.

10 Department of Higher Education, Ministry of Human Resources Development, government of India, *All India Survey of Higher Education (2010–2011)*, 2013, 10.

11 Pawan Agarwal, Indian Higher Education: Envisioning the Future (New Delhi: Sage Publications India Pvt. Ltd., 2013), 10.

12 Anurag Behar (vice chancellor of Azim Premji University), in discussion with the author, November 2014.

13 Ira Pande, ed., *Beyond Degrees: Finding Success in Higher Education.* (New Delhi: HarperCollins, 2008), 76.

14 Abhay Bhushan (serial entrepreneur and investor), in discussion with the author, September 2014.

15 Pranab Bardhan (professor, UC Berkeley), in discussion with the author, October 2014.

16 Rajiv Bajaj (managing director, Bajaj Auto), in discussion with the author, November 2014.

17 N. S. Rajan (chief human resources officer, Tata Group), in discussion with the author, November 2014.

18 Akanksha Srivastava (graduate student at the University of Oxford and IIT alumna), in discussion with the author, July 2015.

19 Jandhyala B. G. Tilak, *Higher Education in India: In Search of Equality, Quality, and Quantity* (New Delhi: Orient Blackswan, 2013), 7

20 Gautam Thapar (founder and chairman, Avantha Group) in discussion with the author, October 2014.

21 Aniket Panda (graduate student at Duke University and IIT alumnus), in discussion with the author, August 2015.

22 Shweta Sangewar (Imperial College London and IIT alumna), in discussion with the author, July 2015.

23 Shouvik Chatterjee (PhD student at Cornell University and IIT alumnus), in discussion with the author, August 2015.

24 Govind Swarup (professor, TIFR), in discussion with the author, December 2014.

25 Krishna Kumar (professor, Delhi University), in discussion with the author, November 2014.

26 Pranab Bardhan (professor, UC Berkeley), in discussion with the author, October 2014.

27 Bharath Bhat (Stanford University and IIT alumnus), in discussion with the author, July 2015.

28 Arijit Chakraborty (PhD student at the University of Auckland and BITS Pilani alumnus), in discussion with the author, June 2015.

29 Sreeja Nag (MIT and IIT alumna), in discussion with the author, July 2015.

30 Jagori Saha (PhD student at Washington University and alumna of Presidency College and the University College London), in discussion with the author, July 2015.

31 Center for World-Class Universities of Shanghai Jiao Tong University, *Academic Ranking of World Universities 2014,* http://www.shanghairanking.com/ARWU2014.html.

32   Sunil Kant Munjal (joint MD, Hero MotoCorp) in discussion with the author, October 2014.

33   Janat Shah (director, IIM Udaipur) in discussion with the author, September 2014.

34   J. R. Achyuthan (PhD student at George Mason University and IIT alumnus), in discussion with the author, July 2015.

35   Deepak Phatak (professor, IIT Bombay), in discussion with the author, November 2014.

36   Ashok Jhunjhunwala (professor, IIT Madras), in discussion with the author, October 2014.

Chapter 3: Bottom Line: A Hefty Price Tag For All

1   http://www.legallyindia.com/Pre-law-student/clat-2015-gets-busy-but-not-so-old-40k-candidates-most-from-up-but-only-400-mature-applicants

2   http://www.newindianexpress.com/cities/bengaluru/Private-tuitions-now-a-multi-billion-rupee-industry-Survey/2013/06/26/article1653569.ece

3   Sudhir Jain (director, IIT Gandhinagar), in discussion with the author, October 2014.

4   S. Ramadorai (chairman, National Skill Development Agency), in discussion with the author, December 2014.

5   Keerthana Kumar (UT Austin alumna), in discussion with the author, March 2015.

6   http://wenr.wes.org/2013/12/indian-study-abroad-trends-past-present-and-future/; http://www.uis.unesco.org/EDUCATION/Pages/international-student-flow-viz.aspx; http://www.iie.org/Services/Project-Atlas/United-States/International-Students-In-US

7   Gautam Thapar (founder and chairman, Avantha Group) in discussion with the author, October 2014.

8   Manas Kaushik (Harvard University, LSE, and AIIMS alumnus), in discussion with the author, July 2015.

9   Sampriti Bhattacharya (PhD student at MIT and OSU and West Bengal University of Technology alumna), in discussion with the author, July 2015.

10 Stuti Misra (University of Auckland and Bharati Vidyapeeth, Pune alumna), in discussion with the author, July 2015.

11 Vinod Maseedupally (University of New South Wales and Bausch & Lomb School of Optometry, Hyderabad alumnus), in discussion with the author, July 2015.; Moneisha Gokhale (University of New South Wales and Bausch & Lomb School of Optometry, Hyderabad alumna), in discussion with the author, July 2015.

12 Hetal Parekh (London School of Commerce and St. Francis College, Hyderabad alumna), in discussion with the author, July 2015.

13 Arijit Chakraborty (PhD student at the University of Auckland and alumnus of BITS Pilani), in discussion with the author, June 2015.

14 Rajiv Ratn Shah (PhD student at NUS and alumnus of DCE, JNU, and BHU), in discussion with the author, July 2015.

15 Smitha Tipparaju (University of Auckland and Calicut University alumna), in discussion with the author, July 2015.

16 Pradeep Lukka (postdoctoral researcher at the University of Tennessee Health Science Center and UCSF and alumnus of the University of Auckland and Rajiv Gandhi University of Health, Bangalore), in discussion with the author, July 2015.

17 http://www.nasscom.in/NASSCOM-PERSPECTIVE-2020-Outlines-Transformation-Roadmap-for-The-Indian-Technology-and-Business-Services-Industries-56269

18 G. Deshpande (trustee of Deshpande Foundation, life member of MIT Corporation), in discussion with the author, October 2014.

19 Ibid.; Neelam Maheshwari (director, grant making and partnerships, Deshpande Foundation, India), in discussion with the author, November 2014.

20 Anil Sachdev (founder, the School of Inspired Learning) in discussion with the author, October 2014.

21 Gautam Thapar (founder and chairman, Avantha Group) in discussion with the author, October 2014.

22 http://economictimes.indiatimes.com/tech/ites/cisco-adds-129-crorepatis-in-a-year-to-retain-talent/articleshow/45904316.cms?intenttarget=no&utm_source=newsletter&utm_medium=email&utm_campaign=Dailynewsletter&ncode=ebb02c295cd25bfe28bb7ca3c3b82be4

23 Sujit Baksi (CEO of business services, Tech Mahindra), in discussion with the author, November 2014.

24 Mukesh Aghi (former CEO, L&T Infotech), in discussion with the author, December 2014.

25 Ajay Bakaya (executive director, Sarovar Hotels), in discussion with the author, October 2014.

26 http://www.commerce.nic.in/eidb/Default.asp

27 http://scroll.in/article/720463/Rafale-deal:-How-'make-in-India'-becomes-'made-in-France'

Chapter 4: Contributing Factors: An Inside Job

1   Roddam Narasimha (professor, Jawaharlal Nehru Centre for Advanced Scientific Research, Bangalore), in discussion with the author, December 2014.

2   Pawan Agarwal, *Indian Higher Education: Envisioning the Future* (New Delhi: Sage Publications India Pvt. Ltd., 2013), 304–356.

3   National Knowledge Commission, *Report to the Nation (2006–2009)*, 62.

4   Ibid., 71.

5   Ibid., 71.

6   http://articles.economictimes.indiatimes.com/2007-03-31/news/28413639_1_institutes-aicte-norms-aicte-act

7   http://articles.economictimes.indiatimes.com/2014-08-09/news/52620584_1_undergraduate-programme-delhi-university-fyup

8   Nandan Nilekani (co-founder, Infosys; former chairman, Unique Identification Authority (UID) initiative), in discussion with the author, October 2014.

    Aromar Revi (executive director, IIHS), in discussion with the author, November 2014.

9   T.V. Mohandas Pai (chairman, Manipal Global Education), in discussion with the author, October 2014.

10 Gurcharan Das, India Unbound: From Independence to the Global Information Age (New Delhi: Penguin Books India, 2002), 95.

11 Pawan Agarwal, Indian Higher Education: Envisioning the Future (New Delhi: Sage Publications India Pvt. Ltd., 2013), 10.

12 http://www.dailymail.co.uk/indiahome/indianews/article-2969503/Madhya-Pradesh-Governor-quits-multi-crore-Vyapam-scandal.html; http://indianexpress.com/article/india/india-others/vyapam-jobs-scam-720-students-and-parents-booked-in-mp/; http://indianexpress.com/article/explained/across-the-board-vyapams-spread/

13 http://www.ndtv.com/india-news/supreme-court-transfers-vyapam-scam-probe-to-cbi-779682

14 http://www.vyapam.nic.in/e_default.htm

15 Pawan Agarwal, *Indian Higher Education: Envisioning the Future* (New Delhi: Sage Publications India Pvt. Ltd., 2013), 307.

16 Nandan Nilekani, *Imagining India: The Idea of a Renewed Nation* (New York: The Penguin Press, 2009), 332.

17 Philip G. Altbach and N. Jayaram, "India's Effort to Join 21st-Century Higher Education", Center for International Higher Education, 2009

18 Devesh Kapur and Pratap Bhanu Mehta, *Mortgaging the Future? Indian Higher Education.* (Brookings–NCAER India Policy Forum 2007–08), 32 https://casi.sas.upenn.edu/sites/casi.sas.upenn.edu/files/bio/uploads/Mortgaging%20the%20Future.pdf.

19 N. R. Narayana Murthy, *A Better India: A Better World.* (New Delhi: Penguin Books, 2009), 10.

Chapter 5: Nalanda University: The View From 1,400 Years Ago

1 R. K. Mookerji, *Ancient Indian Education: Brahmanical and Buddhist* (New Delhi: Motilal Banarsidas Publishers Pvt. Ltd., 1989), 557–586.

2 http://www.unibo.it/en/university

3 http://www.ox.ac.uk/about/organisation/history

4 D. N. Jha, *Ancient India: In Historical Outline* (New Delhi: Manohar Publishers & Distributors, 2015), 71–72.

5 Radha Kumud Mookerji, *Ancient Indian Education: Brahmanical and Buddhist* (New Delhi: Motilal Banarsidas Publishers Pvt. Ltd., 1989), 557–558.

6 D. N. Jha, *Ancient India: In Historical Outline* (New Delhi: 1978 Manohar Publishers & Distributors, 2015), 81–95.

7 R. K. Mookerji, *Ancient Indian Education: Brahmanical and Buddhist* (New Delhi: Motilal Banarsidas Publishers Pvt. Ltd., 1989), 557.

8 Ibid., 565.

9 D. N. Jha, *Ancient India: In Historical Outline* (New Delhi: Manohar Publishers & Distributors, 2015), 164.; R. K. Mookerji, *Ancient Indian Education: Brahmanical and Buddhist* (New Delhi: Motilal Banarsidas Publishers Pvt. Ltd., 1989), 554.

10 R. K. Mookerji, *Ancient Indian Education: Brahmanical and Buddhist* (New Delhi: Motilal Banarsidas Publishers Pvt. Ltd., 1989), 532.

11 Ibid., 528.

12 Ibid., 565.

13 A. L. Basham, *The Wonder That Was India* (London: Pan Macmillan Ltd, 2004), 166.

14 R. K. Mookerji, *Ancient Indian Education: Brahmanical and Buddhist* (New Delhi: Motilal Banarsidas Publishers Pvt. Ltd., 1989), 530–31.

15 Ibid., 549.

16 Ibid., 551.

17 Ibid., 565.

18 Ibid., 548.

19 A. L. Basham, *The Wonder That Was India* (London: Pan Macmillan Ltd, 2004), 166, 268.

Chapter 6: The United States: Leading The World

1   http://www.iie.org/Services/Project-Atlas/United-States/
    International-Students-In-US; http://www.iie.org/Research-and-
    Publications/Open-Doors/Data/International-Students/Infographic;
    http://www.uis.unesco.org/EDUCATION/Pages/international-
    student-flow-viz.aspx

2   Center for World-Class Universities of Shanghai Jiao Tong
    University, *Academic Ranking of World Universities 2014,* http://www.
    shanghairanking.com/ARWU2014.html.

3   http://data.uis.unesco.org/index.aspx?queryid=142&lang=en

4   http://nces.ed.gov/programs/digest/d13/tables/dt13_301.20.asp

5   Clark Kerr, *The Uses of the University* (Cambridge: 1963 Harvard
    University Press, 2001), 7–14.

6   Ibid., 36.

7   http://www.loc.gov/rr/program/bib/ourdocs/Morrill.html

8   http://www.1890universities.org/history

9   http://nifa.usda.gov/program/hatch-act-1887; http://www.
    archivesfoundation.org/documents/smith-lever-act-1914/; Frank H.
    T. Rhodes, *The Creation of the Future: The Role of the American University*
    (Ithaca: Cornell University Press, 2001), 6–7, 195.

10 https://www.jhu.edu/about/history/

11 Clark Kerr, *The Uses of the University* (Cambridge: 1963, Harvard
    University Press, 2001), 10–11.

12 http://www.benefits.va.gov/gibill/history.asp; http://www.history.
    com/topics/world-war-ii/gi-bill

13 https://www.nsf.gov/od/lpa/nsf50/vbush1945.htm

14 http://www.nsf.gov/about/

15 http://www.nih.gov/about/

16 http://www.darpa.mil/about-us/about-darpa

17 http://www.darpa.mil/about-us/budget

18 http://www.ucop.edu/ott/faculty/bayh.html

19 Clark Kerr, *The Uses of the University* (Cambridge: 1963 Harvard University Press, 2001), 118.

20 http://carnegieclassifications.iu.edu/descriptions/basic.php

21 https://www.brynmawr.edu/about

22 Frank H. T. Rhodes, *The Creation of the Future: The Role of the American University* (Ithaca: Cornell University Press, 2001), 105.

23 http://www.forbes.com/sites/halahtouryalai/2014/02/21/1-trillion-student-loan-problem-keeps-getting-worse/

24 http://www.ucop.edu/acadinit/mastplan/ProjectL.pdf

25 http://financialaid.berkeley.edu/cost-attendance

26 http://www.mercurynews.com/california/ci_27634630/uc-cap-out-state-students-at-berkeley-ucla

27 http://www.nobelprize.org/nobel_prizes/medicine/laureates/2013/schekman-speech_en.html

28 https://nces.ed.gov/fastfacts/display.asp?id=40

Chapter 7: California: A Vibrant And Integrated System

1   Digest of Education Statistics, US Department of Education, Table 304.10 and 304.15https://nces.ed.gov/programs/digest/2014menu_tables.asp.

2   Clark Kerr, *The Gold and the Blue: A Personal Memoir of the University of California 1949–1967* (Berkeley: University of California Press, 2001), Vol. 1, 172–190.; http://www.ucop.edu/acadinit/mastplan/mpsummary.htm

3   University of California, *Annual Accountability Report* 2014, http://accountability.universityofcalifornia.edu/documents/accountabilityreport14.pdf.

4   Office of the Chancellor, California State University, *Working for California: The Impact of the California State University System* (May 2010). http://www.calstate.edu/impact/docs/CSUImpactsReport.pdf

5   California Community Colleges, Chancellor's Office *Student Success Scorecard: 2014 State of the System Report*, http://californiacommunitycolleges.cccco.edu/Portals/0/FlipBooks/2014_StateOfSystem/2014_State_of_the_System_FINAL.pdf.

6   Digest of Education Statistics, US Department of Education, Table 317.2, https://nces.ed.gov/programs/digest/d13/tables/dt13_317.20.asp.

7   Ibid.

8   http://www.washingtonpost.com/blogs/govbeat/wp/2014/07/08/californias-economy-is-large-enough-it-could-be-admitted-into-g-8/

9   Nancy Scott Anderson, *An Improbable Venture: A History of the University of California, San Diego* (San Diego: UCSD Press, 1993), 16–90.; Pradeep Khosla (chancellor, UC San Diego), in discussion with the author, December 2014.; Suresh Subramani (executive vice chancellor, UC San Diego), in discussion with the author, November 2014.; Mary Walshok (associate vice chancellor, UC San Diego), in discussion with the author, December 2014.

10 Richard C. Atkinson (president emeritus, University of California), in discussion with the author, December 2014.

11 Center for World-Class Universities of Shanghai Jiao Tong University, *Academic Ranking of World Universities 2014,* http://www.shanghairanking.com/ARWU2014.html.

12 http://ucsdnews.ucsd.edu/pressrelease/2015_research_funding_at_uc_san_diego_again_surpasses_billion_dollar_mark

Chapter 8: UC Berkeley: The Dna Of Excellence And Impact

1   Robert Tjian (president of Howard Hughes Medical Institute and professor at UC Berkeley), in discussion with the author, November 2014.

2   https://www.hhmi.org/about

3   Center for World-Class Universities of Shanghai Jiao Tong University, *Academic Ranking of World Universities 2014,* http://www.shanghairanking.com/ARWU2014.html.

4   http://berkeley.edu/about/

5   Ibid.

6   Center for World-Class Universities of Shanghai Jiao Tong University, *Academic Ranking of World Universities 2014,* http://www.shanghairanking.com/ARWU2014.html.

7   http://news.berkeley.edu/2010/09/28/nrc-rankings/

8   Tsu-Jae King-Liu (chair, department of electrical engineering and computer sciences and professor, UC Berkeley), in discussion with the author, September 2014.

9   http://engineering.berkeley.edu/about-berkeley-engineering

10 https://www.law.berkeley.edu/about-us/

11 Sreeta Gorripaty (PhD student at UC Berkeley and alumna of IIT), in discussion with the author, June 2015.

12 Raj Shekhar Singh, "UC Berkeley–IIT Kharagpur Summer Research Program Survey," July 1, 2015.

13 Anindya De (UC Berkeley and IIT alumnus), in discussion with the author, June 2015.; Avinash Nayak (PhD student at UC Berkeley and alumnus of IIT), in discussion with the author, June 2015.; Aamod Shanker (PhD student at UC Berkeley and alumnus of IIT), in discussion with the author, June 2015.

14 http://www.webometrics.info/en/node/58

15 http://academic-senate.berkeley.edu/about-senate

16 http://academic-senate.berkeley.edu/committees/BIR

17 http://academic-senate.berkeley.edu/committees/coms

18 David Patterson (professor, UC Berkeley), in discussion with the author, October 2014.

19 Jasper Rine (professor, UC Berkeley), in discussion with the author, September 2014.

20 http://teaching.berkeley.edu/dta-recipient/jasper-rine

21 Jasper Rine (professor, UC Berkeley), in discussion with the author, September 2014.

22 Randy Schekman (Nobel laureate; professor, UC Berkeley), in discussion with the author, October 2014.

23 http://news.berkeley.edu/2013/10/07/randy-schekman-awarded-2013-nobel-prize-in-physiology-or-medicine/

24 Randy Schekman (Nobel laureate; professor, UC Berkeley), in discussion with the author, October 2014.

25 http://www.berkeley.edu/news/media/releases/2006/04/27_fermiaward.shtml

26 http://www.berkeley.edu/about/history-discoveries

27 UC Berkeley, *Serving California, the Bay Area, and the Community: The Economic Impact & Social Benefits of the University of California, Berkeley 2005–2006*, http://www.berkeley.edu/news/media/releases/2007/09/13_EconomicImpact.shtml

Chapter 9: Stanford University: An Innovation Powerhouse

1 http://www.marconisociety.org/press/2014paulrajannouncement.html

2 Ibid.; Arogyaswami Paulraj (Marconi Award Winner and professor, Stanford University), in discussion with the author, December 2014.; http://web.stanford.edu/~apaulraj/pdf/VSM.pdf; http://web.stanford.edu/~apaulraj/pdf/AVSM.pdf

3 Arogyaswami Paulraj (Marconi Award Winner and professor, Stanford University), in discussion with the author, December 2014.

4 http://facts.stanford.edu/index

5   C. Stewart Gillmor, *Fred Terman at Stanford: Building a Discipline, a University, and Silicon Valley* (Stanford: Stanford University Press 2004), 17–39, 492–493.; http://www.stanford.edu/about/history/

6   Stanford University, *Stanford Facts 2015, 9* http://facts.stanford.edu/pdf/StanfordFacts_2015.pdf.

7   Center for World-Class Universities of Shanghai Jiao Tong University, *Academic Ranking of World Universities 2014,* http://www.shanghairanking.com/ARWU2014.html.

8   http://www.stanford.edu/about/

9   Gillmor, *Fred Terman at Stanford: Building a Discipline, a University, and Silicon Valley* (Stanford: Stanford University Press 2004), vii.

10 http://electronicdesign.com/communications/fred-terman-father-silicon-valley-raises-industry

11 Gillmor, *Fred Terman at Stanford: Building a Discipline, a University, and Silicon Valley* (Stanford: Stanford University Press 2004), 2.

12 Ibid., 253.

13 Ibid., 9, 85, 285, 428, 436–441, 500.

14 Ibid., 139.

15 Ibid., 326–327.

16 Tom Kailath (US National Medal of Science winner and professor at Stanford University), in discussion with the author, February 2015.

17 Arogyaswami Paulraj (Marconi Award winner and professor at Stanford University), in discussion with the author, December 2014.

18 Krishna Saraswat (professor, Stanford University), in discussion with the author, September 2014.

19 Gillmor, *Fred Terman at Stanford: Building a Discipline, a University, and Silicon Valley* (Stanford: Stanford University Press 2004), 121.

20 Ibid., 167, 282–284, 324.

21 Ibid., 305–311.

22 Ibid., 327–331.

23 Ibid, 257, 267, 290.

24 Ibid., 347.

25 Raghu Mahajan (graduate student at Stanford University), in discussion with the author, July 2015.

26 Arpit Goel (graduate student at Stanford University and alumnus of IIT), in discussion with the author, July 2015.

27 Bharath Bhat (alumnus, Stanford University and IIT), in discussion with the author, June 2015.

28 Stanford University, *Stanford Facts 2015, 29,* http://facts.stanford.edu/pdf/StanfordFacts_2015.pdf.

Chapter 10: Next Steps: A Gray Revolution

1   R. Gopalakrishnan (director, Tata Sons Limited), in discussion with the author, November 2014.

2   http://www.britannica.com/topic/broken-windows-theory; http://www.ci.missoula.mt.us/881/Broken-Window-Theory

3   R. Gopalakrishnan (director, Tata Sons Limited), in discussion with the author, November 2014.

4   National Knowledge Commission, *Report to the Nation (2006–2009),* 65.

5   Philip G. Altbach and N. Jayaram, "India's Effort to Join 21st-Century Higher Education", Center for International Higher Education, 2009

6   https://www.psychologytoday.com/basics/bystander-effect

7   Sudhir Jain (director, IIT Gandhinagar), in discussion with the author, October 2014.

8   https://www.class-central.com/report/swayam-india/

9   Anant Agarwal (CEO of edX and professor at MIT), in discussion with the author, August 2015.

10 Krishna Kumar, *Politics of Education in Colonial India* (New Delhi: Routledge, 2014), 54–61.

11 Ira Pande, ed., *Beyond Degrees: Finding Success in Higher Education.* (New Delhi: HarperCollins, 2008), 98.

12 Donald Kennedy, *Academic Duty* (Cambridge: Harvard University Press, 1999), 127.

13 Henry Rosovsky, *The University: An Owner's Manual* (New York: W. W. Norton & Company, Inc., 1991), 33.

14 Donald Kennedy, *Academic Duty* (Cambridge: Harvard University Press, 1999), 107.

15 Frank H. T. Rhodes, *The Creation of the Future: The Role of the American University* (Ithaca: Cornell University Press, 2001), 243.

16 Sam Pitroda (former chairman, National Knowledge Commission), in discussion with the author, September 2014.

17 Ramachandra Guha, *India after Gandhi: The History of the World's Largest Democracy* (New York: HarperCollins, 2007), 401–402

Chapter 11: The Journey: Must Start Now!

1   D. N. Jha, *Ancient India: In Historical Outline* (New Delhi: Manohar Publishers & Distributors, 2015), 22.; Romila Thapar, *The Penguin History of Early India: From the Origins to AD 1300* (New Delhi: Penguin Books, 2002), 17, 280–282.

2   A. L. Basham, *The Wonder That Was India* (London: Pan Macmillan Ltd, 2004), 59–71.

3   D. N. Jha, *Ancient India: In Historical Outline* (New Delhi: Manohar Publishers & Distributors, 2015), 149–173.

4   R. K. Mookerji, *Ancient Indian Education: Brahmanical and Buddhist* (New Delhi: Motilal Banarsidas Publishers Pvt. Ltd., 1989), 500.

5   D. N. Jha, *Ancient India: In Historical Outline* (New Delhi: Manohar Publishers & Distributors, 2015), 173.

6   Ben Wildavsky, *The Great Brain Race: How Global Universities Are Reshaping the World* (Princeton: Princeton University Press, 2010), 3.

7   Jamil Salmi, *The Challenges of Establishing World-Class Universities* (Washington, DC: The World Bank, 2009), 40.

8   http://en.people.cn/90001/6381319.html

9   https://www.timeshighereducation.co.uk/news/eastern-stars-universities-of-chinas-c9-league-excel-in-select-fields/415193.article; Ben Wildavsky, *The Great Brain Race: How Global Universities Are Reshaping the World* (Princeton: Princeton University Press, 2010), 71–74.

10 Pranab Bardhan (professor, UC Berkeley), in discussion with the author, October 2014.

11 Ministry of Human Resources Development, government of India, *Taking IITs to Excellence and Greater Relevance: Report of Dr. Anil Kakodkar Committee* (April 2011), 27–28.

12 Ben Wildavsky, *The Great Brain Race: How Global Universities Are Reshaping the World* (Princeton: Princeton University Press, 2010), 72–73.

13 Ibid., 10

14 Ibid., 73–74.

15 Center for World-Class Universities of Shanghai Jiao Tong University, *Academic Ranking of World Universities 2014*, http://www.shanghairanking.com/ARWU2014.html.

16 Brijendra K. Syngal (former chairman and MD, VSNL), in discussion with the author, September 2014.

17 OECD, *PISA 2012 Results in Focus: What 15-Year-Olds Know and What They Can Do with What They Know,* http://www.oecd.org/pisa/keyfindings/pisa-2012-results-overview.pdf.

18 Center for World-Class Universities of Shanghai Jiao Tong University, Academic Ranking of World Universities 2014, http://www.shanghairanking.com/ARWU2014.html.

19 Ben Wildavsky, *The Great Brain Race: How Global Universities Are Reshaping the World* (Princeton: Princeton University Press, 2010), 80–81.

20 World Economic Forum, *Global Competitive Index 2014–15,* http://reports.weforum.org/global-competitiveness-report-2014-2015/rankings/.

21 Ibid.

22 Ben Wildavsky, *The Great Brain Race: How Global Universities Are Reshaping the World* (Princeton: Princeton University Press, 2010), 83.

23 Center for World-Class Universities of Shanghai Jiao Tong University, *Academic Ranking of World Universities 2014,* http://www.shanghairanking.com/ARWU2014.html.

24 Ben Wildavsky, *The Great Brain Race: How Global Universities Are Reshaping the World* (Princeton: Princeton University Press, 2010), 196.

25 Hang Chang Chieh (executive director of the Institute for Engineering Leadership and Professor, NUS), in discussion with the author, November 2014.

26 Paul Matsudaira (head of the department of biological sciences and professor, NUS), in discussion with the author, November 2014.

27 John Thong (head of the electrical and computer engineering department and professor, NUS), in discussion with the author, November 2014.

28 http://www.ndtv.com/india-news/pm-modi-launches-skill-india-initiative-that-aims-to-train-40-crore-people-781897

Bibliography

1. Agarwal, Pawan. *Indian Higher Education: Envisioning the Future.* New Delhi: Sage Publications India Pvt. Ltd., 2013.

2. Altbach, Philip G. and N. Jayaram. "India's Effort to Join 21st-Century Higher Education." Center for International Higher Education, 2009.

3. Anderson, Nancy Scott. *An Improbable Venture: A History of the University of California, San Diego.* San Diego: UCSD Press, 1993.

4. Atkinson, Richard C. *Research Universities and the Wealth of Nations.* A speech at the US–China Forum on Science and Technology Policy. Beijing, October 16–17, 2006.

5. Basham, A. L. *The Wonder That Was India.* London: Pan Macmillan Ltd, 2004. First published 1954 Sidgwick & Jackson, London.

6. Cole, Jonathan R. *The Great American University: Its Rise to Preeminence, Its Indispensable National Role, Why It Must Be Protected.* New York: PublicAffairs, 2012.

7. California Community Colleges, Chancellor's Office. *Student Success Scorecard: 2014 State of the System Report.*

8. Center for World-Class Universities of Shanghai Jiao Tong University. *Academic Ranking of World Universities 2014.*

9. Das, Gurcharan. *India Grows at Night: A Liberal Case For a Strong State.* New Delhi: Penguin Books, 2012.

10. Das, Gurcharan. *India Unbound: From Independence to the Global Information Age.* New Delhi: Penguin Books India, 2002.

11. Department of Higher Education, Government of Odisha. *Report of the Task Force on Higher Education.* (constituted on Oct. 7, 2009).

12. Department of Higher Education, Ministry of Human Resources Development, government of India. *All India Survey of Higher Education (2010–2011)* 2013.

13. Department of Higher Education, Ministry of Human Resources Development, government of India. *Report of the Committee to Advise on Renovation and Rejuvenation of Higher Education* (the Yashpal Committee) 2009.

14. Douglass, John Aubrey, C. Judson King and Irwin Feller, editors. *Globalization's Muse: Universities and Higher Education Systems in a Changing World.* Berkeley: Berkeley Public Policy Press, 2009.

15. Dreze, Jean and Sen, Amartya. *An Uncertain Glory. India and Its Contradictions.* London: Penguin Books, 2014.

16. Durant, Will. *The Case for India.* Mumbai: Strand Book Stall, 2011. First published 1930 by Simon and Schuster, New York.

17. EY. *Global Venture Capital Insights and Trends 2014.*

18. Gillmor, C. Stewart. *Fred Terman at Stanford: Building a Discipline, a University, and Silicon Valley.* Stanford: Stanford University Press, 2004.

19. Guha, Ramachandra. *India after Gandhi: The History of the World's Largest Democracy.* New York: HarperCollins, 2007.

20. Guha, Ramachandra, editor. *Makers of Modern India.* New Delhi: Penguin Books, 2010.

21. *Higher Education in Maharashtra: Preparing for the Future – New Ideas and Pathways.* July 2011.

22. Jha, D. N. *Ancient India: In Historical Outline.* New Delhi: Manohar Publishers & Distributors, 2015. (First published 1977 under the title *Ancient India: An Introductory Outline.*)

23. Kalam, A. P. J. *Ignited Minds: Unleashing the Power within India.* New Delhi: Penguin Books, 2003.

24. Kapur, Devesh and Mehta, Pratap Bhanu. *Mortgaging the Future? Indian Higher Education.* (Brookings–NCAER India Policy Forum 2007–08).

25. Kennedy, Donald. *Academic Duty.* Cambridge: Harvard University Press, 1999.

26. Kerr, Clark. *The Uses of the University.* Cambridge: 1963 Harvard University Press, 2001.

27. Kerr, Clark. *The Gold and the Blue: A Personal Memoir of the University of California 1949–1967.* Berkeley: University of California Press, 2001.

28. Kumar, Krishna. *Politics of Education in Colonial India.* New Delhi: Routledge, 2014.

29. National Knowledge Commission, *Report to the Nation (2006–2009).*

30. Nilekani, Nandan. *Imagining India: The Idea of a Renewed Nation.* New York: The Penguin Press, 2009.

31. McKinsey Global Institute. "The 'Bird of Gold': The Rise of India's Consumer Market." May 2007.

32. McKinsey & Company, editor. *Reimagining India: Unlocking the Potential of Asia's Next Superpower.* New York: Simon & Schuster, 2013.

33. Mookerji, R. K. *Ancient Indian Education: Brahmanical and Buddhist.* New Delhi: Motilal Banarsidas Publishers Pvt. Ltd., 1989. (First published in 1947 in London.)

34. Murthy, N. R. Narayana. *A Better India: A Better World.* New Delhi: Penguin Books, 2009.

35. OECD, *PISA 2012 Results in Focus: What 15-Year-Olds Know and What They Can Do with What They Know.*

36. Office of the Chancellor, California State University. *Working for California: The Impact of the California State University System* (May 2010).

37. Pande, Ira, editor. *Beyond Degrees: Finding Success in Higher Education.* New Delhi: HarperCollins, 2008.

38. PanIIT Alumni. *PanIIT Panch Ratnas: Five Actions to Reform Higher Education in India.* July 2009.

39. PRS Legislative Research, *Swaminathan Committee on Farmers (October 2006).*

40. Rangnekar, Sharu. *In the Wonderland of Indian Managers.* Noida: Vikas Publishing House Pvt. Ltd, 2010.

41. Rhodes, Frank H. T. *The Creation of the Future: The Role of the American University.* Ithaca: Cornell University Press, 2001.

42. Rosovsky, Henry. *The University: An Owner's Manual.* New York: W. W. Norton & Company, Inc., 1991.

43. Salmi, Jamil. *The Challenges of Establishing World-Class Universities.* Washington, DC: The World Bank, 2009.

44. Sen, Amartya. *The Argumentative Indian: Writings on Indian Culture, History, and Identity.* London: Penguin Books, 2006.

45. Sukhatme, S. P. *Some Perspectives on Technical Education in India.* Professor V. G. Kulkarni Memorial Lecture. September 12, 2011.

46. Stanford University. *Stanford Facts 2015.*

47. Ministry of Human Resources Development, government of India. *Taking IITs to Excellence and Greater Relevance: Report of Dr. Anil Kakodkar Committee.* April 2011.

48. Tilak, Jandhyala B. G. *Higher Education in India: In Search of Equality, Quality, and Quantity.* New Delhi: Orient Blackswan, 2013.

49. Thapar, Romila. *The Penguin History of Early India: From the Origins to AD 1300.* New Delhi: Penguin Books, 2002.

50. UC Berkeley. *Serving California, the Bay Area, and the Community: The Economic Impact and Social Benefits of the University of California, Berkeley 2005–2006.*

51. University of California, *Annual Accountability Report 2014.*

52. Wildavsky, Ben. *The Great Brain Race: How Global Universities Are Reshaping the World*. Princeton: Princeton University Press, 2010.

53. World Economic Forum, *Global Competitive Index 2014–15.*

About the Author

Shail Kumar

Shail Kumar is Past-President of the IIT Foundation; co-founder of Pan IIT alumni movement in the USA; former administrator at UC Berkeley and UC San Diego; co-founder and CEO of two start-ups; and was an executive in several Fortune 500 and Silicon Valley-based corporations. He has an MBA from Indiana University, Bloomington and a bachelor's degree in engineering from the Indian Institute of Technology (IIT), Kharagpur.

For this book, Shail has drawn from his over thirty years of student, alumni leadership, and professional experiences. He also read thousands of pages of national and state level committee reports and numerous non-fiction books. Finally, he conducted over hundred interviews with a diverse group of stakeholders in India and across four continents.

Son of an Indian Army officer, Shail grew up around India. He currently resides in the Silicon Valley with his wife and two children. He enjoys traveling, yoga, and spending time with his family.

Have questions, comments, or suggestions for the author?
You can reach him via:
    Twitter: @ShailendraIIT87
    Facebook: www.facebook.com/ShailendraIIT87
    Website: www.ShailKumar.com